WEEKEND GARDENER

Contributing writer: Wayne S. Ambler
Consultant: C. Colston Burrell

Publications International, Ltd.

Wayne S. Ambler is a horticulture writer, teacher, and lecturer. He is an active horticulturist who has completed a masters degree thesis in Horticulture Education. He was a contributing writer to *Treasury of Gardening* and he served as volume consultant for the Time-Life Gardener's Guide. He owns and operates a wholesale perennial nursery in Virginia.

C. Colston Burrell is a Master of Landscape Architecture, has an M.S. in Horticulture, and is a garden designer, writer, consultant, and photographer. He is president of Native Landscape Design and Restoration, Ltd. He coauthored the *Illustrated Encyclopedia of Perennials* and contributed to the *New Encyclopedia of Organic Gardening* and *Landscaping with Nature.* He is a member of the American Association of Botanic Gardens and Arboreta and the Perennial Plant Association.

Photo Credits

Contents

Landscape Design

Getting Started with Gardening

Contents *continued*

Introduction

There's no doubt about it—gardening takes work. But the payback is immeasurable when you develop your property into a comfortable, outdoor living area. The yard or garden is an extension of your home and yourself—with your signature on every detail. And building a harmonious space for leisure and function can be easier than you think.

With today's busy lifestyles there's little time for gardening chores, so it's crucial to make the most of your time. By devoting a few hours a week to the garden, it is possible to build a practical, usable space in which you can spend your precious leisure time.

The focus of this book is to learn how to build a garden for perpetual pleasure, not work. We concentrate on low-maintenance gardening; however, low maintenance does not have to be boring. You can rely on trees and shrubs with interesting year-round characteristics and long-living perennials and bulbs to set the framework for an ever-changing landscape. You'll be able to have lush borders with continual bloom that are practically self-maintaining.

This book will begin by taking you one step at a time through the stages of creating your own carefully planned space. We'll show you how to observe and evaluate your property, how to use your site to your advantage, and how to identify what your personal needs are in terms of an outdoor living space.

With that information in hand, you'll then begin the building process. Some of the work may seem to be labor intensive, but the return on your initial investment will be appreciated for years to come. Your garden should require minimal tending while keeping an artistic flair. Anyone who takes pleasure from gardening but has little time to spare will enjoy each step of the *Weekend Gardener* creation process.

You'll discover time-saving tips and techniques that can be applied throughout the lifetime of your garden. Gardening can be fun and even simple, without the drudgery of daily watering, weeding, and grooming. You may even choose to develop naturalized plantings, which provide long-term interest for much less effort than most formal borders. Without all the fuss, we'll suggest ways to reduce pruning chores, deal with pests, and simplify fertilizing. Many problems can be prevented with some basic, well-planned attention—saving you countless hours of maintenance.

Weekend Gardener also includes handy directories that outline the characteristics of many plant species, each chosen for their ease of care. You'll find advice for choosing the best quality plants that will practically provide for themselves. After all, you want to enjoy your garden without becoming a hostage to it! With thoughtful planning, selection, and treatment, your gardening goals can be realized.

🌱 *All it takes is a few hours a week, and you can have a gorgeous garden!*

Landscape Design

1

Planning Your Garden

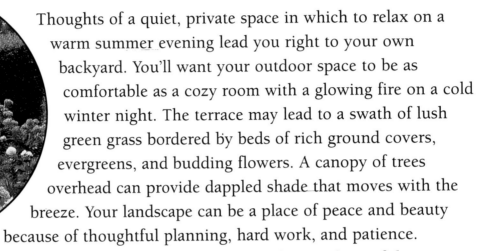

Thoughts of a quiet, private space in which to relax on a warm summer evening lead you right to your own backyard. You'll want your outdoor space to be as comfortable as a cozy room with a glowing fire on a cold winter night. The terrace may lead to a swath of lush green grass bordered by beds of rich ground covers, evergreens, and budding flowers. A canopy of trees overhead can provide dappled shade that moves with the breeze. Your landscape can be a place of peace and beauty because of thoughtful planning, hard work, and patience.

Whether you're looking to screen an eyesore or frame a beautiful vista, you'll become personally involved in developing a garden that suits your needs and desires. Any way you look at landscaping, you can choose the style that best reflects your own tastes.

A simple assessment of your personal landscape needs is your first step in planning your property. Make a list of what you want to incorporate in your design. Take notes of special functions or service areas your landscape will need to provide. Then consider the tips in the following pages as you build your landscape. You'll discover ideas that you can enjoy for a lifetime.

Assessing Your Landscaping Needs

A beautifully designed landscape may be attractive to view, but if it doesn't accommodate the needs of the people who use the property, the design is not practical. Before finalizing the plan for your space, discuss with the members of your household the needs and plans for use of the landscape. Make a list of the functions that you'll want each area of your property to serve. Some considerations include: sitting/dining area, clothesline, barbecue, dog pen, wind protection, lawn recreation, children's play area, and firewood storage. Draw a simple sketch showing the general location of the elements needed in relation to the house and to one another. For instance, if an outdoor eating area is needed, sketch it near the kitchen. The relationship diagram will help you in the beginning steps of putting a plan together. Your considerations should include the amount of maintenance time you're interested in spending in the yard.

If your house is visible from a road, you have a public view area. Think of your house, or front door, as the focal point of a picture. You'll want to frame the view, to draw attention to your house. Typically, foundation plantings are set at the base of the house to create a transition between the house and the landscape. Foundation plantings can be a simple mix of small evergreens and flowering shrubs, ornamental trees, ground covers, and herbaceous plants. Consider shade when choosing trees; deciduous trees will shade the house in the summer while allowing sunlight in during the winter. Be sure to screen service areas—trash cans, laundry lines, and the like—from the public view area.

You'll want to develop other sections of your landscape for outdoor living. You may decide to incorporate a service area—a tool shed or clothesline. It should be convenient to the house yet tucked away from private entertaining and out of public view. If children will be using the landscape, plan for a play area: A swing set or sandbox may be in your plans. You'll want this area set aside from heavy traffic yet still in full view for easy supervision. Separate the dining and entertaining area from the children's area with a low shrub border, and you'll achieve a feeling of individual outdoor rooms.

A private entertaining and dining area is among the most common functions of a well-planned landscape. Design it as you would a comfortable room in your house. The size of the area should be determined by the number of people who will be accommodated. A patio with an adjacent lawn for occasional spillover works well. Shade, as well as privacy, can be achieved through proper selection and placement of screening materials and a canopy of trees.

A combination of flowering plants and shrubs can create a delightful border or spruce up an unsightly spot in your yard.

Create a Functional Sketch

When you plan for outdoor activities and traffic patterns, related functions should be grouped together. For example, parking and an entrance to the house go together. With a sketch pad and a bird's-eye view, simply plot the relationship between the indoor space—windows and doors—with the outdoor space—public, private, and service. From the list of functional areas you need, designate space to accommodate each function.

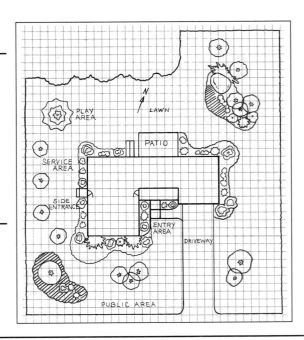

Traffic Flow Design

Paths direct and move traffic from place to place. The heavier the traffic, the sturdier, wider, and more permanent the path should be. Make entrance walks comfortable enough for at least two people to walk abreast (four to five feet wide). Rear-entry paths should be three to four feet wide. All paths should be flush with the ground for safety; make steps stable and well-lighted. A sturdy walkway will save time, as it requires little regular maintenance.

HOW MUCH GRASS DO YOU NEED?

Although everyone appreciates the beauty of a well-manicured, stately lawn, maintenance tasks are time-consuming and expensive. Determine exactly how much open space is needed for such things as lawn games and spillover from patio entertaining. You can also use low maintenance plantings such as ground cover beds to keep lawn space to a minimum.

Paving, Patios, and Privacy

One economical way to expand your living space is to go outdoors—patios and decks are functional and are significant design elements in the landscape. Calculate how large your outdoor living area needs to be to accommodate the people who will use it on a regular basis. Also think about the type of furniture you'll be using (outdoor furniture takes up a lot of space). Study potential locations throughout the seasons and at different times of the day. You'll have to decide whether you want the deck or patio in sun, shade, or both. If a shady site is not available, the planting of a single tree as an overhead canopy is a solution.

The shape of your patio depends on your creativity. Complement the shape and style of the surrounding garden and the style of the house. Squares and right angles tend to look formal and traditional; wide sweeping curves can soften the lines of a small yard. Integrate plantings to help soften lines, increase privacy, and add interest. Most of all, be creative—grid patterns and paving combinations are almost unlimited. Because the choice of paving materials is the most important element in the design, choose a low-maintenance material that complements your landscape and home. Brick and stone are the easiest to use.

Screening, whether by plants or fencing, is sometimes necessary for wind and noise reduction or for privacy. A deck at a high level tends to be exposed to excess wind. Planting trees or shrubs can reduce a gust to a gentle breeze. Vine-covered lattice or fence sections work well for protecting seating areas from wind. Where noise is a problem, a dense planting of shrubs will significantly absorb sound. (Thick-leaved, dense conifers work best.)

A patio or deck is most comfortable when it provides privacy and the feeling of an outdoor room. Small trees and shrubs are effective in building the "walls," and large trees provide a canopy for the ceiling. Keep part of the patio or deck open for easy traffic flow into the lawn space and other surrounding areas. Fencing can be effective in providing privacy as well as adding elements of texture, color, and interest to the garden. A simple eight-foot section of fence can screen an unpleasant view and provide privacy.

Edgings are used to permanently outline and separate garden beds and borders from lawns. They help define and organize space and make mowing easier; they keep garden maintenance low by preventing creeping grasses from invading the bed; and they restrain mulch from washing into the lawn. When planning, use a string line to mark straight edgings. Lay a garden hose for long sweeping curves. Keep curves wide for easy mowing.

You can naturalize a patio or deck with a few well-placed plants, creating a transition zone between your house and the landscape.

Paving with Brick

A brick-surfaced patio is long-lasting and easy to build. Mark the area and remove six inches of soil. To carry rainwater away, grade the slope two inches for every six feet of distance. Build a wood or brick edge along the perimeter of the patio. Spread two inches of gravel and a sheet of landscape fabric to prevent weeds from growing through. With a screed, flatten a two-inch layer of sand. Firmly tamp the sand to prevent bricks from settling into an uneven surface. Lay the bricks flat and tap each one lightly into place. Sweep sand into the joints.

USING BRICK PAVERS

Four-inch by eight-inch brick pavers are twice as long as they are wide to take advantage of pattern possibilities without the use of mortar joints. The pavers are one-and-a-half to two inches thick and each brick paves 32 inches of area.

Size of paved area	Number of pavers required
10' × 10' patio	450
20' × 4' walk	360

Using Fences for Privacy

Using ready-made fence panels from a building supplier, a screening fence can be installed easily in a matter of a few hours. Decide the function of the fence and determine the style needed to fit that purpose and position. Fence panels need not be completely solid to provide privacy. Long sections of solid-board fencing can be monotonous. Integrate lattice or patterns into panels and use plants to soften the space.

Garden Accents and Special Needs

🍂 *Benches serve a dual purpose in a garden as a decorative accent and as a peaceful spot to sit and relax.*

Garden accents are designed to lead the viewer's eye to something special. When strategically placed, accents provide points of interest in the garden. Trellises, arbors, and gates, in addition to becoming the focal points of a view, can create a transition from one part of your garden to another. Individual plant specimens, or plant groupings with contrasting texture, color, or form, can serve as centers of attraction. When planning your garden, consider how different plants will become the highlight of your garden as the seasons change. The white bark of birch trees in front of a dark evergreen backdrop is dramatic in winter. A golden-rain tree might go unnoticed without the brilliant yellow flowers in early summer.

You can incorporate smaller accents as the garden becomes established and you've assessed the area after the major construction and planting have been completed. The assortment of garden accents is almost endless. Statuary can add interesting spotlights when integrated with the overall design of a garden. A simple birdbath or bird-feeding station can be used to lead the eye to individual points of interest. Use planters to beautify an unused corner of a patio or to serve as a focal point at the end of a garden path. Planters with brightly colored foliage, radiant flowers, or interesting shapes can brighten up dark spaces. Two or more planters can be used to frame an area of particular interest. Freshen up containers with potted annuals and seasonal flowering plants for renewed accent in the garden. A bench with a style that fits the fashion of your landscape can serve as a focal point in addition to being functional.

Among the many ways to deal with grade changes in your landscape, one method is to construct a retaining wall. Use materials that will not decay; once the garden is planted it's almost impossible to replace a wall without destroying the planting. A stone drywall (a wall without mortar) is a permanent, attractive solution that can be built in stages. Stone is natural and fits well with practically every style of garden. Railroad ties and treated lumber are also good, but they will eventually deteriorate and need repair.

Outdoor lighting is used mainly for safety (to illuminate steps or a path), but it can also extend the hours you'll enjoy your garden. Ordinary spotlights and floodlights can be too obtrusive in the garden. Easy-to-assemble in an afternoon, low-voltage lighting kits are available in many styles. You'll be amazed by the results you can achieve with these simple and versatile lights. Use low-voltage lighting to highlight special features and add a dramatic effect to your landscape. Uplight a structurally interesting tree or shrub to create a statuary appearance. Direct lights downward from the branches of a tree to create a moonlight effect. Wash a wall or fence with soft lighting to silhouette plants against the wall. Mushroom-type, low-level lighting along a garden path invites visitors to enjoy the quietness of the garden at night.

Specimen Plants

Shrubs are usually used in massed plantings to provide a backdrop or screen, but a single shrub can be used effectively as a specimen or an accent. Although the plant need not be evergreen, the specimen should be attractive and appealing throughout the seasons. Colorful autumn leaves, intriguing trunk or bark patterns, and summer flowers are some characteristics to consider. A single flowering tree or shrub set against a backdrop of dark evergreens provides an all-season point of interest.

Vine-Covered Arbor

An arbor is an attractive way to support vines and provide shade. Whether a freestanding style or an arbor large enough to shade an entire patio, be sure the structure is high enough for people to walk through comfortably. A ready-made trellis can be installed in little time, becoming immediately available to plant your favorite vine. Train young vines, such as clematis and wisteria, by tying them to the structure with loose string or plastic ties.

Using Ornamental Grasses

Ornamental grasses add grace to any garden. With their array of colors, textures, and sizes, ornamental grasses add year-round interest to a garden. Whether as a specimen or a massed planting, grasses can be used for screening, accenting, as a focal point, or to frame a view. Grasses are found over the entire earth—in many different environmental conditions—so you're certain to find a variety to suit your decorative and cultural needs.

Ornamental grasses are categorized as cool-season and warm-season grasses. Many ornamental grasses are perennials, but some are treated as annuals. Certain grasses actively grow during the cool parts of the year. In early spring, these varieties burst into quick, lush growth. You can plant these types behind spring-flowering bulbs for a fine-textured background. When frost comes, the foliage and seed heads turn a bright golden-tan and continue to offer a fine display through winter.

Other grasses can remain dormant during the winter, beginning their growth when the weather and soil have warmed sufficiently.

Needing little maintenance, they're best left alone except for an annual cutting back at the end of winter. These grasses thrive on hot, long days and, once established, are highly tolerant of drought conditions.

Ornamental grasses are also grouped by how they grow. Some grasses form dense clumps, others spread by stolons or rhizomes. Grasses that spread will quickly invade the space of other nearby plantings unless they are planted in an area where you can contain their growth. Clumping varieties will stay where you plant them as they thicken with age. Determine each variety's space needs and expect a well-tended grass to mature in three years. Ornamental grasses require little maintenance. Most varieties prefer well-drained soil in full sun; some varieties tolerate partial shade. Fertilizer needs are low; over-fertilization can result in tall, lush growth that may require staking. In late winter, cut the grasses down to allow for new growth, but be careful not to cut too low since damage to the growing shoots may occur. Two to six inches, depending on the size of the grass, should be sufficient.

Designing with grasses is easy. Use small grasses as edging plants or ground covers; they're often hardier than many commonly used plants. They have appeal throughout the year, and there are many varieties from which to choose. When planted in mass, larger grasses become effective wind and privacy screens. Ornamental grasses make effective screens from early summer through winter. Choose varieties that will grow to at least eye level, and space the plants so they will form an impenetrable mass at maturity. Perennials mixed with grasses tie materials together during interim periods when one season's blooms have finished and the next season's blooms have yet to begin. Any single, large ornamental grass can be used as a specimen plant, a focal point in an open garden, or to break up expansive spaces. Many types of grasses are also well suited to container growing, as long as they receive the moisture and nutrients necessary for continual growth.

🌿 *An ornamental grass specimen can really stand out as a stark contrast to flowering plants in a garden.*

Four Seasons of Interest

Winter

This is the time of the year when the ornamental grasses come into their own. After the last of the fall flowers are gone to frost, grasses reach their peak with their bold masses of tans, golds, and buff colors. They'll hold their seed stalks and heads until the snow becomes heavy.

Spring

The basal leaves of many cool-season grasses remain green through the winter, ready to jump at the first sign of spring. These fast-growing grasses provide your garden with a transitional period between early-flowering bulbs and later-arriving perennials and annuals.

Summer

Warm-season grasses grow with a sudden burst of energy. Their textures are still soft and the colors of variegated types add interest to your garden. Near the end of the summer, the large varieties of warm-season grasses soon grow to massive proportion as they display their large, downy plumage.

Autumn

Most garden plants begin to look ragged by now, but many grasses are at their peak. Their flowers turn to seeds, taking on many shades of beige and gold. Leaves may turn a brilliant yellow, red, or purple. Tall seed stalks and drying foliage sway in the breeze, creating the quiet rustling sound of autumn.

2

Analyzing Your Landscape

Conscious thought and observation—not hard work—is the weekend gardener's guide to an accurate analysis of a property. Before you spend hours of unnecessary manual labor, study your unique situation so that a practical plan requiring little long-term maintenance can be followed.

Develop a sense of how your house fits into nature's space. Is your property nestled in a damp woodland or on a small urban lot? Which features of the property must be worked around, such as utility wires, and which features can be eliminated or rearranged, such as an entrance path that is too narrow? How can you use to your advantage the amenities that attracted you to the property? Was it the peaceful, private backyard or the vista from the dining room window?

Watch the shade as the sun moves overhead; you may discover a better spot to build a patio. Observe where the snow drifts from a windy winter storm; note the natural flow of traffic in and around your garden; look for the earliest dandelions to identify a possible microclimate. Soon you'll be able to interpret the conditions on your site. Use your property plat to note any hidden utilities or easements.

As you compare your list of needs with your analysis notes, you'll be able to customize a design to match your household's needs with your existing plot.

Sizing Up Sun and Shade

When designing your garden, the position of sunlight and shade at different times of the day and year is an important piece of information. You'll need a basic knowledge of the movement of the sun in relation to the garden's features. Understanding this movement will help in deciding the placement and choice of plants.

As you analyze your garden site, observe existing trees and structures, noting how they will affect the sun and shade in your space. On your garden sketch, take note of hot, sunny areas that can be cooled down by the proper placement of trees or overhead structures. Also, indicate the areas that are permanently shaded by trees or structures of which you have no control.

A plant needing full sun may do well even if it has to endure shade for a few hours in the late afternoon, but a shade-loving plant might burn if it receives a few hours of sun during the day. Plants that perform well in the full sun of New England may need protection from the summer afternoon sun of the Southern states. Choose deciduous trees to cool the house in the summer. At the end of the growing season, the leaves will fall as the house receives the advantage of additional sunlight for winter warmth.

Plants and other garden features and accessories appear to take on different textures as the angle of the sun changes. The low, afternoon sun of a winter day seems to highlight the interesting bark of a birch or the subtle colors of ornamental grasses, which might go unnoticed during another season or even a different time of day. Sun and shade are constantly changing patterns, varying the feel of the garden from hour to hour and season to season.

Within your garden, you will discover special niches where some plants may bloom earlier or longer into the season. These niches, or microclimates, may be desirable for certain varieties of plants, but may be detrimental to others. Microclimates are unique to special sections of your garden. South-facing slopes tend to have a slightly longer growing season, as the earliest of spring flowers may bloom a week or two before those located in a cooler part of the garden. Consider the effects on plants in your landscape as you discover its microclimates. Although the south-facing wall is warm on sunny winter days, the rapid drop in temperature from a bright winter day to a cold night might be too extreme for many plants. Plants that are marginally hardy and those that are prone to winter drying are best suited to the cooler, shadier north-facing exposure.

Salvia performs well in both sunny and partially shaded conditions, which makes it an excellent choice for wooded areas. This mass planting showcases a dramatic use of color.

Environmental Influences

The sun rises directly from the east on the first day of spring. But the sun rises north of the east-west line in the summer, exposing all sides of a house to a certain amount of sunlight: It's height in the sky produces short shadows from buildings and plants.

In the wild, each plant fits perfectly into its own niche. Some trees rise high into the air, basking in the sun while being pummeled by harsh, drying winds—and they thrive under such conditions. At the feet of these tall trees, small trees and shrubs live in a different environment: no rough wind and no brilliant sun. These plants trade abundant solar energy for protection from the elements.

The same pattern occurs in your garden. Some parts are shady much of the day, while others are mostly sunny. Some parts are exposed to dominant winds, others are protected. These elements are in constant flux. As trees and shrubs grow, they modify the environment around them, creating more shade and a greater barrier against the wind.

Most woody plants are surprisingly adaptable to varying degrees of sun and wind exposure. That's because they rarely get to live in the same environment throughout their entire lives. They may sprout in full sun but have to cope with increasing shade as other plants around them also grow; or a much larger tree may topple over, suddenly exposing to harsh sun a tree or shrub that has grown in shade all its life. Despite this great adaptability, plants do have preferences.

🌿 *Buildings cast shadows, trees grow in size, and the sun shifts in the sky, creating an ever-changing environment.*

Plants gather energy from sunlight. It seems reasonable that most plants would grow faster and denser with full sun. But with nearby walls, fences, and trees, full sun may be rare in the average backyard. Most woody plants grow almost equally well in full sun or partial shade. Full sun tends to stimulate increased flowering and helps bring out more brilliant fall colors. Some protection from hot afternoon sun is good for even "full sun" plants.

The best shade for most plants is dappled shade, which is sunlight piercing through the leaves of tall trees. This type of shade provides good light all day while shielding tender plants from the burning effects of full sun.

Strong winds can do severe damage to plants, especially during the winter months. As the wind blows through the leaves and buds, it dries the air, causing leaves to burn on the edges and flower buds to abort. The windier it is, the more damage cold temperatures will do: This is the "wind chill factor." Plants that are borderline hardy in a given zone should always be planted where they won't be affected by strong winds.

The best protection from strong winds is offered by other plants. They buffer the wind rather than cut it off entirely. Conifers and wind-resistant broad-leaf evergreens are the best choices for softening wind year-round, although even the leafless branches of deciduous trees are surprisingly efficient at screening strong winds. Fencing can also help buffer winds.

Soil, Water, and Drainage Needs

When we look at a tree or shrub, we generally only consider the aspects above ground: shape and size, leaf color, flowers, and the like. We rarely stop to think that at least half the plant—its extensive root system—is underground. The underground portion, more than anything else, determines whether the plant will thrive or fail. Before you begin choosing the proper trees, shrubs, or vines for your yard, analyze the soil, water, and drainage conditions. You must then determine whether any changes should be made. It is always easier, less costly, and best of all, less-time consuming to do this before you begin planting.

The soil in which your plant grows serves four basic purposes. It helps, through its structure, to hold the plant upright, and it supplies food, water, and air to the roots. Most soils are already capable of meeting these purposes and can be used with little amendment. Called loam soils, they contain a mixture of different sized soil particles and organic matter.

Some soils, however, may be extremely dense, with little air space between the particles. This type of soil, called clay, is made up of particles of rock so tiny and close together they allow little air circulation. Clay holds water well, perhaps too well. Sandy soil contains larger particles of rock. Air is present in abundance in sandy soils, but water runs straight through. This creates dry growing conditions.

To determine which type of soil you have, squeeze some slightly moist soil in your hand. Clay soils will form a compact lump and retain their shape. Loam soils will form a ball but fall apart if poked at. Sandy soils won't hold their shape at all.

Both sandy and clay soils can be improved in the same way—by adding organic amendments. Add about one-third each of peat, compost, and well-rotted manure or other organic matter, and mix carefully into the planting area.

Before planting, have your soil's pH level tested. This is a measure of acidity and alkalinity. Most soils in North America fall in a pH range of 6 to 7, from slightly acidic to neutral. This is ideal for most plants. Garden centers and local Cooperative Extension offices usually offer an analysis service and will explain how to collect a soil sample. If the results indicate that your soil is on the alkaline side (7 or above), consider either choosing plants that tolerate alkaline soils or amending the soil with peat moss or sulfur. If your soil is very acidic (below 5.5), try either planting acid-loving plants or adding ground limestone. The exact quantities of amendment needed to change your soil's pH depend on a great many factors, notably its original pH and the type of amendment used. A professional soil analysis will also indicate the levels of other essential nutrients in your soil. If a deficiency is identified, the institution will indicate the exact type and amount of fertilizer needed to remedy the problem.

Gravel can be used to prevent weeds and promote better drainage.

Water makes up about 90 percent of the tissue in leafy plants. Woody plants have an advantage over herbaceous ones in that they generally have extensive root systems that reach down and out for great distances. Thus, woody plants can seek out moisture and continue to grow even as other plants suffer from lack of water. But there are limits to this ability. Most woody plants prefer soils that are evenly moist, meaning soils that may dry out on the surface but remain slightly moist underground.

If your area is subject to regular or prolonged droughts, you should consider planting naturally drought-tolerant varieties. Newly planted trees and shrubs need extra care in watering since their root systems are quite limited, especially during the first year. Some soils suffer from chronically poor drainage. They are spongy and moist at all times. Choose plants that are suited to such soils to prevent having to alter the soil's drainage ability (which may be time-consuming and expensive). It may still be necessary to improve the drainage of your yard before you begin to plant. You can solve the problem by planting woody plants in raised beds or mounds to give them a few extra feet of soil in which to grow. This will provide enough well-draining soil for good air circulation, and the moist soil beneath will ensure that roots never lack water.

Soil Profile
The soil your plants grow in serves many purposes. Be sure to analyze your soil before purchasing any plants. Take samples from the lower level of the topsoil region.

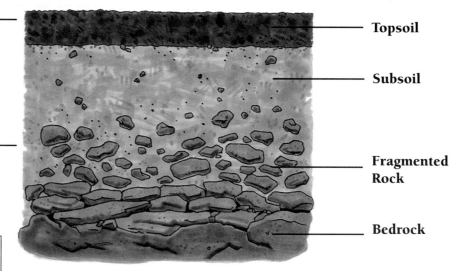

Topsoil

Subsoil

Fragmented Rock

Bedrock

OPTIMUM pH FOR SOME COMMON PLANTS

4.5–5.5	6.0–7.5
Azalea	Abelia
Rhododendron	Ash
5.5–7.0	Arborvitae
Holly	Barberry
Magnolia	Forsythia
Redbud	Juniper
Weeping Willow	Lilac
Crape Myrtle	Privet
Spirea	Pyracantha

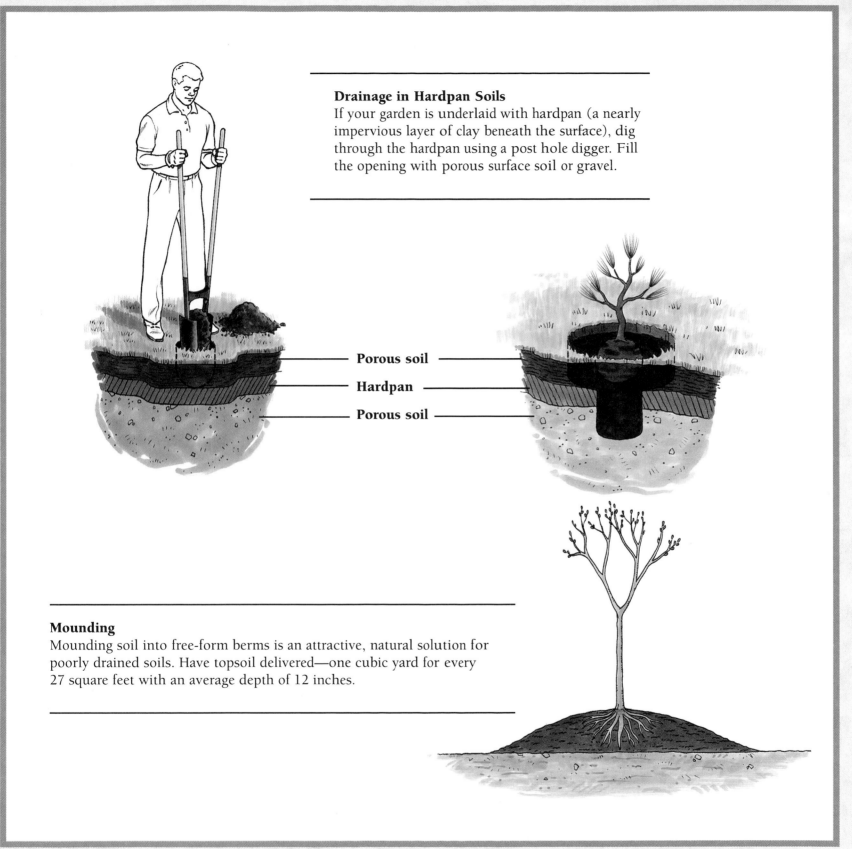

Drainage in Hardpan Soils

If your garden is underlaid with hardpan (a nearly impervious layer of clay beneath the surface), dig through the hardpan using a post hole digger. Fill the opening with porous surface soil or gravel.

Porous soil

Hardpan

Porous soil

Mounding

Mounding soil into free-form berms is an attractive, natural solution for poorly drained soils. Have topsoil delivered—one cubic yard for every 27 square feet with an average depth of 12 inches.

Planting Lawns and Ornamental Grasses

🌿 *Turf grasses can endure more traffic than ornamental varieties. A footpath is one solution for alleviating some of the wear.*

Some species of grass tolerate wear and regular mowing; these are the grasses that are used for lawns. Other species of grasses, while not durable enough to serve as a lawn, are wonderful garden plants. Ornamental grasses can serve as long-living ground covers, specimen plants, or privacy screens with year-round interest and low maintenance requirements.

Whether you're starting a new lawn or renovating an old one, some important elements should be considered before just throwing some grass seed around. First, decide what type of grass you'll want to grow. There are basically two types of lawn grasses; those that bunch and those that creep. Many cool-season grasses are the bunching type. They continue to grow from new shoots at the base of the plant. Creeping grasses, as most warm-season varieties are, spread by sending out rhizomes or stolons—stems that creep along or are just below ground level, forming a new plant at the tip. Both grasses form thick mats if they're properly cared for. Creeping grasses form a better turf for high-traffic areas. You'll also have to consider the climatic zone you live in, because not all varieties will grow under all conditions. (See the turfgrass hardiness zone map on page 26.)

Once the soil is graded, you're ready to sow seed. Sow cool-season grass in the early fall so the grass will have four to six weeks to establish itself before frost. Spread the seed with a hand spreader at the recommended rate found on the package. Use a garden rake to gently work the seed into the top ⅛ inch of soil; seed that is planted too deeply will not germinate. Roll the area with a lawn roller to ensure good contact between the soil and the seed. Using clean, weed-free straw, lightly mulch the seedbed, just enough so that half the soil is left exposed. The straw will help shade the soil and your seedlings, preventing them from drying too quickly. Keep the top layer of soil evenly and constantly moist. Water with a fine spray several times a day until the seedlings become strong enough to withstand regular irrigation. If you're renovating small patches of an old lawn, follow the same steps on a lesser scale.

You can also plant sod for an instant high-quality lawn. Though the initial cost is higher than starting a lawn from seed, the time saved is advantageous to a busy gardener. It is available in cool-and warm-season varieties. Cool-season sod can be installed any time of the year that the ground isn't frozen. Warm-season sod should be installed in spring or summer, when the grass is actively growing.

Starting a Lawn From Seed

Proper soil preparation is critical. Remove rocks, lumps, and grass clods after the ground has been graded and the pH adjusted. Use a hand spreader to apply the seed at the recommended rate. Scratch the seed into the soil with a garden rake and tamp with a lawn roller; the close contact between the seed and the soil will aid in sprouting. Apply a light mulch of clean straw and regularly water without allowing the soil to dry out.

Installing Sod

Purchase high-quality, certified turf from a reputable source. Final grade one inch lower than the grade for seeding. Unroll strips of sod and tuck them into place. Cut irregular pieces with a spade or knife; don't overlap or stretch the strips. Fill in any visible joints with topsoil. Roll with a lawn roller so the roots come in contact with the soil. Keep a newly sodded lawn well-watered until its roots become established.

Ornamental Grass Ground Cover

Rapidly spreading ornamental grasses—such as ribbon grass—are easily established by planting young starts. Use a 1-inch by 12-inch board to space plants 12 inches apart. Lay out the board and plant a row of grasses flush with the soil level; tamp each plant into the soil. Start the second row 12 inches away from the first row. Keep the bed watered until it becomes well established. Once established, grasses mat together, forming a bed impenetrable to weeds.

Turfgrass Hardiness Zone Map

Generally, the hardiness of a particular plant refers to its ability to survive certain minimum low temperatures. Other factors, however, do play important roles. Soil-moisture availability, wind conditions, and length of growing season are factored in for recommended hardiness zones. Some plants do not tolerate excessive heat, especially high nighttime temperatures.

A specific hardiness zone map is usually followed to determine turfgrass hardiness. The continental United States is divided into three sections. Cool-season grasses grow best in Zone A. Zone B is a transition zone, where both cool-season and warm-season grasses grow. Warm-season grasses are hardy in Zone C.

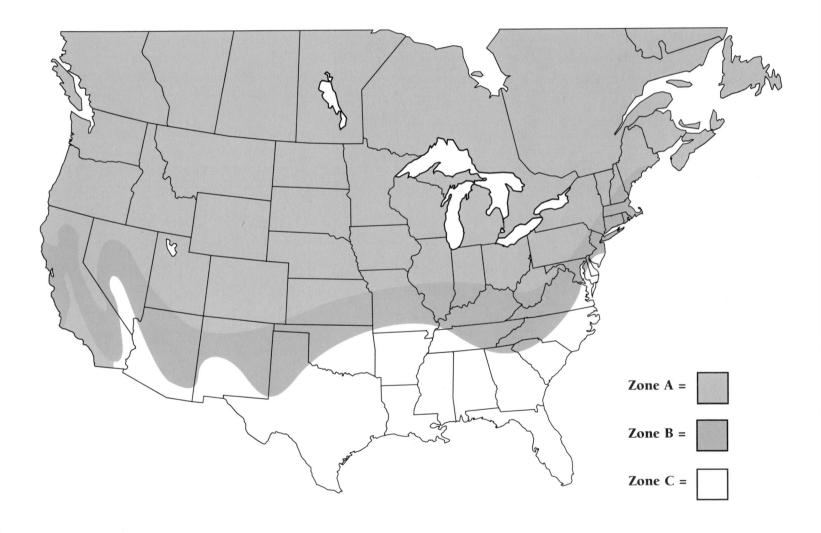

Zone A =

Zone B =

Zone C =

3

Pests and the Rest

Some type of pest is sure to arrive when it's least expected, no matter how much effort you put into a landscape's design, planting, and care. Stunted plant growth, yellow patches in the lawn, or tiny holes in the leaves of a new planting of ground cover may seem mysterious, but the next few pages will show you how to identify the cause and determine a control method. You may discover that the more you fertilize and water, the more you play host to pests. In other instances, diseases and insects may make an already neglected area worse. Don't despair; once the problem is identified, the cure is sometimes as simple as changing the height on your lawn mower. The presence of pests doesn't always indicate a need for a spray. A small insect population may be easily picked off the plant. If you decide to use chemicals, some safety tips are included. You'll also find an illustrated section for easy identification of the most common weeds, diseases, and other pests of lawns and ground covers. Included are recommendations for dealing with each problem. Finally, plan for a trouble-free landscape. Select plants wisely, lay out beds and plantings that require minimal maintenance, and keep your plants healthy by supplying them with all of their cultural needs.

Growth and Overgrowth

It's always difficult to visualize how large a plant will grow once it becomes part of your landscape. For instance, an eight-inch high Chinese juniper will grow to eight feet tall and eight feet wide in a few short years. Plants mature at varying rates. Plants labeled as "dwarf" may become large with time, but establish themselves slowly. Other plants will grow rapidly when young and produce less new growth later on. While planning, you'll need to determine how large you want the plant to be within a particular time frame. If you're planning a patio and need a quick source of shade, a fast-growing tree may be just what you need. Foundation plantings need a different solution. Slow-growing dwarf shrubs and ground covers can accommodate the needs of a foundation garden around a home where space is limited.

As you plan your design, think about the plant characteristics you want before you determine which variety to grow. Would a round or vase-shaped shrub suit the area best? Think about the size: Do you need a tall shade tree or a short, round ornamental one? Choose plants according to their position in the landscape. Consider the natural shape and ultimate height and width of plants before you install them. Improper plant selection often disappoints the homeowner when drastic renovation measures are required. For instance, by choosing a columnar variety of flowering dogwood, which may grow only eight feet wide rather than the usual 20 feet, you'll spend less time with shears in hand.

Existing soil conditions, wind, sun exposure, and hardiness are also serious considerations when picking plants. Do you need a plant that can tolerate wet soils or one that will thrive in dense shade? Once you've answered these questions, find a plant that is suited to all of your requirements and success will almost be guaranteed.

Pruning to keep plants inbounds is an integral part of landscape upkeep. The weekend gardener has little time to keep a formal hedge immaculately groomed. When possible, choose plant varieties that will separate garden spaces without constant pruning. Take advantage of natural growth habits—shape and density—that will suit your needs as you plan your garden. Some plantings, such as formal hedges, are sheared to maintain a formal appeal. Most shrubs require minimal thinning to maintain their natural shape while reducing their size.

Choose vines wisely. Some vines need expansive room to grow; others do well with limited space. Boston Ivy, for instance, puts on a glorious show with its brilliant-colored fall foliage, but its growth is so rapid that you may find yourself spending too much time keeping the plant within bounds. Annual vines—Morning Glory and Scarlet Runner Bean—and slower-growing perennials—Clematis and Carolina Jessamine—may help you achieve the same effect without the vine becoming invasive.

🐚 *There is virtually no limit to the size, shape, and color of plants you can choose to suit your unique situation and taste.*

Ground Cover

Once woody ground covers become established, they seem to creep up on you. Before a drastic renovation job becomes necessary, spend a warm winter afternoon pruning some of the previous year's growth by following the plant's natural growth pattern. If too much of the plant is removed, the plant's health is at risk and an unsightly effect will be the result. If space is limited, choose clumping varieties of ground cover rather than horizontal or trailing types.

A Formal Sheared Hedge

As new growth appears from the base of the hedge, use a hedge shear to uniformly cut the ends of the branches. Keep the bottom of the plants wider than the top, allowing plenty of sun to reach all sides of the row. As the hedge matures, a concentration of small branches will develop among the outer shell. Renovate the hedge again by cutting the top and side lower so sunlight can increase branching from the inside of the plants.

Renovation by Thinning

Flowering shrubs look their best when maintained by thinning. Thinning allows the plant to keep its natural shape. After the plant has matured and the size of the plant needs reduction, annually remove up to one-third of its oldest stems at ground level. Remove shoots that will not destroy the shape of the shrub. This will promote new growth from the base of the plant. Newer growth generally flowers heavier than mature growth.

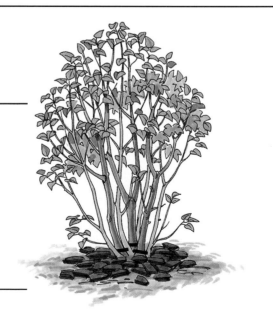

Pests and Other Problems

Plant pests are inevitable, but you're liable to see fewer pests if you're taking care of your plants. Luckily, a well-maintained lawn develops less weed growth than a poorly cared for lawn. Weeds have difficulty establishing themselves where the soil is covered with healthy turf.

The list below will help you identify the most common pests of lawns and ground covers. If you feel uncertain about what is causing symptoms of damage, take a sample to your local garden center or your county Cooperative Extension office to have it identified.

Once you've identified the cause of the problem, you'll need to know how to control it. A change in cultural maintenance—less water for instance—may be the best control, or the use of chemicals may be necessary. If chemical control is required, choose a chemical that is recommended for use on your species. Study the label and follow the directions for use.

🌿 *The best safeguard against weeds and pests is a healthy, well-maintained lawn and garden.*

LAWN AND GROUND COVER WEEDS

WEED	DESCRIPTION	CONTROL
Black Medic. *Medicago lupulina.*	Annual. Spreading plants form a dense mat of dark green foliage that resembles clover. Small yellow flowers appear in spring, forming black seeds. It is a particular problem during dry periods.	Use a postemergent systemic herbicide when turf is not water stressed.
Common Chickweed. *Stellaria media.*	Cool-season annual. It is low-growing with branching stems and small, pointed yellow-green leaves with small starlike white flowers. It grows actively from autumn through spring. Thin turf and bare soil are where it grows best.	Use a preemergent herbicide in fall or early spring.
Crabgrass, Smooth and Hairy. *Digitaria ischaemem and D. sanguinalis.*	Both are summer annuals that germinate in late spring. Thick clumps of smooth (or hairy) leaves with a spreading habit crowd out desirable turf grass.	Use a preemergent herbicide in spring when forsythia is in bloom.

LAWN AND GROUND COVER WEEDS

WEED	DESCRIPTION	CONTROL
Dandelion. *Taraxacum officinale.*	Perennial. Leaves are broad with deep notches, forming a rosette. Flowers are yellow and develop into fluffy white seed heads.	Use a postemergent systemic herbicide when plants appear, or dig by hand, taking care to remove the entire taproot.
Ground Ivy. *Glechoma hederacea.*	Perennial. This creeping plant has round, scalloped edges; stems are squared. Bright purple flowers appear in spring.	Weed is easily removed by hand, or a postemergent systemic herbicide can be used when plants appear.
Knotweed. *Polygonum aviculare.*	Summer annual. Stems spread across the ground, forming dense mats of small blue-green leaves. Small white flowers appear in late summer.	Use a postemergent systemic herbicide when plants appear.
Purslane. *Portulaca oleracea.*	Summer annual. Small yellow flowers appear on thick mats of small, succulent green leaves with reddish stems. It grows vigorously in the heat of summer where lawns are thin or soil is bare.	Weed is edible and easily pulled. Use a preemergent herbicide in spring or a postemergent contact herbicide when plants appear. It is especially troublesome in new plantings.
Oxalis. *Oxalis stricta.*	Annual or perennial. Yellow-green leaves resemble clover. Flowers are yellow and develop seedpods that eject mature seeds throughout the lawn or garden.	Use a postemergent systemic herbicide when plants appear; some control is gained from preemergent herbicide use in spring.
Red Sorrel. *Rumex acetosella.*	Perennial. Green leaves are arrow-shaped; reddish brown flowers appear in late spring. The plant has a taproot and spreads rapidly by rhizomes. It is evergreen in mild climates.	Use a postemergent systemic herbicide when plants appear.

LAWN AND GROUND COVER WEEDS

WEED	DESCRIPTION	CONTROL
**Plantain—Broadleaf and Buckhorn.** *Plantago major; P. Lanceolata.*	Perennial. Both plantains form a rosette of leaves, either wide or lancelike; they produce slender stalks on which the seed heads develop. Both species develop long taproots.	Dig plants to remove entire taproot or use a postemergent systemic herbicide when plants appear.
**Wild Garlic, Wild Onion.** *Allium* species.	Perennial. Narrow, tall, green, hollow stems appear in early spring. Plant forms clumps and multiplies by underground bulblets.	Use a postemergent systemic herbicide.

PESTS THAT ATTACK GROUND TURF

SYMPTOM	CAUSE	CONTROL
Lawn becomes spotted with yellow or brown patches in late spring or summer. The patches become large if left untreated.	***Black insects, ¼ inch long.*** These insects feed on grass and lay eggs on turf stems. Larvae feed on stems, then on underground roots, killing the turf.	Apply insecticide in spring and when larvae are feeding on stems. Water lawn to wash insecticide into the soil.
Round or irregular yellow patches in turf during hot, dry summer weather. Dead patches rapidly become quite large.	***Chinch bugs.*** These small, reddish brown or black insects suck plant sap from blades and stems. They are particularly active during the hot summer months.	Apply an insecticide labeled for chinch bugs as soon as symptoms appear. Re-treat lawn at three-week intervals until control is obtained.
Stunted clumps of yellow grass appear throughout the lawn.	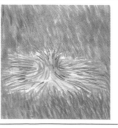***Downy mildew.*** This fungus attacks turf in cool, humid climates. Spores are spread by water.	Apply fungicide labeled for downy mildew in early spring or when symptoms appear. Mow lawn when grass is dry.

PESTS THAT ATTACK GROUND TURF

SYMPTOM	CAUSE	CONTROL
Patches of dead turf appear in early spring and again in late summer.	 **Grubs.** As larvae of beetles—Japanese, June, Asiatic Garden—they live in the soil and feed on roots.	Apply soil insecticide labeled for use on grubs in turf in early spring and late summer. Control adult beetle population in trees, shrubs, and flowers by hand-picking or with recommended insecticide when they appear in late spring and early summer.
Hollow, long trailing ridges of soil appear across the lawn, followed by decline of turf. Holes that lead to underground tunnels are visible. Tunnels are most prominent during cool seasons.	**Moles and voles.** These are small, tunneling rodents. Moles feed on grubs and insects, while voles feed on plant roots–often from mole tunnels.	Control soil insect population to deplete food source of moles. Use spike-traps when pests are active.
Large patches of St. Augustine grass decline and turn yellow; individual leaves become mottled with yellow. Turf becomes thin.	**St. Augustine Decline (SAD).** The virus spreads through insects and infected lawn-cutting equipment.	Plant SAD-resistant varieties of St. Augustine grass. Control aphids that transmit the virus. Keep lawn-cutting equipment clean.
Patches of yellow or brown turf appear as winter snow melts. Deteriorating grass mats together, turning pink or gray, while white, cottony growth develops.	**Snow mold.** This fungus is active when turf is wet and cold. It can reappear in late fall.	Apply a fungicide in early spring to prevent spread. Reduce water and fertilizer in the fall to prevent recurrence.
Small patches of dead grass in spring, enlarge throughout the summer. Grass blades appear to have been cut off in affected areas. Small tunnel holes are visible in affected areas.	 **Sod webworm.** These larvae of moths lay eggs on turf. The larvae tunnel into the soil, feeding at night on grass blades. Webs are formed within affected areas.	Spray with insecticide in the evening when feeding larvae are out of their tunnels. Repeat applications until adult moths, larvae, and symptoms disappear.

PESTS THAT ATTACK GROUND COVERS

SYMPTOM		CAUSE	CONTROL	PLANTS
Growing tips become distorted. Leaves curl and begin to wither. A clear, sticky substance that may attract ants appears on leaves.		**Aphids.** Small, sucking insects of various colors: green, yellow, red, brown, and gray. Aphids appear in masses on tender growing shoots and new foliage.	Wash insects from plants with a strong jet of water or apply insecticidal soap or insecticide labeled for control of aphids.	Ajuga, English Ivy, Turfgrass.
Leaves turn yellow, and tiny, elongated white bumps appear along stems and leaves. Small, round brown bumps also appear. The plant becomes stunted and loses its leaves.		**Euonymus scale.** The dark brown shelled female and white males multiply rapidly. Infestations rob plant of nutrients by sucking plant sap.	Use a dormant oil spray in early spring for prevention. Cut out infected parts, and spray with recommended insecticide until signs of insects are gone.	*Euonymus* species.
Plants show decreased vigor, and leaves become speckled from loss of color. The undersides of leaves are covered with small black specks.		**Lace bugs.** Infestations of small, lacelike insects on the undersides of leaves suck plant sap.	Spray the undersides of foliage when symptoms appear. Use an insecticide recommended for lace bugs on the plant being attacked. Apply three times at 7- to 10-day intervals.	Azaleas, Cotoneaster.
New growth is distorted, and foliage is covered with white a powdery substance.		**Powdery mildew.** This fungus attacks plants during warm, humid periods with cool nights.	Spray with a lime-sulfur fungicide at 10- to 14-day intervals.	Ajuga, Candytuft, Euonymus, Periwinkle.
Foliage has irregular-shaped holes, especially near the base of the plant.		**Snails and slugs.** Pests feed at night on foliage; they leave a slimy trail. Slugs look like snails without shells.	Pick pests when visible; lay a board near the infested areas for slugs and snails to hide under and collect them during the day. Shallow pans of beer will lure the pests and drown them.	Ajuga, Daylily, Hosta.
Leaves lose their green color and are speckled with white. A fine white webbing appears between leaves and stem, especially on young tips.		**Spider mites.** Tiny pests suck plant sap during hot, dry periods. They are difficult to detect until the population is large.	Spray with an insecticidal soap or apply a miticide three times at three-day intervals.	Cotoneaster, English Ivy, Juniper.

4

Directory of Popular Turf Grasses

Lawns have been cultivated in America since colonial times. Since then, great strides have been made in cultivating varieties of grass that will withstand adverse conditions. Turf specialists have divided the United States into two distinct climatic regions and a third of transition, or overlap (see page 26). Some varieties of grasses native to a climate similar to the northern region will grow best only in the North; other species and their hybrids will only grow well in the southern region, which is similar to their native habitat. The overlap zone, or transition zone, can accommodate some varieties from either the northern zone or the southern zone.

Turf grasses today can tolerate heavier wear, colder weather, and drier conditions than their native counterparts. Toughness and hardiness have been "fixed" into the plant variety through selective breeding and hybridizing.

A beautiful lawn is not a low-maintenance project. It takes careful planning to control weeds and diseases. It takes effort to keep the mower sharp and the lawn regularly cut. So the best way to cut maintenance time is to choose a variety well-suited to your needs. This plant directory will help you select the right grass for a successful lawn.

Bermudagrass
Cynodon dactylon

Bermudagrass, a warm-season grass that forms a dense mat, spreads by rhizomes. This turf grass is grown in the South and the Southwest. Bermudagrass tolerates wear and can withstand drought conditions. Bermudagrass is a high-maintenance turf that grows vigorously in warm weather but turns brown in the winter if temperatures drop below 50°F.

How to grow: Bermudagrass grows well in most soils but must have full sun. Plant sprigs or plugs of named varieties purchased from a reputable nursery or sod producer in your area. (Bermudagrass from seed is unreliable and will produce an inferior lawn.) Bermudagrass must be planted during the warm growing season for it to become established before winter dormancy begins. Fertilize during the season when growth is active. Feed in early spring with one pound of nitrogen per 1,000 square feet, followed by late spring and midsummer applications each of one pound per 1,000 square feet.

Related varieties: 'Midiron' is medium-textured, dark green, and cold-tolerant. 'Tiflawn,' medium-fine textured, bright green, and highly tolerant to foot traffic, is often used on playing fields.

Buffalograss
Buchloe dactyloides

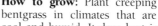

Buffalograss is a warm-season turf grass grown mostly in the Great Plains and the southern Rockies. It's a fine-textured, low-growing grass with curly leaf blades that grows into dense sod by spreading stolons. It is used for lawns and banks, and is exceptionally drought resistant.

How to grow: Plant buffalograss in full sun where soils are dry. It will thrive in the alkaline soils of the West. Buffalograss resists wear from foot traffic and is commonly used for nonirrigated lawns. Fertilize in spring with 1½ to 2½ pounds of nitrogen per 1,000 square feet. This grass grows slowly and should be mowed to a height of ½ to 1½ inches. Plant buffalograss from seeds, sprigs, or plugs.

Related varieties or species: There are currently no developed varieties or related species used for turf.

Creeping Bentgrass
Agrostis stolonifera palustris

Creeping bentgrass is a cool-season transition zone turf that grows best from the Midwest to the Pacific Northwest and in the Northeast. It's a fine-textured, high-maintenance turf that is used for golf putting greens. It spreads by creeping stolons. Creeping bentgrass will not generally survive heavy foot traffic.

How to grow: Plant creeping bentgrass in climates that are cool and humid. It does best in full sun but will tolerate partial shade. Creeping bentgrass may be propagated by seed, but named varieties are propagated by plugs. Sow seeds or plant plugs in well-drained, fertile, acidic soil. Fertilize in spring and again in summer with two pounds of nitrogen per 1,000 square feet. Keep the soil well watered during dry conditions. Creeping bentgrass needs a low mowing height, from ¼ inch to 1 inch; otherwise, thatch will build up quickly. Creeping bentgrass is susceptible to several turf diseases.

Related varieties: 'Emerald' is dark green and heat-tolerant. 'Arlington,' a fine-textured medium green, is tolerant of drought conditions and foot traffic. 'Pencross' is medium green, heavier textured than other varieties, and adapts to foot traffic.

Creeping Red Fescue
Festuca rubra rubra

Creeping red fescue, also called fine fescue, is a densely clustered, fine-textured, medium to dark green turf grass that spreads by creeping stolons. It grows well in shaded areas and is tolerant of drought. It is often mixed with bluegrass or turf-type fescue blends. Grow creeping red fescue in the North and in the transition zone.

How to grow: Plant creeping red fescue from seed and grow it in shaded areas where drought conditions are expected. When it becomes established, it tolerates drought but does not tolerate heavy wear. It grows best in cool-season and high-altitude areas. Fertilize in the fall with 2 to 4 pounds of nitrogen per 1,000 square feet. Mow to 2 inches. This is the most shade-tolerant turf for northern gardens.

Related varieties: 'Pennlawn' is medium dark green with fine texture and disease resistance. 'Illahee' is dark green, medium-textured, and vigorous. Chewing fescue, *Festuca rubra commutata,* is similar to creeping red fescue, although it tends to form clumps. 'Jamestown' is dark green, fine-textured, and tolerant of low mowing. 'Wintergreen' keeps good winter color.

Tall Fescue

Festuca arundinacea

Tall fescue is a cool-season grass that grows in the North and is especially suited to the transition zone. It is a coarse-textured, clumping turf that remains medium green all year. Since it is tolerant of wear and drought, tall fescue is used for play areas.

How to grow: Tall fescue prefers fertile, moist, slightly acidic soil and a full sun or partial shade location. Soil should be moderately well-drained, but tall fescue can tolerate wet soils. Plant seed in the fall or early spring so turf becomes established before hot weather. It is one of the most drought-tolerant and wear-resistant turf varieties for cool seasons. Use tall fescue in the transition zone and in the northern zone for playing fields and lawns with heavy traffic. Fertilize in the fall with 4 to 6 pounds of nitrogen per 1,000 square feet. Mow from 2 to 2½ inches.

Related varieties: 'Kentucky 31' is the standard tall fescue variety. It is coarse, medium green, and tolerant of drought and wear. 'Kentucky 31' is rapidly being replaced by turf-type fescues, which have a finer texture and display better wear-resistance and drought-tolerance than tall fescue.

Kentucky Bluegrass

Poa pratensis

Kentucky bluegrass is a cool-season turf grass that grows in northern regions. It spreads by rhizomes and forms a dense, medium-textured, medium green turf. A Kentucky bluegrass lawn is the standard to which other grasses are compared.

How to grow: Kentucky bluegrass grows best in full sun in moist, fertile soil with a pH between 6.0 and 7.0. Some varieties are more tolerant of partial shade conditions. Consistent irrigation during dry periods is necessary as Kentucky bluegrass is not tolerant of prolonged drought. Plant Kentucky bluegrass from seed. Fertilize annually with 2 to 4 pounds of nitrogen per 1,000 square feet. Mow from 1 to 2 inches.

Related varieties: 'Aldelphi' is dark green, dense, medium-textured, and resistant to disease. 'Baron,' a heavy feeder, is dark green, medium-textured, and disease-resistant. 'Fylking' is dark green with a finer texture; it can be mowed to 1½ inches. 'Merion,' disease-resistant and tolerant of heat, forms a dense mat of medium-textured dark green turf. 'Touchdown' is dense, medium dark green, with a fine texture. It tolerates low mowing and is resistant to disease.

Japanese Lawngrass

Zoysia japonica

Japanese lawngrass is a fine-textured warm-season grass that spreads by rhizomes and stolons. It grows best in the transition zone and in the South. It forms a dense, low-growing lawn of high quality. It is relatively pest free and, when established, is resistant to weeds.

How to grow: Grow Japanese lawngrass in full sun to partial shade where summers are long and hot. The soil should be well-drained and fertile. Plant plugs or sod in spring to allow for development before the onset of winter. It is a heavy feeder during the warm season. Fertilize with one pound of nitrogen per 1,000 square feet in spring, midsummer, and early fall. Since the leaves of Japanese lawngrass are wiry, mow regularly; remove grass clippings from the lawn since thatch builds up quickly. Mow from ½ to 1½ inches. Japanese lawngrass is tolerant of wear during the growing season but less so in winter. When temperatures drop below 50°F, the grass turns brown.

Related varieties: 'Meyer' is fine-textured and dark green. *Zoysia tenuifolia* is light green and the finest textured of the Zoysias.

St. Augustine Grass

Stenotaphrum secundatum

St. Augustine grass, a warm-season, coarse-textured grass, is best suited to the Southeast coast and Florida. It is aggressive and spreads by branching stolons. St. Augustine grass develops into a thick spongy mat as stolons grow on top of one another. This grass is blue-green in color.

How to grow: St. Augustine grass will grow in full sun to full shade in humid climates. It is the most shade-tolerant of all the warm-season grasses. It prefers fertile, well-drained, sandy soil and is tolerant of salty conditions. It is moderately tolerant of wear. St. Augustine grass requires frequent watering to keep its vigor. Fertilize annually with 3 to 6 pounds of nitrogen per 1,000 square feet. Mow from 1½ to 2½ inches. The grass turns brown in winter if temperatures drop to 55°F. St. Augustine grass is started by cuttings; plant sprigs, plugs, or sod in spring or early fall.

Related varieties: 'Bitter Blue' is medium-textured and holds better color in cool weather. 'Floratine' is fine-textured and holds good winter color. 'Seville' is the most shade-tolerant variety. There are also variegated specimens that can be cultivated as basket plants.

Master Gardener Q & A

Commonly Asked Questions

Q: How should I raise the soil pH from a 5.0 to 6.5?
A: Apply lime in granular form as ground limestone at a rate of 4 to 5 pounds per 1000 square feet. Repeat in about six months; season is unimportant since lime (calcium) won't burn the plants. It takes a year or so to raise the pH to the desired level, and gradual application works better than one heavy treatment. Have the soil tested again the following year for further recommendations.

Q: What are the most common lawn weeds about which I should be concerned?
A: Naturally, the weeds you'll deal with will be different from those in another region, but general problems will be similar. The best weed control is prevention. A thick, healthy lawn has no bare soil where weeds can become a problem. Broad-leaved weeds—like dandelion and plantain—and annual grassy weeds—like crabgrass—can be kept under control with herbicides. Annual weeds will die in winter, scattering thousands of seeds for next year's onslaught. Use a preemergenct herbicide in spring to prevent those seeds from sprouting.

Q: How should I eliminate existing moss to rejuvenate the lawn?
A: The presence of moss indicates lack of sunlight and poor soil. Soils where mosses grow tend to be acidic, compacted, poorly aerated, and low in fertility. Remove the moss and freshly prepare the soil. Raise the pH with lime and add a complete fertilizer. Deeply cultivate the soil, adding organic matter and sand if necessary to improve drainage and aeration. Reseed or install sod of a shade-resistant turf species.

Q: When should I cut back my ornamental grasses?
A: Part of the beauty of ornamental grasses is their attractiveness in a winter garden—the seed stalks and foliage can be enjoyed throughout the winter. Then, just before the grasses begin their new growth, cut the dead part down. Cool-season varieties begin their growth in late winter; warm-season varieties begin when the soil has warmed significantly. To prevent damage to the emerging leaves, cut back the grasses before your plants break dormancy.

Q: How can I sketch my property to scale?
A: First, make a non-scaled sketch of your area, noting the dimensions of existing details. Next, use graph paper to sketch the plan to scale using each square to represent a certain distance (for example, one square equals one foot). Photocopy your sketch so you're able to try several different ideas without having to repeat the process. Remember that plants will grow, so sketch your layout as it would look, say, 10 years from now. By using scale during the planning process, you'll get a better perspective on your garden design.

Q: When shopping for a building lot, what characteristics should be considered to make my landscape planning easier?
A: First, consider your outdoor living areas. Do you need a large, flat area for the children to play? If so, don't buy a steep lot. Perhaps you'll want to plant a vegetable garden, or want another area that requires full sun; a wooded lot might not suit your needs. Use a list of your household's requirements for the property to determine if the lot can fill those needs.

Master Gardener Q & A

Q: It will be years before our trees grow large enough to shade our deck. Is there anything to do in the meantime?

A: A simple open trellis or arbor overhead will provide support for fast growing vines, annuals such as morning glories, or perennials such as clematis. An overhead structure identifies a comfortable living space while affording protection from the sun. Be sure to build the structure high enough for comfort, while realizing that cascading vines will take space.

Q: I need to make our backyard more private. Should I enclose the yard with a privacy fence?

A: Unless you need to keep people out, or keep children and pets in, you probably don't need the entire yard enclosed. Strategically placed sections or panels of fence in combination with small trees and large shrubs, for example, make for a more aesthetically pleasing atmosphere. An enclosure will make the yard seem small. Take advantage of neighboring trees and gardens to make your yard feel larger.

Natural borders brighten and seem to enlarge your yard.

Q: Is it important to collect the grass clippings when cutting the lawn?

A: Remove excessive amounts of clippings from tall grass, as they will smother and kill the grass underneath. A few species of turfgrass produce a heavy thatch buildup (matted, dead grass) that can prevent water, fertilizer, and air from getting into the soil, thus weakening the health of the lawn. Regular cutting will usually produce only light clippings that will quickly deteriorate—adding valuable nutrients back into the lawn.

Q: What time of year should I start a new lawn from seed?

A: It depends on the type of grass you plan to grow. Most likely, if you're planting seed, you'll be using a cool-season grass. It's best to prepare the soil at the end of the summer and sow seed about six weeks before the first average frost in your area. The seed will sprout during the remaining warm weeks and continue to develop deep roots through autumn and into winter. By mid-spring the lawn will be well established.

Q: Does it really matter whether I use fresh barnyard wastes and compost as opposed to old, seasoned organic matter?

A: Microorganisms that break down the vegetative matter use much of the available nutrients (especially nitrogen) from the soil. Material will decompose in a compost pile faster than if the matter is directly cultivated into the soils, as the microorganisms also need air. If fresh organic matter is used in or on top of the garden, you will need to apply additional nitrogen to protect plantings from a nutrient deficiency.

Getting Started with Gardening

1

Beginning with the Basics

The basic chores of gardening can be quite enjoyable, given the proper planning and the proper tools. Imagination, creativity, and knowledge are the best gardening tools available. This chapter contains the basic knowledge of how to garden. Creativity is limited only by your imagination. Outfit your garden shed with the basic essential equipment and you'll discover that only simple supplies are necessary. You'll learn from this chapter how to use these tools to properly prepare the soil to meet the needs of your new plantings.

Strong, healthy plants are better able to survive such difficulties as drought, insect infestations, and diseases. Less time will be needed for troubleshooting and nursing your garden if healthy soil is developed before planting. Getting your garden off to a good start means less work in the long run!

Also included is information about how to properly handle pregrown nursery plants. The hints in these sections will help you to reduce plant loss during the critical transplanting stages. You'll also learn what to look for when selecting plants at the nursery or garden center, so that you can be sure that the plants you buy are in good, healthy condition.

Study the information contained here before laying out and tilling your planting areas or purchasing any plants. You'll find the time spent studying this information in advance will save much future effort.

Tools for Gardening Projects

In any enterprise, the proper tools make the work much easier to accomplish. You don't necessarily need a large array of tools to garden successfully. The basic hand tools you will need include a hand trowel, a cultivator, a spading fork, a square-ended spade, an iron bow rake, a narrow-bladed hoe, a pair of small pruning shears, and a narrow-bladed paring knife or jackknife. Several additional tools worth considering are a hoe with a small blade that will fit into narrow spaces, a scuffle hoe, and a sprayer. Another piece of equipment that's handy, and saves a lot of time, is a large-wheeled garden cart for hauling.

When selecting tools, it's important to invest in good quality at the outset. Buying cheap tools is false economy. Not only do they make the work harder, they're likely to break as soon as stress is exerted on them. Thus, you save money by paying a higher price for one shovel every ten years than buying two or three at a marginally lower price over that same period.

Carefully study the construction of several different brands of each tool you're buying to determine which are most solidly built. Details to look for include wooden handles made of hickory or ash with the grain running straight along the full length of the handle; the metal portion fitted and securely attached to the wood portion—avoid those where a single rivet holds the entire tool together; a rolled edge along the top of the blade to allow more pushing surface for your foot; blade shanks that are reinforced rather than of a single thickness; and blade shanks that extend along the wooden handle for added strength.

Consult garden center employees. Ask them to point out the comparative advantages and disadvantages of each brand they carry. Confer with experienced gardening friends about which features they've found to be important.

In addition to the basic tools listed here, many other garden tools and gadgets are available. A wheelbarrow, for instance, can save lots of time. Invest in these tools only after you own the basics and gain quite a bit of hands-on gardening experience. Over time, you may conclude that some of these specialty tools would make your work easier; more often than not, you'll find that the basic tools you already have do the job satisfactorily. Buy others only as you experience a need for them.

Keep tools in top condition by storing them carefully in an area protected from the weather. Remove dirt and mud after each use, wiping the metal parts with a lightly oiled cloth. Periodically sharpen the blades on shovels and hoes, as well as on knives and shears. Hanging tools for storage helps keep blades sharp longer while also cutting down on storage area clutter.

Tools come in many shapes and sizes. Knowing which one is right for the job will prevent unnecessary purchases and save you time.

Necessary Garden Tools

Illustrated here are some basic tools and gardening equipment. Start with these, adding others only if you find a need for them. Items such as a garden cart, for example, may prove useful, but certainly are not essential. Prolong tool life by keeping them properly stored when not in use; wooden handles shrink from weathering, resulting in a loose tool-head that is impossible to use.

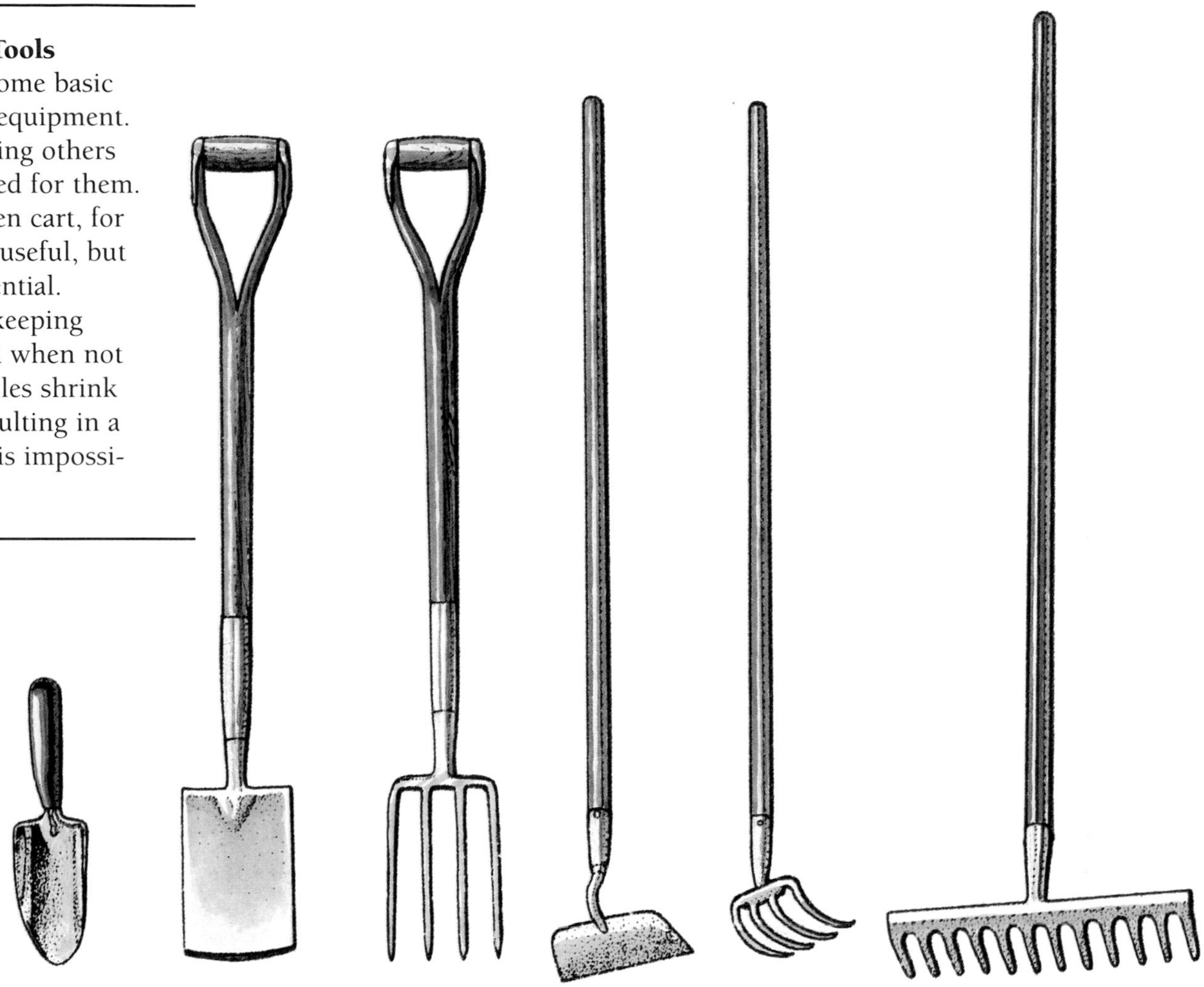

| Trowel | Spade | Fork | Hoe | Cultivator | Rake |

SHARPEN CUTTING TOOLS

Using a metal file, periodically sharpen the inside surface of your garden hoe and the underside surface of your spade. Sharp tools make for an effortless job when time is limited.

Zone Map

The United States Department of Agriculture Plant Hardiness Zone Map divides the United States into ten zones based on average minimum winter temperatures, with Zone 1 being the coldest in North America and Zone 10 the warmest. Each zone is further divided into sections that represent 5-degree differences within each 10-degree zone.

This map should only be used as a general guideline, since the lines of separation between zones are not as clear-cut as they appear. Plants recommended for one zone might do well in the southern part of the adjoining colder zone, as well as in the neighboring warmer zone. Factors such as altitude, exposure to wind, and amount of available sunlight also contribute to a plant's winter hardiness. (Because snow cover insulates plants, winters with little or no snow tend to be more damaging to marginally hardy varieties.) Also note that the indicated temperatures are average minimums—some winters will be colder and others warmer.

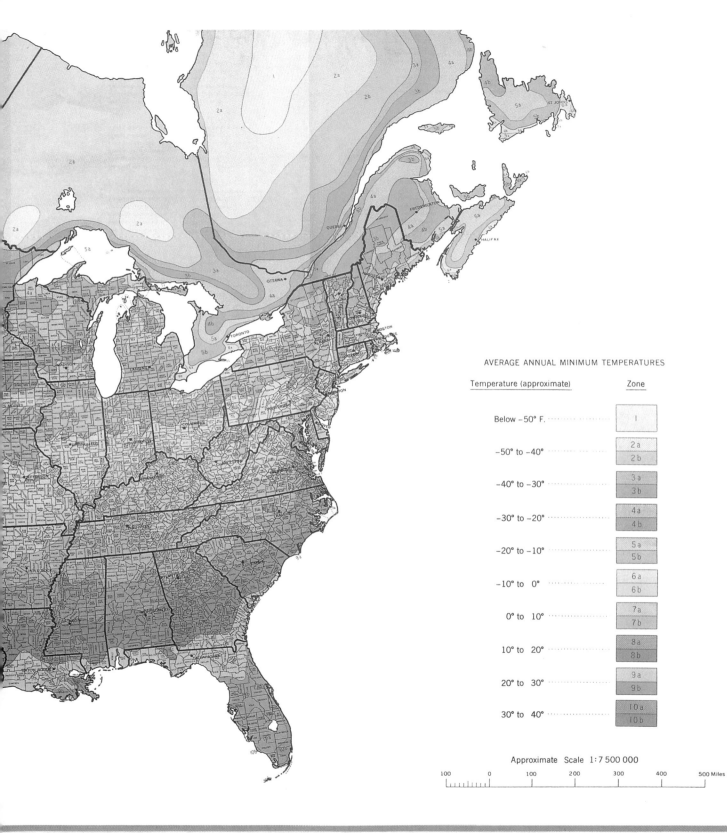

AVERAGE ANNUAL MINIMUM TEMPERATURES

Temperature (approximate)		Zone
Below −50° F.	....	1
−50° to −40°	....	2 a 2 b
−40° to −30°	....	3 a 3 b
−30° to −20°	....	4 a 4 b
−20° to −10°	....	5 a 5 b
−10° to 0°	....	6 a 6 b
0° to 10°	....	7 a 7 b
10° to 20°	....	8 a 8 b
20° to 30°	....	9 a 9 b
30° to 40°	....	10 a 10 b

Approximate Scale 1 : 7 500 000

100   0   100   200   300   400   500 Miles

Preparing the Soil

If you have a garden with rich, fertile soil, consider yourself lucky. Good garden soil is not easy to find. Most gardeners must improve on one or more conditions of their soil. If the results of your soil test indicate a lack of certain nutrients, you should follow the recommendations made by the testing company. If the imbalance is slight, organic fertilizers can be used. Because they generally contain a low percentage of nutrients that are slowly released into the soil, organic fertilizers are inadequate when fast results are needed or if the imbalance of nutrients is great. In these situations, inorganic fertilizers are the better choice.

Fertilizer is commonly formulated in some combination of the three major nutrients: nitrogen, phosphorous, and potassium (NPK). The numbers featured on each bag represent the percentage of each of these nutrients in the mix. The NPK formula should be listed on each container of organic fertilizer.

It's also possible to purchase fertilizers separately rather than in a three-nutrient mix. These are useful when there's a deficiency in a single nutrient. Consult your Cooperative Extension office or garden center staff if you have questions or feel uncertain about solving nutrient deficiency problems.

Adjusting the nutrient and pH levels in your soil will not make any difference in its consistency. Improving soil texture requires the addition of "soil conditioners." The most commonly used conditioners are leaf mold, well-rotted cow manure, peat moss, and compost. Vermiculite, perlite, and coarse builder's sand can also be added.

Although soil preparation can be an extensive job, the time and effort for treatment is well spent. Trees, shrubs, and perennials are long-term investments; proper installation will safeguard against the need for additional soil improvement. Without thorough preparation, you may sacrifice the health of your investment.

To properly prepare a planting bed, first remove any sod from the area, then rototill or hand dig the soil, turning it over thoroughly. If the area is rocky, remove as many stones as possible as you till. Next, spread the necessary fertilizer, soil conditioners, and pH-adjusting products over the area. Till again. You should be able to till the soil more deeply the second time. Ideally, you want to loosen and improve the soil to a depth of more than 8 inches (bad soils may require 10-12 inches).

Now is the perfect time to install some kind of mowing strip around the garden bed. Patio squares or slate pieces laid end-to-end at ground level will keep grass and flowers from intermixing. Other options can include landscape logs, poured concrete strips, or bricks laid side-by-side on a sand or concrete base. The mowing strip must be deep enough and wide enough so grass roots cannot tunnel underneath or travel across the top to reach the flower bed, and the top of the strip must not extend above the level of the adjacent lawn.

Ground limestone, used to raise the pH level of acidic soil, should be spread evenly and then tilled into the soil.

Planting Preparations

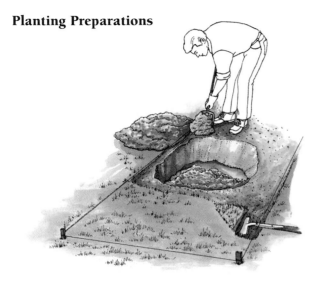

1 Mark the boundaries with string or a garden hose. Cut with a spade and remove the sod from the entire bed. Till and remove rocks as you proceed. For individual trees, use a spade to prepare an area at least two times the size of the root ball.

2 Spread organic matter to improve soil quality. If the soil needs greatly improved drainage, other soil conditioners, such as perlite or sand, should be added. The volume of soil will increase; mound the bed slightly—the organic matter will eventually deteriorate and the bed will settle to its original level.

3 Cultivate the bed a second time to thoroughly incorporate these additions. This second digging will allow the tiller to loosen soil to a greater depth than could be achieved by tilling only once. The more permanent your planting will be, the more important deep preparation becomes.

4 Install an edging strip around the bed. The top of the strip should be at ground level to allow the wheel of the lawn mower to run along it. Correct installation will save many hours of maintenance each year by preventing grass from spreading into the landscape bed.

Selecting Quality Plants

Landscape plants available in the United States are generally of high quality. Whether you make your purchases through a local greenhouse or nursery, a chain store, or a roadside stand, you'll usually find vigorous, insect- and disease-free plants. What's more, with rare exceptions, these offerings can be relied upon to be correctly labeled.

Because of this consistently good quality, it's possible to buy plants wherever you find the best price on the variety you want. However, before buying, be sure that it really is the lowest price. Bedding plants and perennials are generally sold in packs and small containers. Unless you need to evaluate the color of the flowers, the presence of blooms is unimportant. In fact, annuals that are not flowering in the pack tend to establish root systems quicker than those that are in bloom, resulting in side branching and abundant flowering. To ensure an easy transition from the greenhouse to the garden, purchase plants at nurseries or garden centers at the proper planting time. Young annuals are tender. If these plants need to sit for a few days before planting, be sure to attend to their needs. Keep them outside in bright light, but protected from the afternoon sun and wind. Check the soil moisture daily; bedding plants dry out quickly and will need regular watering. Each time bedding plants wilt down some of their strength is lost.

Trees, shrubs, and vines that have been grown in containers may be purchased and planted any time the ground isn't frozen. Moving a plant from a container to the garden does not shock the plant as does digging from a nursery row. Look for plants with vigorous growth, that are well-rooted but not crowded in the container, and no visible signs of pests or damage.

Landscape plants that have been dug from the nursery, with root-ball wrapped in fabric, are known as "balled and burlapped" (B&B). Purchase B&B plants only during spring and fall—their root systems are most actively growing and are able to overcome the shock of disturbance. Pick plants that appear to have been freshly dug. A loose ball of roots indicates damage—choose another specimen. Choose trees carefully; the trunk and branching habit has been determined and may not be reversible.

❧ *Multiplant packs are often cheaper than individual plants, but don't be lured into buying more than you need for your garden.*

What to Look for in Container-Grown Plants

Look for these signals when selecting plants grown in containers. They'll go a long way toward indicating how long the plant has been in the container and how it's been cared for during that time. Strong, vital plants that have been given good care have a far better chance of surviving when transplanted into the garden. It's always best to transplant as soon as possible—just a few days of neglect will cause damage.

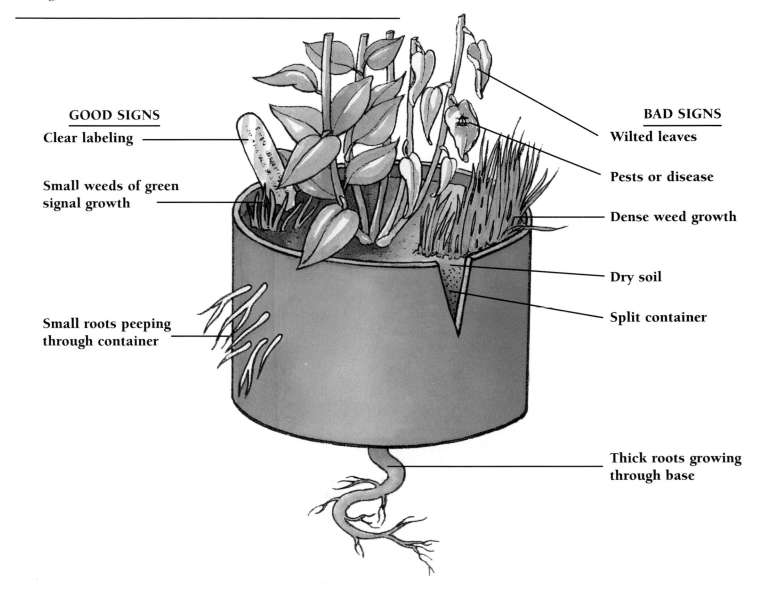

GOOD SIGNS

Clear labeling

Small weeds of green signal growth

Small roots peeping through container

BAD SIGNS

Wilted leaves

Pests or disease

Dense weed growth

Dry soil

Split container

Thick roots growing through base

Shopping the Nursery Versus Buying Mail-Order

Once you've studied the situation in your garden and have a good idea of the trees, shrubs, and other plants you wish to purchase, it's time to go shopping. The question is where.

Most amateur gardeners look no further than local nurseries for their plants. These growers offer a wide variety of sizes of the most popular plants, and you can pick exactly the specimen you feel would look best on your property. Furthermore, nursery employees are usually very knowledgeable about which plants do best in your area. Don't hesitate to ask questions.

🌱 *Local nurseries usually stock common plants (like these impatiens). The exotic may have to be found elsewhere.*

The main difficulty with local nurseries is a lack of choice. They tend to stick to the tried and true. If you are looking for a specific species or variety, the nursery may not be able to help you. If you live near a major urban center, you may find among the local nurseries a few that specialize in less common trees, shrubs, vines, and perennials. Those nurseries are good places to shop for more unusual varieties.

It may surprise novice gardeners to discover that many nurseries operate by mail order. Mail order is an excellent way to find particular species and varieties that are not available locally. Mail-order nurseries are generally reputable companies with many years of experience in serving customers. But beware of those that seem to offer too much for your money. They often fail to mention the original size of the tree, which may be barely more than a rooted cutting, or they may offer seedlings of unproven value. When dealing with this sort of nursery, you may find the money you saved would have been better spent on a smaller number of larger or better-quality plants bought from a more trustworthy source.

Some mail-order nurseries are specialists that deal only in dwarf conifers, windbreaks, trees with variegated foliage, or some other unique category. Their plants are often expensive (some of the offered plants are extremely rare and hard to multiply), but they are often the only source of many less common trees, shrubs, vines, and perennials. They usually offer a wide range of sizes. If you are looking for a rare but expensive plant, you might be willing to buy a smaller specimen and watch it grow.

Whenever possible, try to buy from a mail-order nursery that is located in a climate similar to yours. The plants you buy will already be well-adapted to your growing conditions. Spring is the best time to order outside of your area. Plants ordered in the fall, especially from Southern nurseries, may not go dormant in time for early autumn freezes in the North.

Be sure to check state regulations regarding plant purchases. You may find some plants cannot be sent to your area. Most citrus-producing states, for example, will not allow citrus produced in other states to be brought within their borders. Such information is usually printed in the catalog.

Plants will be shipped to your home via mail or some other carrier. Upon arrival, open the package and inspect your purchase. Little time is given for damage claims on perishable items. Woody plants are often shipped "bare-root;" soil removed, the roots system is wrapped in damp moss or wood shavings and packaged in plastic. The plant will be dormant, so you won't notice much life. Plant according to the instructions with your package. The weekend gardener may have to postpone planting for several days. Don't despair; plants can be safely stored for several days until planting. Dormant plants—perennials and small woody plants—can be repackaged in plastic and put in the refrigerator. Larger plants and those with visible growth can be opened and placed in a cool shed; keep roots moist but don't submerge the roots for any longer than a day.

You'll receive potted perennials and annuals when they are in an actively growing state. If you can't plant them immediately, treat them as you would treat tender annuals purchased early in the season. Unpack the plants to provide good air circulation, water regularly, and protect them

BUYING WILD COLLECTED WILDFLOWERS AND BULBS

The increasing popularity of gardening with wildflowers has stepped up the demand for many of these rare beauties. Unfortunately, because many beautiful species are slow to grow and difficult to propagate for nursery production, wildflowers and native plants are being collected from native stands and sold to gardeners. When purchasing wildflowers, investigate their origin—whether nursery propagated and grown, or collected. By cutting the demand for collected plants, our rapidly decreasing stands of native plants will survive for future generations to enjoy.

❧ *While it might be tempting to pick a few wildflowers along the roadside to add to your garden—don't. The natural supply is dwindling.*

Chapter
2
Care and Feeding

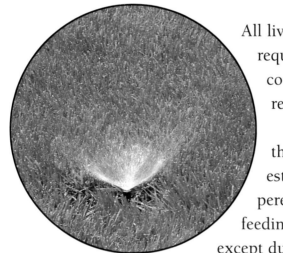

All living plants need to be tended to, though some species require more care than others. You may not be able to control the sunshine and weather, but the gardener can regulate the plant's nutritional and moisture supplies.

Water is as necessary to plant growth and health as the availability of plant nutrients. For most of your established plantings—trees, shrubs, vines, and perennials—an annual application of fertilizer is all the feeding you'll need, and nature will supply their water needs except during cases of extreme drought. Annuals and container plantings require a more regulated watering and feeding program. You'll find ideas in the next few pages that will make the feeding and watering tasks easier—in fact, you may actually enjoy trying some of these suggestions.

Weeds, being plants, have the same requirements as your ornamental plants. Thus, weed establishment creates a competition for the essential water and nutrients—with fast-growing weeds often winning. This chapter suggests ways to eliminate the need for hand weeding by weed prevention. Once weeds begin to compete for water and nutrients, the garden plants begin to suffer. With little effort, an aggressive weed prevention plan will prohibit their establishment.

Quenching a Plant's Thirst

🌺 *A steady supply of water is as essential for a healthy, growing plant as sunlight and good soil.*

If plants receive the water they need—whether from nature or irrigation—they'll respond with vigorous growth and numerous blooms. It's not easy, especially at first, to gauge exactly when plants require water—so much depends upon current weather and soil conditions. How do you judge when to water and how much water to give? The one sure way to test is by poking your finger several inches into the soil and feeling how moist or dry it is. Don't rely on a visual test: Leaves begin to wilt after drought damage has begun, and surface soil can appear dry though ample moisture is present underneath.

It's especially necessary to water new plants the first season after planting whenever nature doesn't supply enough rain. The new root systems need a little extra care to become reestablished in their new location. After the first year, most perennial plants can sustain themselves without watering, except during exceptionally dry spells. Annual flowers may require more frequent watering—the soil surface dries first and their root systems don't extend as deeply as most perennial plants. Mulching the plant bed helps retain moisture in the soil by preventing excessive evaporation.

When you do water, water deeply. Generally, actively growing garden plants need about an inch of water per week—less of a concern when plants are dormant in winter. If not supplied by nature, the watering job is yours. A good approach is to use an automatic watering sprinkler, letting it gently "rain" for an extended period of time. Set up an empty can to collect irrigation water to determine the time it takes for your sprinkler to deliver an inch of water. Additionally, check at half-hour intervals to see how deeply the water has penetrated. Turn the water off when the soil is moistened to a two-inch soil depth. Don't water again until your testing indicates the need.

One problem with sprinkler water is that the foliage becomes very wet, creating an ideal environment for the spread of fungus diseases. In addition, flower clusters heavy with water are more likely to bend and break or to become mildewed.

The best way to water is with a soaker hose, which can be snaked through beds, hidden by a light layer of mulch, and kept in place for the duration of the growing season. The water slowly oozes from the hose's many tiny holes for several hours—even overnight. All of the water soaks directly on the soil and down to the plant roots without any waste or damage.

Drip irrigation is another excellent slow-soaking system that is a sensible alternative for those who have large plant beds or who garden in climates where irrigation is constantly needed for cultivated plants to survive. Once the system is laid out, it can remain in place year after year. In areas that freeze, however, a drip irrigation system must be drained for the winter.

Soaker Hose Watering

An easy way to provide deep watering of landscape beds is to weave a soaker hose through the bed, leaving the connector end near the outside edge. Mulch can conceal a soaker hose without disruption. A quick connector on the soaker hose allows speedy attachment to the regular garden hose whenever watering is needed. When soil is well-soaked, the garden hose can easily be disconnected and stored out of the way until it's needed again.

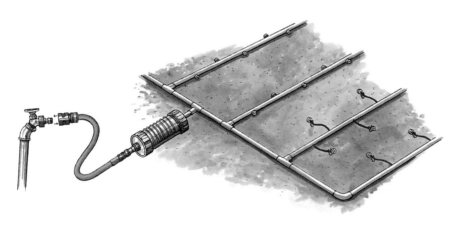

Drip Irrigation Watering

In areas where there is little natural rainfall, a drip irrigation system run by a timer may be the appropriate, carefree watering method. Suitable for beds, individual plants, and container gardening, it allows slow, deep watering directly to each plant's roots. Tiny tubes or sprinklers apply the water to each individual plant, or small groups of plants, with minimal water wastage. This helps keep foliage dry, thus reducing the possibility of the spread of diseases.

Plants with Water Dams

As plants are being put in the garden, build a collar of soil encircling each plant. Rain and irrigation water will collect rather than immediately run off, giving the water time to soak in around the plant's roots. Where flower beds are level, this isn't essential, but when planting on a slope, a dam is a great help. The dam disappears after time and is not necessary to rebuild.

Benefits of Deep Watering

When plants are watered infrequently but heavily, they'll develop large and deep root networks. Frequent light waterings cause plants to develop shallow root systems just below the soil surface. This causes plants to be poorly anchored, subject to toppling in heavy wind or rain, and prone to wilting unless they're watered daily. Therefore, slow, deep-soak watering produces stronger and hardier plants. Whenever possible, water during the cool part of the day.

Bubbler Wand for Watering Individual Plants

To water a few individual plants rather than the entire flower bed, a bubbler wand can be connected to the garden hose. This device breaks the pressure of the water as it leaves the hose, allowing slow watering without water runoff or soil erosion. Water under the plant at the root zone, keeping the leaves and flowers dry as wet foliage promotes the spread of mildew.

Benefits of an Automatic Sprinkler

You'll benefit from using an automatic sprinkler on lawns and large plant beds—especially after fertilizer has been recently broadcasted or side-dressed. The water covers a large area, ensuring that the fertilizer is evenly dissolved and worked into the soil. Although the leaves and flowers of most landscape plants prefer to stay dry, a sprinkler is a portable and convenient method of irrigation without a major expense. When not in use, the sprinkler is easily stored.

Keeping Weeds at Bay

The weekend gardener doesn't have much time to spend pulling unwanted weeds. The most time-efficient weed control is prevention—get them before they get you! Weed seeds are quick to germinate and they grow rapidly. As soon as they're brought to within an inch of the soil surface through digging and cultivating, they'll begin to sprout.

In established garden beds, where you're not planning on sowing flower seeds, the use of a preemergent herbicide (which prevents weed-seed germination) is recommended. Sprinkle the granules on the freshly prepared soil or around the already planted flowers, ground covers, shrubs, or trees. Apply preemergent weed control to established lawns to prevent annual weeds, such as crabgrass, from invading. Take care not to apply the chemical to newly seeded lawn areas, as it will prevent your grass seed from germinating. Be sure to keep any pets away from areas that have been treated with chemicals.

Weeds that have been previously established—especially deep-rooted perennial weeds—are controlled most easily by spraying a contact herbicide. These herbicides, available in a ready-to-use spray formulation, can be sprayed directly on the foliage when there is no threat of rain for 24 hours. Within a week or two, the weeds will have died.

The most popular way of dramatically reducing weed problems is by using some kind of mulch. Mulch is a layer of organic or inorganic material laid on the soil surface to shade out weeds, retain soil moisture, and have a moderating effect on soil temperature.

Many materials can achieve these results, but some are more practical, less expensive, easier to handle, and more attractive than others. The list of organic mulches includes: pine needles, leaves, straw, dried seaweed, tree bark strips, bark chunks, sawdust, wood chips, cocoa bean hulls, and cotton seed hulls. Inorganic mulches include "blankets" made from sheets of porous landscape fabric disguised with a thin layer of decorative, organic mulch.

Perhaps the choice of which kind of mulch to use isn't as important as the decision to use some kind of mulch. If it's an organic mulch, it will improve the quality of the soil as it breaks down and adds to what gardeners call "soil tilth."

Some mulching material is not very pleasing to the eye. Other organic mulches may alter the soil chemistry as they break down (annual soil tests will detect these changes so you can adjust fertilizer applications to compensate). Still other types have an odor when they're fresh or may prove too expensive for use in large quantities.

Still, there must be at least one among all of the alternatives that will satisfy your needs. The use of a mulch will dramatically reduce the weed problems in any garden. However, if for some reason a mulch is not used, continued hand cultivation of the top inch of soil will be necessary to expose roots of young weeds to the sun's drying rays.

Wood chips make a simple and attractive organic mulch. They are easy to handle and blend well with the landscape.

Using a Preemergent Chemical

Granules of a preemergent chemical can be scattered on the soil to prevent weed seeds from sprouting. Because it kills all seeds, do not use a preemergent treatment in any area where you have recently planted, or plan to plant, flower seeds.

Planting in Landscape Fabric Mulch

Landscape fabric mulch can be laid before planting. Spread landscape fabric over prepared soil and dress it with decorative mulch. Cut holes to plant individual plants. The landscape fabric will allow water to seep into the ground while preventing weeds from growing to the surface.

Mulching

Mulching keeps weeds down, almost entirely eliminating the need for weeding. It helps retain moisture in the soil, reducing the need for watering, and gives the garden a neat, cared-for appearance. It also evens out soil temperatures so plants suffer less damage from extremes of heat and cold.

Cultivation of Nonmulched Areas

Where no mulch is used, frequent cultivation of the top inch of soil is the best way to control weeds. Newly germinated weed seedlings die quickly when stirred up this way.

Feeding Alternatives

🐚 *A pleasing balance can be reached by placing taller plants behind shorter ones. Set against a backdrop of trees, these snapdragons overlook zinnias.*

As mentioned in the Landscape Design section, the best course to follow is to have your garden soil tested each year, then follow the recommendations given with your test results. Knowing which nutrients are needed helps cut down on the number of choices, but still leaves the decision of whether to use an organic or inorganic source up to you.

As you study the NPK formula on each plant food, you'll notice that organic fertilizers contain much lower percentages of nutrients per pound than do inorganic fertilizers. This can become a problem when you're trying to adjust a large garden bed's nutrient content at the beginning of a new planting. You may find that, in order to raise the nutrients to the recommended level, you'll have to add four inches of the organic material. This can be done if the area to be covered is small, but for large areas, it could become unwieldy. In these cases it's more practical to make major adjustments with inorganics, then proceed with organics for minor adjustments in future years.

Fertilizers are applied in a dry granular form or mixed with water for a liquid application. Regular granular forms, such as 5-10-10, are good, but only last in the soil for about four weeks. Slow-release, pelleted fertilizers are better because they dissolve into the soil over an extended period of time, releasing essential nutrients throughout the growing season. Although slow-release fertilizers may cost more, a single application in the spring is all that is necessary. The granular types should be broadcast over the soil surface and dug in. Liquid applications can be made with a hand sprayer or a siphon-proportioner (a special mixing attachment for your garden hose).

Applications of liquid fertilizers are good for a quick-fix situation. The nutrients are dissolved in water and directly available to the plant. To supply food for immediate use by new transplants, a weak solution of water-soluble fertilizer (either fish emulsion or an inorganic type) can be poured from a watering can directly around each plant. Thereafter, a couple of side-dressings of granular plant food sprinkled around each plant at two-week intervals should carry annuals through the end of summer.

For best absorption, fertilize when the soil is moist. Take care to apply it on the soil rather than on the plant leaves. The plants, your hands, and the fertilizer should be dry when you fertilize. Caution: Always wash your hands after handling fertilizer.

Even though the level of nutrients in compost is low, the addition of organic matter to your soil will drastically improve its workability. Compost is made by combining plant wastes with soil and fertilizer, allowing them to decompose for several months, then mixing them back into the garden.

Composting

Because making your own compost takes several months, many gardeners find it easier to purchase bagged compost. Either way, compost is a good additive for soils low in organic materials. Added to clay soil, compost lightens the soil and improves aeration; added to sandy soils, compost improves water-holding capacity.

Side-dressing

Granular fertilizers release nutrients more quickly than organic fertilizers. Sprinkling a handful of 5-10-5 around each plant (known as side-dressing) in spring and again in midsummer will give annuals a feeding boost that will keep them in top growing and flowering condition through the summer. Use slow-release fertilizers once in the spring.

Liquid Fertilizer Solution

Liquid fertilizer is an immediate source of nutrients. The concentrated form is diluted by mixing with water according to the manufacturer's directions. Use a mild solution on new transplants to help them quickly recover from the shock. Liquid fertilizer can be applied in place of granular side-dressings.

Keeping Ahead of Pests

You'll probably meet many kinds and sizes of pests as they visit your garden. Some will be as obvious as a rabbit finding your tender hosta leaves a delicacy. Other pests, such as fungi, can multiply invisibly until it covers your favorite phlox. Pests come in many shapes. Everyone is familiar with insects and mites—those tiny creatures who chew the leaves, leaving a Swiss cheese effect; or pierce the stem, sucking the essential nutrients from the plant. But these aren't the only garden nuisances. Rodents will burrow under plants and eat their roots; slugs and snails will invade a cool, moist garden, leaving holes in every plant in sight; weeds can consume an untended bed, choking out the finer flowers or ground covers. You know you need to rid your garden of these problems; however, using a chemical pesticide is not always the best solution. In many instances, the onset of a garden pest can be prevented by some simple and inexpensive preventive cultural practices.

There is much the gardener can do to prevent pest problems. It's important to know that complete eradication of a pest is neither practical nor wise. With eradication of one species, a more damaging species may overpopulate. The first measure is to determine the amount of control that is necessary.

Since plants that are weakened by drought and poor cultural practices are most susceptible to pests, give your garden the necessary care to keep the plants strong and healthy. Preventing pest problems is the easiest and most economical approach.

Choose pest-free plants when shopping and swapping plants with your gardener friends. Careful plant selection could make the difference between a healthy, hassle-free garden and one that is trouble-ridden. Inspect under the plant's leaves for insects, mites, or eggs, and check the pot for invasive species of weeds. There is no sense inviting difficult-to-control pests into the garden.

Garden sanitation also plays an important role in plant pest prevention. Remove diseased plants and their debris from the beds. If a bed of annuals had a particularly difficult pest problem, remove all evidence of that planting, and plan on using a different type of annual the following

Slugs and snails leave little behind after they prey upon your plants. It's important to detect pests early.

year. Otherwise, some of the insects or disease organisms may overwinter and start the infestation again. Because many pests specifically attack a certain type of plant, avoid using that type of bedding plant for a year or two. You may discover that certain trees or shrubs are prone to a particular pest in your area. Avoid using such plants in your garden and you'll prevent the disappointment of having to nurse a plant back to health.

To prevent leaf and flower diseases, overhead watering should be finished early in the day so the foliage and flowers have time to dry before nightfall. Disease organisms thrive on damp foliage, and they're much easier to prevent than to control once established.

Safety with Pesticides

When maintaining a landscape, whether lawns, flower beds, or trees, there is no doubt you'll use some sort of pesticide. It's wise to understand some basics about pesticides, as well as using common sense for safety when around pesticides.

Pesticides are substances that are used to control pests. They include insecticides, herbicides, and others. For a pesticide to be effective, it must interfere with the normal development of the pest without doing harm to the host. This doesn't mean all pests will be eliminated. In fact, your pest problem might not be severe enough to warrant the use of a chemical. For instance, a few dandelions in the lawn or beetles on a shrub can easily be removed by hand. Non-chemical controls are often feasible, without risk to the gardener or the environment.

Safety when handling, mixing, applying, and storing pesticides is critical. Most poisoning occurs during the mixing process. Splashing concentrated chemical on the skin or in the eyes, for instance, can be prevented by wearing long sleeves and trousers, rubber gloves, and safety goggles. Read the pesticide label and follow the directions each time the pesticide is used. Follow the directions precisely—the proper dose and calibrations have already been scientifically calculated for the most effective use. The instructions will list which plants it may be safely applied to, and which individual pests it will control. Don't assume that all insecticides will control all insects, and likewise with weed-killers—they are formulated very specifically.

Insecticides are pesticides that are used to control insect pests. You'll first need to accurately identify the pest in order to choose the best means of control. Insecticides that control root-feeding insects may be applied as granules with a lawn spreader or as liquid with a sprayer. Top-feeding insects, which feed on the leaves of turf and ornamental plants, are best controlled by spraying the pesticide and allowing it to dry on the foliage.

Selective herbicides—pesticides that control weeds—are chemicals used on lawns and, to a lesser degree, in beds of newly planted ground covers and shrub borders. Weeds are divided into two main categories. Perennials live for many years; annuals live for one season and then reseed. Preemergent herbicides are used to prevent the germination of many weed species, mostly annuals. They are usually used early in the spring to prevent weeds, such as crabgrass, from germinating in late spring. Postemergent herbicides are directly applied to newly germinated or established weeds. Broad-leaf weeds and perennial grasses are most often treated with a postemergent herbicide.

Nonselective herbicides kill any green plant the chemical comes in contact with. When using a nonselective herbicide, keep the spray nozzle close to the weeds and never apply during breezy or windy weather.

🌿 *Use extra caution when applying chemicals near entrances, windows, or living spaces.*

Master Gardener Q & A

Commonly Asked Questions

Q: Which type of pruning shears is best?

A: There are basically two types of pruning shears: anvil and scissors. A good quality pair of shears should last many years. An advantage the scissors type has over the anvil is that it won't crush the stem while cutting. Good shears can be taken apart for sharpening, and replacement parts can be easily obtained for high quality models. Long-handled lopping shears are helpful when thinning shrubs and cutting larger stock than hand pruners can cut.

Q: Although I understand the benefits of using compost in the garden, I will probably never be disciplined enough to build and maintain a pile. What can I use instead?

A: Many municipalities have old piles of leaf mold—from autumn collection—that is free for the taking. Arm yourself with a few plastic bags and a shovel and head for the lot. Another option is purchasing composted manure from a stable or barnyard. You can also buy dehydrated manure or compost and incorporate it into the soil as you would with fresh compost.

Q: My neighbors have no problem growing a beautiful camellia, but after many failures, I've stopped planting them. Their soil seems the same as mine.

A: The successful camellia is probably growing in a microclimate that may not exist on your property. A protected microclimate is a good situation to try marginally hardy plant species, since it's protected from extreme daily temperature changes and winter winds. Visit your neighbors' site and try to determine the origin of the unique location—you may have a site that is equally suitable.

Q: I'm looking for a particular cultivar that I can only find through mail order. Is it safe to buy plants from another temperature zone?

A: If you know the type of plant will grow in your climate, you should have no problem—if it's a spring purchase. If the nursery's zone is warmer than yours, specify a safe ship date for your area. The newly installed plant will have all summer to acclimate to your seasons, and should survive the upcoming winter.

Q: There are a bewildering number of varieties available of the kind of plant I'm looking for. How do I make a wise decision as to which variety to purchase?

A: Sometimes the color of the bloom is the only difference in variety, making the choice one of personal preference. Other times the differences are more drastic, such as a resistance to a disease that may be prevalent in your area; and still other times the difference may be in the ultimate height, width, or form of the plant. Read nursery catalogs and talk to garden center salespeople to determine which varieties interest you and best suit your conditions.

Q: What does it mean to have "well-drained soil"?

A: Although it's necessary for your soil to have water available for your plants, too much water held for long periods of time will disturb the balance of air that is necessary for healthy root growth of most plant species. Without air in the soil, many plants will likely drown. Loam, a balance of sand, clay, and organic matter, is usually well-drained. Heavily compacted clay soils are often poorly drained.

Master Gardener Q & A

Commonly Asked Questions

Q: Being a weekend gardener, I'm not sure I want to spend the energy necessary to double-dig my new perennial bed. What are the advantages?

A: Double-digging provides a better quality soil for the deep roots that many perennials develop. Remember, perennials are long-lived plants, and the time and effort you use to develop a perfect growing environment is well spent. Imagine your investment withering up a few years after planting because the soil 12 inches under the surface is too compact for the roots to develop properly!

Q: How can proper site and plant selection make insect management easier?

A: There are many types of landscape plants that are virtually pest free (or at least pest resistant). Find out which pests are a problem in your area, and steer clear of plants that attract such pests. Additionally, a plant that is growing out of its optimal environment—full sun as opposed to partial shade—may not be able to support the beneficial insect predators that normally keep the pests at bay.

Q: I have seen collections of perennials, trees, and bulbs advertised so inexpensively that it's hard to resist purchase. Are such bargains worth the price?

A: Beware of such bargains—you get what you pay for. The trees, shrubs, and perennials are often no more than rooted cuttings, six inches tall—and sometimes they're species that won't thrive in your climatic conditions. Bulb collections are often an inferior quality of small size or outdated cultivars; they may take several years to become large enough to bloom.

Q: How do I select which shade tree is the right one for our property?

A: Determine the height, width, and density of shade needed for the site. Also decide how important the rate of growth is to your plan. Consider the environmental conditions—temperature zone, soil type, light exposure of your proposed tree site, and how much pest control you are willing to use. Take this information and compile a list of possibilities—with help from catalogs or by talking to local gardeners. Then go to a local garden center or botanical garden to see your choices.

Ornamental trees (such as this prunus*) can provide shade in the summer, as well as a brilliant display of flowers in spring and dazzling color in fall.*

Annuals

1

Planning a Seasonal Kaleidoscope of Color

Annuals are those plants that go through an entire life cycle—germinate, grow, flower, produce seed, and die—all in a single growing season. Generally, they reach the point of flower production within six to eight weeks after sprouting and continue in abundant bloom until they're killed by frost. In some parts of the United States, perennials that would not survive a severe winter are used as annuals for seasonal color.

It's no wonder, then, that annuals are such a boon to gardeners! Most grow quickly and easily, provide a long season of color, and require minimal special care at very low cost. They also offer a wondrous variety of sizes, flower forms, and leaf types from which to choose. A gardener's problem is not whether to grow annuals—it's how to narrow the choice to those few that space allows.

In this first chapter, we'll discuss some of the important factors to be considered when planning the planting of annuals. Subjects include how soil and light conditions affect plant choices; the palette of colors, forms, and textures available from annuals; and the attractive ways in which various plantings of annuals can beautify your landscape. We'll also suggest ways the gardener with limited time can use color—from annuals—throughout the seasons to set and change the mood.

Color, Form, Texture, and Scale

🌿 *With so many colors and types of annuals available, your choices are limited only by your imagination.*

Annual plantings will have more impact if, as part of the planning process, you consider everything that each variety has to offer. Frequently, we think only about the color of the flowers annuals produce: Will a pale pink petunia look best beside blue ageratum, or would a bright one pink be better?

Color is an important factor, but many plants have even more to offer. Keep in mind that color comes not only from bloom. It can come from foliage and seedpods as well. Annuals may have both colorful blooms and foliage of an unusual texture or color: bold-leaved geraniums and nasturtiums; heart-shaped morning glory and moonvine foliage; purple-red cockscomb leaves; or feathery cosmos and baby's breath.

Some annuals are grown primarily, or even exclusively, for their foliage. Outstanding examples are silvery gray dusty miller, rich purple basil and perilla, and the myriad colors of coleus. Finally, there are those annuals primarily treasured for their seedpods. This group includes decorative peppers, ornamental eggplants, and purple-beaned dolichos.

Another decorative aspect of plants is their texture or surface. Compare the large, coarse texture of the sunflower to the fine, soft bachelor's button. Fill masses with fine-textured plants and reserve heavier-textured annuals for contrast or accent. Most often we think of foliage as the sole textural source, when texture can be added equally often by flowers.

Besides color and texture, the form of flowers and of the overall growth habit of the plant needs to be considered. Flower forms include tall spikes, round globes, sprays, and clusters. Plant forms range from tall and skinny to low and spreading.

In addition, scale (the size of the plant) must be kept in mind. Miniature plants are great to use in small spaces and where people are close enough to see them, but in a large area they can become completely lost. On the other hand, large-growing plants such as spider plants, cosmos, and nasturtiums may dominate and even smother out smaller neighbors when space is limited. In general, plant taller, spike-type annuals in the background of mixed beds, while reserving closer foreground seats for smaller, delicate beauties.

When selecting plants to be combined in a garden, all of these factors should be taken into consideration at the time of planning. The design will be more effective if a pleasing mixture of contrasting textures, colors, and plant and flower forms is used.

Learn to look for the bonus a plant may offer. Try to discover the best plant for a given location, rather than settling for one that happens to be readily available. Above all, don't worry about making a bad choice. The beauty of gardening with annuals is that you get another chance every growing season!

The Varied Characteristics of Annuals

Color

Flowers are not the sole source of color in annual gardens. Many plants such as this dramatic purple perilla and more muted silver-gray dusty miller are treasured for their foliage alone. Others (such as cockscombs) have both colorful foliage and flowers. Still others—ornamental peppers, eggplants, and dolichos, for instance—provide garden color with their attractive fruits.

Scale

A variety of scale can be provided by both flowers and plants. Here, a large, wide-spreading cosmos and compact coreopsis provide similar flowers on different-sized plants. Other species (zinnias, for example) offer a wide range of flower sizes and forms on plants that are all similar in form and size.

Form

The broad, velvety leaves of this flowering tobacco, as well as its tall spikes of trumpet-shaped flowers, are a complete contrast in form to the low-spreading impatiens. Try interplanting tall, open annuals with a spreading carpet of contrasting form. A garden is more visually stimulating when a variety of forms are used.

Texture

This cloud of baby's breath illustrates the role that texture can play in a garden. A bed planted with open, airy plants would appear to be a floating mist. By contrast, a bold, massive planting such as these marigolds would be heavy and solid-looking. Mixing plants of differing textures provides a pleasant variety and balance.

Massing Colors

It's only natural for the gardener—who has few free hours to putter in the yard—to want the most dramatic result from the least amount of effort. Like a mountainside dressed in autumn glory, who can resist the abundance of color from a river of red and blue salvia?

The easiest, most straightforward way to use annuals is to select one favorite and flood the entire planting area with it. This approach eliminates deciding where to plant a particular variety, selecting which colors and textures blend together effectively, or learning the cultural requirements for more than one kind of plant. Once you've determined the soil preparation requirements of a particular species, the entire bed can be prepared and planted in a day.

Certainly, the impact of all one kind and color of bloom can be dramatic. Imagine an entire garden awash with fiery red geraniums or bold, yellow marigolds; fluorescent-pink fibrous begonias or cooling white petunias!

Variations of this approach are also possible. For those who prefer variety of color, but the same kind of plant, a checkerboard design would allow the use of large clumps of several different colors from a single species. The lipstick shades of impatiens work well in this kind of massing—geraniums would, too.

Alternatively, some species come in an abundant variety of flower and plant sizes. A bed filled with zinnias, for example, could include everything from dwarf 10- to 12-inch mounds in front to giant three- to four-foot-tall background clumps, with a wide range of flower colors and sizes in single, double, and spider forms. Marigolds are another species that grow in great variety, all of which are extremely vigorous and practically foolproof.

Another way to mass annuals is to keep to a single color but use several different plant varieties. The resulting garden would contain plants of different forms and heights with a variety of different flower shapes, all in varying shades of one color. A unique option for this style of massing would be a silver-gray garden!

Whichever design option is selected, massed plantings are generally rather formal looking—bold and dramatic rather than homey or quaint. They're the perfect complement to a large or formal house. Massing can also provide a clean, uncluttered look where garden space is severely limited.

For something simple, easy, and different, consider the massed approach. Using annuals for this purpose allows the added option of changing the entire look of your yard every growing season simply by selecting a different plant or color. However, if that's too much bother, you can always repeat the same theme year after year.

❧ *Bold stripes of color (as in this massed planting of sweet alyssum, marigolds, and lobelia) can have a dramatic impact.*

Simple Massed Layout

This simple massed garden layout uses bedding geraniums of several varieties. All of the bed sections are the same size plant. This selection of varieties requires a similar culture, so bed preparation and plant care is easy. Note that white varieties have been used as buffers between flower shades that might clash. This garden is full of color all at one height.

			15'				
3'	Orbit Apple Blossom	Orbit Violet	Sprinter White	Orbit Cherry	Hollywood Star	Orbit White	Elite Salmon

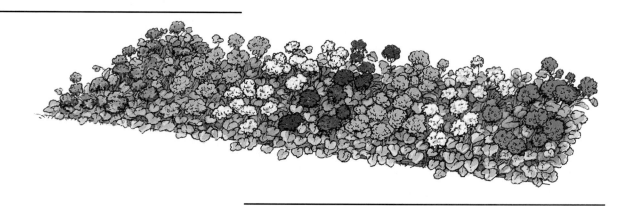

Elaborate Massed Layout

Illustrated here is a more elaborate massed layout for the same garden bed, using the same geranium varieties. Two "standard" or tree geraniums have been added as focal points that will stand above the rest of the flowers in the bed. Potted plants on pedestals could be substituted for the tree geraniums to break the monotony of a large bed. Other possible substitutes include a pair of dwarf columnar evergreens, small boxwood bushes, or clumps of tall, decorative grasses.

Tree Geranium   15'   Tree Geranium

Sprinter White	Elite Salmon	Orbit Cherry	Elite Salmon	Sprinter White
Orbit Violet	Orbit Apple Blossom	Orbit White	Orbit Apple Blossom	Orbit Violet

3'

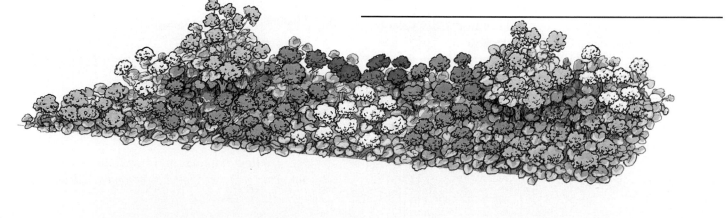

Gardening in a Single Color

This all-yellow garden plan utilizes many different annuals. Diversity of plant and flower forms, as well as different plant heights, add interest to this planting. As the color-coding shows, the tallest varieties are located in the center back of the bed and the low-growing varieties at the front, with intermediate heights filling in between. As a result, none of the plants will be hidden from view.

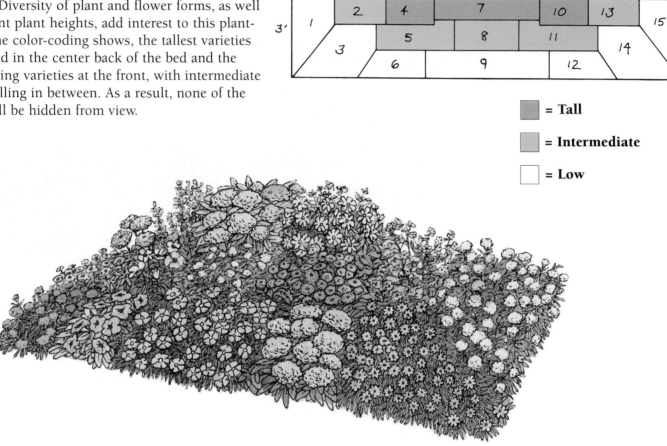

☐ = **Tall**

☐ = **Intermediate**

☐ = **Low**

All-Yellow Garden:

1. **Pot Marigold**
   Yellow

2. **Zinnia**
   Yellow Zenith

3. **Marigold**
   Gold Lady

4. **Snapdragon**
   Golden Rocket

5. **California Poppy**
   Sunlite

6. **Petunia**
   California Girl

7. **Crested Cockscomb**
   Yellow

8. **Marigold**
   Yellow Fireworks

9. **Marigold**
   Signet Lemon Gem

10. **Dahlia**
    Sunny Yellow

11. **Feverfew**
    Gold Ball

12. **Crested Cockscomb**
    Yellow

13. **Nasturtium**
    Golden

14. **Cosmos**
    Sunny Yellow

15. **Marigold**
    Yellow Nugget

2

Annuals in the Landscape

Any visitor to public gardens such as Disney World or Busch Gardens can tell you just what a fantastic display annuals provide. Bare walls are decorated with half-baskets full of flowers; large massed plantings line sidewalks and fill sitting areas; huge planters are jammed with color; baskets of blooms hang from tree limbs and archways; and window boxes decorate balconies and roof edges. The versatility of annuals makes them the perfect choice in many planting situations. After all, they bloom for a long time and come in a wonderful variety of colors, sizes, and forms—all producing an abundance of blossoms or decorative leaves. Most of them thrive with minimal care, and they're certainly inexpensive to grow. Best of all, if garden space is limited, annuals give you the flexibility to change your display every year.

Whether you plan to tuck annuals into a few open spots to brighten the summer yard or to plant in containers with color for the deck, there is information in this chapter to help you save time.

Whether you have a large yard or a small one, you'll find ideas here for ways to appreciate the beauty of annuals. Above all, you can enjoy the experience of planning your own garden, keeping in mind that there is no "right way" or "wrong way," there's just your way. If you're happy with the garden you create, that's what's important.

Laying Out an Annuals Garden

It is seldom possible to create an attractive garden of annuals without a plan or simply by planting out young plants. More often than not, this approach will produce unsatisfactory results.

The best way to plan is with a simple sketch. Draw a quick outline of your garden bed, noting its approximate dimensions and the amount of sun the area receives each day. If you predict that you'll be using the same areas for annuals beds each year, save future time by filing your notes as a reference for next year's plantings. Also list the names of your favorite annuals so you'll be sure to include most, if not all, of them in your plan.

The next step is to study your favorite bedding plants and to note the colors they come in and their growth habits. Mark down whether they prefer full sun, partial shade, or full shade. Also specify how tall they grow. Check to see if any of your favorites prefer more or less sun than your site has available—cross out those that aren't suitable.

If you have few favorites and a large space to fill, add a second list of annuals that you find attractive and that fit the light and color limitations of your site. Use seed catalogs to help you choose. Be sure to note several variety names and sources if a plant comes in more than one desirable color.

Plan your garden on paper using colored pencils to represent sections of various plant varieties within the bed outline. A more interesting and informal design can be achieved if, by following natural shapes, you vary the size and shape of these sections. Then decide which plants should go into various sections of your plan. Remember to keep tall plants in the back and low plants up front, filling in with intermediate heights. If a bed is going to be in an area where it will be seen from all sides, the tallest plants should be in the center of the bed with low ones around the outer edges.

As you plan, be sure flower colors in adjacent sections vary but don't clash. Maintain a balance of color in the bed. In large beds, repeat the same variety in several sections, making the sections much larger than you would in smaller beds.

Once the plan is in its final form, you can then figure out approximately how many plants you'll need of each kind. Using the spacing information contained in the "Directory of Popular Annuals" (see pages 90–101) calculate the number of plants needed to fill your area.

🐾 *A breathtaking garden does not happen by accident. It will take a little advanced planning to bring out the best in your landscape.*

Annuals Garden Against a Wall or Fence

This plan shows how to lay out a garden bed so all of the plants will be well displayed against the backdrop of a wall, fence, or building. Note that space has been left between the wall and the rear of the flower bed so gardening work—such as weeding and watering—can be done from both sides of the bed.

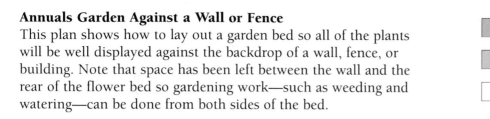

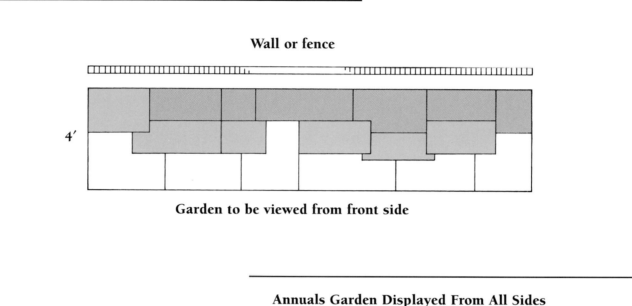

Garden to be viewed from front side

= Tall

= Intermediate

= Low

Annuals Garden Displayed From All Sides

When planting an island-type flower bed that will be viewed from all sides, plant taller varieties toward the middle and plant shorter varieties gradually toward the edge. If the bed is eight feet or wider, a simple stepping-stone pathway through the middle of the bed allows easy access to all parts of the bed for plant care.

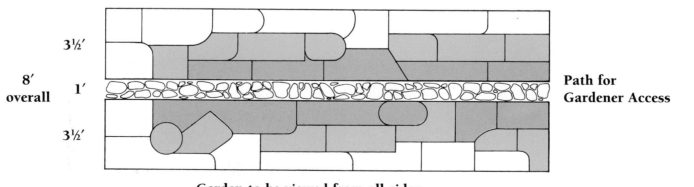

Garden to be viewed from all sides

Planning an Annuals Garden

To plan a flower bed, sketch its shape, noting its dimensions and exposure to sun. List your favorite bedding plants, and note their height and colors. For guaranteed success, include some of the tried and true varieties that you've noticed in your region. Once you've found niches for all of your favorites, make a second list of other plants you'd like to try—use some of these to fill any empty spots in your plan.

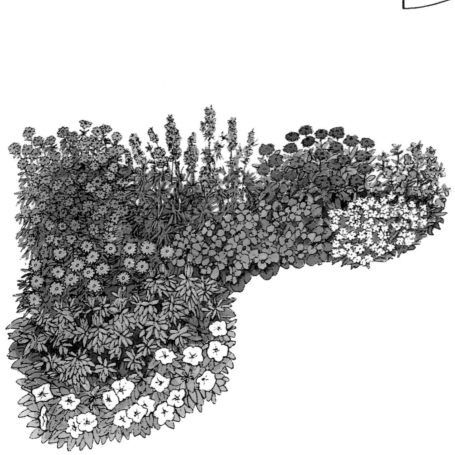

Scale
  1' = 2"

Colors
  Blue = B
  Pink = P
  White = W

Height
  Low = L
  Intermediate = I
  Tall = T

Favorites — *must* have:
  ✓ Sweet Alyssum   W; L
  ✓ Asters   B, P, W; I
  ✓ Larkspur   B, P, W; T
  ✓ Lobelia   B, W; L
  ✓ Petunia   B, P, W; L
  ✓ Salvia   B, P, W; I

Other possibilities:
  ✓ Begonia   B, P, W; L
  ✓ Cosmos   P, W; T
     Geranium   P, W; I
     Lantana   P, W, B; L
  ✓ Snapdragon   P, W; L, I, T
  ✓ Zinnia   W, P; L, I, T

  ✓ = Those actually used in plan.

Mingling Annuals with Other Plants

Many of us recall the old-fashioned gardens of our grandparents or other relatives and neighbors. These were usually hodge-podges of annuals, perennials, and shrubs. Frequently, there were also trees, vegetables, and small fruits—strawberries, raspberries, or currants—mixed in.

It seemed that gardens, rather than being planned, more or less "happened." More than likely, they evolved. As the gardener fancied something new or was given a plant by a friend, it was inserted into an available blank spot. Where yards were small and space was limited, these mixed gardens combined whatever was at hand. The end result often had an individual eclectic charm that was undeniable and delightful.

There's no reason, of course, why we can't create a similarly informal effect in a modern garden. For those with limited garden space, a mixed garden makes especially good sense. It allows us to have some of our personal favorites, rather than limiting us to only a few kinds of plants—as is the case of massed garden designs.

Although annuals make a splendid display on their own, they also combine effectively with other plants. Any dull spot can be brightened almost immediately with the addition of a few colorful annuals.

If, when you look over your garden, you feel something is lacking, see if you can identify one or more problem areas where accents of color would improve them. For example, although many shrub borders are flower-filled in spring and early summer, they often

provide only a few blooms the rest of the season. In some gardens, shrub plantings provide no summer color at all. It's amazing how much more attractive such an area becomes when just a few groupings of annuals are inserted. The immediate impact of the provided color turns a dull area into a living space. It's not necessary to plant a large, labor-intensive bed in front of the entire length of the shrub border. Several strategically located accent clumps are usually all that is needed. Try to accentuate the curved lines of a bed with a small arc of annuals that follow the line of the bed. Intensify statuary or a specimen plant with annuals and create a strong focal point in the garden.

🌱 *A mixed garden is the perfect choice when open space is limited, as in an urban area.*

Annuals can also provide the perfect midsummer boost to a perennial border. Annuals come into their own in midsummer, when many shrubs and perennials have finished their displays. Plant them in the spaces where spring bulbs and some perennials are dying back, or where biennials, such as foxgloves and English daisies, have been removed—anyplace an empty spot occurs.

If a perennial bed is so heavily planted that there is no free space in which to plant annuals, consider taking a different approach: Place pots or boxes of annuals on small outdoor tables or stools, then tuck these display stands here and there throughout the border. If there is a fence or wall behind the border, use it as a support from which to hang half-baskets or window boxes full of splendid flowering annuals.

A mixed garden is a personal one that truly reflects the individual taste of the homeowners. Rather than being a garden for show, it's a garden designed for the pleasure of those who own it. If others who visit it also find it enjoyable, so much the better.

Some uniquely charming mixed gardens are possible. Fruit trees, such as cherry, peach, pear, or apple, can supply partial shade to flower beds filled with combinations of different-colored annuals and perennials.

If you don't want to be limited to only a few kinds and colors of flowers in your garden, consider planting a mixed garden. With the wonderful array of annuals at your disposal, it's even possible to have an entirely different and unique garden every growing season.

Livening Up a Shrub Border

Most shrub borders have few blooms during the summer months. To liven up what is normally a dull area, add a few sweeps of colorful annuals, using the shrub border as a backdrop. This plan shows how informal groupings can be inserted. Either massed or mixed annuals can be used.

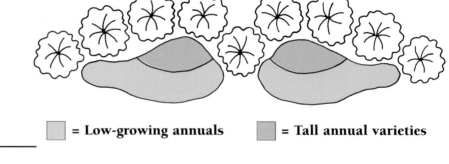

 = Low-growing annuals   = Tall annual varieties

Annuals in a Perennials Border

This plan shows part of a perennial border, indicating where each grouping of perennials, biennials (plants that have a two-year life cycle, blooming their second year), and bulbs may be planted. Areas shaded in gray indicate sections that will be in bloom in the spring months.

Peony	Phlox	Delphinium	Echinops		Hollyhock	Foxglove	Delphinium	Phlox
	Tulip	Bleeding Heart	Shasta Daisy	Iris		Daffodil		Peony
Candytuft	Pansy	Daffodil	Cerastium		Candytuft		Pansy

This overlay of the above plan shows how annuals can add color in those sections of the perennial border where bulbs and early spring flowering biennials have died back or have been removed (shaded in gray). Red-shaded areas indicate where perennials will provide summer bloom.

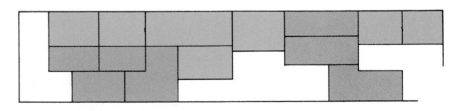

Combining Annuals, Fruits, and Vegetables

This small garden contains a mixture of annuals, fruits, and vegetables. Such a mixture provides year-round interest as well as function. This plan could easily be modified to include your own favorites.

1. Favorite flowering tree
2. Pole beans, snap beans, or raspberries on trellis
3. Rhubarb
4. Blueberry (2 different varieties for cross-pollination)
5. Beets or Swiss chard
6. Herbs or other vegetable favorites
7. Flowering annuals
8. Fountain, statue, or other garden feature

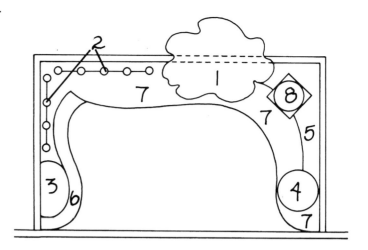

Colorful Annuals in a Small Oasis

The same small space is packed full of color while providing a private, vine-covered sitting area. The birdbath might be replaced with a piece of garden sculpture or an unusual accent plant—perhaps a tree lantana, topiary evergreen, or rosemary. Heavy plantings reduce maintenance because the soil stays shaded, so weeds are less likely to become established.

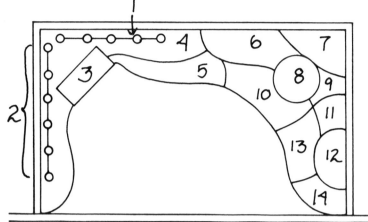

1. Morning glory } over trellis
2. Moon vine
3. Garden seat or other garden feature with impatiens planted around and behind it
4. Marigold
5. Lobelia—blue
6. Cosmos—mixed
7. Hollyhock—mixed
8. Birdbath
9. Marigold
10. Red salvia or red peppers
11. Perilla
12. Pot marigold—yellow
13. Sweet alyssum—white
14. Swan River daisy

78

Container Gardening

Probably no form of gardening allows more versatility than container gardening. Growing plants in containers makes it possible to garden in situations where there is no yard or soil available—on a rooftop, a high-rise balcony, a deck, a fire escape, or even in an area that's covered with concrete.

The containers themselves can be as plain or elaborate as you wish. Clay or plastic pots; wood, plastic, or metal window boxes; decorator pots of ceramic, terra cotta, alabaster, or wrought iron; recycled plastic or metal pails;

🌿 *Container plants can be used to brighten walkways, steps, and other areas where there is little or no soil.*

wire frames lined with sphagnum moss; a child's cast-off metal wagon; hanging planters; a plastic-lined bushel basket—any of these can be used. Here's a chance to give your imagination free rein!

All that's essential is that the container be capable of holding soil as well as allowing excess water to drain away. Keep in mind that plants thrive more readily in larger amounts of soil because the soil temperature and moisture level fluctuate less as soil volume increases. Unless the gardener is extremely vigilant, plants are more likely to suffer frequent drying out and overheating when planted in small pots.

Annuals are particularly well-suited for use in container plantings. They quickly fill and overflow the planters. You can also plant them in masses of a single species or in a mixture of different kinds and colors.

Another advantage to growing plants in containers is their portability. You can move them from one area to another at will, as long as you remember that shade-loving plants can quickly burn if shifted into brilliant sun. Conversely, sun lovers won't flourish if shaded for more than a few days.

Care of container plantings takes little total time, but it does require regular attention. Soil moisture needs to be checked every evening. Ideally, you want to rewater each planter before the soil becomes too dry. On the other hand, the soil should not be constantly soaking wet or the plants will drown. Therefore, it's necessary to conscientiously keep track of the moisture level.

Plant roots grow downward and tend to mass at the bottom of a container. To be sure that water reaches all of the soil in the container, fill the planter to the rim with water allowing it to soak in completely. If no water comes out of the drainage holes, fill again. Repeat this process until water starts to drip from the bottom of the container.

To keep the plantings looking full and to encourage abundant blooming, remove dead flower heads promptly. Once every ten days to two weeks, water with a mild fertilizer solution. That's all it takes to keep container gardens in peak condition.

Drainage in Container Gardens

To grow plants successfully in containers, good drainage is essential. Drainage holes need to be covered to keep soil in place: pieces of broken pottery, fine screening, or a coffee filter are all good choices.

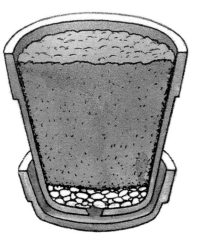

Gardening in Decorative Containers

When using a decorative container with no drainage holes, place a well-drained pot inside of the container. Raise the inner pot on a layer of pebbles to keep it above water level. Peat moss in the space between the inner and outer pots can provide insulation to help stabilize soil temperatures.

ANNUALS THAT DO WELL IN CONTAINERS

Fibrous begonia	Nasturtium
Coleus	Pansy
Dracaena	Ornamental pepper
Geranium	Perilla
Impatiens	Petunia
Lobelia	Phlox
Marigold	Sweet pea
Pot marigold	Verbena

The Versatility of Window Boxes

Window boxes are versatile planters that are not just useful on window ledges. They can also hang from porch rails or fences, perch along the tops of walls, mark the edge of a deck, or line a walk or driveway. Add them wherever you want color without creating a flower bed.

The Many Uses of Hanging Baskets

Hanging baskets provide another almost endless source of color. You can group them at different levels on a porch, add half-baskets to brighten a blank wall, or hang them from tree limbs. With regular watering, feedings, and occasional pinching, baskets are almost care-free.

MIXED CONTAINERS

Mixed garden containers provide all-season interest by combining annuals, bulbs, or perennials with a tree or shrub. A young, single-stem tree gives added height while an underplanting of flowering plants provides color change through the season.

Caring for Annuals

Most weekend gardeners mix business with pleasure. They ramble around their yard regularly, stopping to admire a healthy plant here, snapping off a few dead flower heads there, then pulling out some weeds in another area.

At the same time, they're noticing clues that signal possible problems. If some of the plants have limp-hanging leaves, the gardener will check how dry the soil is and turn on the soaker hose if needed. If some leaves or flowers are peppered with holes or totally eaten away, a closer inspection will be made to discover whether a caterpillar or bug has invaded. This, in turn, will lead to hand removal of the insect or spraying or powdering with the appropriate insecticide.

There are time-saving tips included here that will help make growing annuals in your garden seem elementary. By following the basic principles of pruning, you'll be able to increase the natural bloom period for long-season flowering on neat, compact plants.

An illustrated section that allows easy identification of garden pests and diseases contains recommendations for dealing with each problem. By selecting those plants that are easiest to grow and are best-suited to your garden site, and by following gardening techniques that reduce the need for maintenance, your summer can be both carefree and colorful.

Ways to Increase and Control Growth

🌱 *Proper care and maintenance will keep your flowers blooming and prevent them from overgrowth.*

Annuals will flourish when provided with the best possible growing conditions. However, there are a few simple care techniques that will help increase and control their growth.

PINCHING BACK

To encourage plants to fill out, remove the growth bud at the end of the main stem when the plant is in its rapid growth stage. For bedding plants, the best time to do this is when you're planting them in the garden. They're at a stable stage of growth and, in addition, the removal of some of their foliage will help balance any root damage they may suffer in the transplanting process.

Simply pinch back the last inch or so of the main growing tip. This will redirect the plant's energy from a single shoot to numerous latent side buds. Several days after pinching, you'll see several small shoots pushing from the remaining stem. These will grow into a cluster of stems to replace the original single stem. The plant will be shorter, stockier, and fuller than if no pinching had been done. It will also be neater-looking, more compact, and have many more branches on which to produce flowers. A second pinching can be done several weeks after the first one if an even fuller plant is desired.

DEADHEADING

Once annuals begin to bloom, it's important to remove spent flowers promptly for several reasons. First, once the flower dies, it detracts from the good looks of the garden. Second, even though we say it's dead, it's actually very much alive and continues with its growth toward seed production. This process pulls plant energy that would otherwise be available for new foliage and flower production. Removal of spent flowers helps to quickly redirect plant energy to side shoots for smooth and speedy transfer to new growth.

To make this rerouting most efficient, always cut back to just above the first side bud that is already beginning to grow. If there is no active side bud below the bloom, cut back either to a side branch or immediately above a leaf where a latent bud will be likely to push out new growth. Make a clean cut with a sharp-bladed knife, since ragged cuts take much longer to heal and are likely sites for entry of rot and disease. These rules for cutting apply to the removal of cutting flowers as well.

Occasionally it becomes necessary to cut back growth to keep a plant from becoming leggy or from drowning out neighboring plants. The easiest way to cut back a mass of annuals is to shear the tops with hedge shears. Be sure to keep the bed neat and healthy by discarding the cuttings.

Pinching Back Growth Tips

Pinching back the plant growth tip helps encourage multiple branching. This, in turn, advances the production of more flower buds along these additional branches. At the same time, pinching produces a more sturdy, compact plant that not only looks nice but is also less subject to breakage due to wind, rain, or heavy bloom weight. A second pinch in midsummer will stimulate new growth as well as increase flower production.

Deadheading Flowers

Deadheading should be done soon after the flower dies, so no plant energy is wasted on seed formation. Single flowers should be cut back to the place on the stem where a side shoot is already pushing out. If none is evident, then cut back to above a leaf, a node, or a side branch. Cluster flowers will look fresh and attractive longer if the individual florets are snapped out of the group as they die.

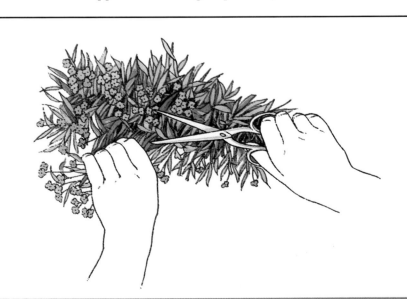

Pests and Other Problems

The following lists are designed to help you identify the most common garden pests and diseases for annuals and perennials. If you feel uncertain about what is causing damage to your plants, take a specimen to your local garden shop or your county Cooperative Extension office.

Once you know what your problem is, you'll need to decide how to control it. When an infestation is slight, it's often possible to simply remove the sick plants or individual insects. For a heavy infestation, you'll probably need to turn to chemical insecticides or fungicides.

Follow manufacturer's instructions precisely and read and follow any cautions on the package label. Apply these chemicals as directed and only when they're absolutely necessary. One final note: new biological and chemical controls are continually being developed. Those listed here are current at the time of this writing, but more effective new ones may well be developed in the future.

When possible, select pest-resistant strains of plants.

INSECTS AND ANIMALS

SYMPTOM	CAUSE	CURE	PLANTS	
Cluster of small, soft-bodied insects appear on buds and growth tips (gray, black, pink, green, red, or yellow in color); sticky secretions may be evident. Leaves are curled.	**Aphids**	Spray with rotenone or malathion[1] in the evening.	**Annuals** Pot Marigold Nasturtium Primrose Sweet Pea	**Perennials** Chrysanthemum Delphinium Lupine
Leaves have been chewed away; hard-shelled beetles of many colors and sizes can be seen on plant and burrowed into flowers.	**Beetles of various kinds**	Pick off by hand and destroy or spray with rotenone or Sevin*[1].	**Annuals** Gourds Hollyhock American/French Marigold Zinnia	**Perennials** Chrysanthemum Mallow

[1] = Inorganic treatment   * = Copyrighted brand name

SYMPTOM	CAUSE	CURE	PLANTS	
Growth tips are wilted or entire plant is wilted; small hole appears in plant stem at point where wilting begins.	Borers	Cut out borer, snap off at level of hole, or destroy entire plant if affected at base of plant; spray with endosulfan[1], pyrethrum, or rotenone.	**Annuals** Gourds American/French Marigold Ornamental Corn Zinnia	**Perennials** Dahlia Delphinium Iris
Leaves and flowers are chewed away; caterpillars appear on plant.	Caterpillars of various kinds and sizes	Pick off by hand and destroy; spray with pyrethrum, malathion[1], or *Bacillus thuringiensis*.	**Annuals** Nicotiana Ornamental or Flowering Cabbage Petunia	**Perennials** Butterfly Weed Chrysanthemum Mallow Yarrow
Entire young plant is wilted and is partially or entirely chewed through at ground level.	Cutworms	Dig in soil around plant base; find rolled up caterpillars and destroy; circle plant with cardboard collar on edge (1" below ground and 1" above ground).	**Annuals** China Pink Nicotiana Ornamental or Flowering Cabbage Petunia	
Foliage turns yellow and begins to curl; leaves are peppered with small round holes; small green-patterned, trangular-shaped winged insects can be seen when disturbed.	Leaf Hoppers	Spray off light infestations with garden hose; spray with malathion[1] or methoxychlor[1]; dust with diatomaceous earth.	**Annuals** Aster Dahlia Pot Marigold	**Perennials** Chrysanthemum Coreopsis Pincushion Flower
Leaves are "painted" with whitish, curling trails—microscopic larvae of tiny flying insects.	Leaf Miners	Remove badly infested leaves; spray with malathion[1].	**Annuals** China Pink Hollyhock	**Perennials** Columbine Pink
White or pinkish fuzzy clumps appear on stems and at base of leaves and are sticky to the touch.	Mealybugs	Spray with malathion[1] or pyrethrum; hand kill by painting each bug with alcohol.	**Annuals** Asparagus Fern Moses-in-a-Boat Transvaal Daisy	

[1] = Inorganic treatment   * = Copyrighted brand name

SYMPTOM	CAUSE	CURE	PLANTS	
Slime trails appear on plants; soft, sticky slugs can be found on plants after dark; irregular holes have been eaten in leaves and lower stems.	***Slugs and Snails***	Shallow containers of beer will attract and drown pests; set out metaldehyde slug bait[1]; pick by hand.	**Annuals** Hollyhock Nicotiana Petunia Primrose	**Perennials** Daylily Hosta Phlox
Yellowing leaves have a speckled look; fine spider webs can be seen on plants, tiny reddish mites appear on the webs and the undersides of leaves.	***Spider Mites***	Spray plants with miticide[1] on backs of leaves; wash or spray with soapy water.	**Annuals** Flowering Maple Impatiens Primrose	**Perennials** Bush Clematis Yellow Coneflower Daylily
Small globs of white bubbles occur on plant stems or leaves; small insects can be found hidden inside.	***Spittlebugs***	Ignore spittlebugs unless very pervasive; spray with malathion[1]; wash off repeatedly with hose.	**Annuals** Bachelor's Button Four O'Clock	**Perennials** Chrysanthemum
Brown or white flecks appear on plant leaves.	***Thrips***	Spray with malathion[1] or dust with sulphur.	**Annuals** Gladiolus	**Perennials** Daylily
Clouds of tiny white insects flutter around plant when disturbed.	***White Flies***	Spray with malathion[1] or diazinon[1]; use yellow sticky traps.	**Annuals** Heliotrope Lantana Morning Glory Vine	**Perennials** Aster Mallow

[1] = Inorganic treatment   * = Copyrighted brand name

DISEASES

SYMPTOM		CAUSE	CURE	PLANTS	
Leaves become mottled, curl, and shrivel; plants become deformed.		*Blights and Viruses*	Remove and destroy plants; buy blight-resistant strains; wash hands before handling plants.	**Annuals** Aster Snapdragon	**Perennials** Japanese Anemone Lupine Peony
Newly sprouted seedlings fall over and die.		*Damping Off*	Start seeds in sterile soil mix; dust seeds with Captan*[1] before planting.	**Annuals** All plants	**Perennials** All plants
Round, dusty brown or black spots appear on leaves; leaves drop from plant.		*Leaf Spot*	Remove badly diseased leaves; spray with benomyl[1] or zineb[1].	**Annuals** Aster Chrysanthemum Foxglove Phlox	**Perennials** Garden Phlox Iris
Lower leaves and stem turn grayish and look slightly wilted.		*Powdery Mildew*	Increase air circulation and keep foliage dry; spray with benomyl[1] or sulphur.	**Annuals** Bachelor's Button Floss Flower Phlox Sweet Pea Zinnia	**Perennials** Boltonia Delphinium Garden Phlox
Orange or reddish-brown raised dots form on backs of leaves; leaves look wilted.		*Rust*	Increase air circulation; keep foilage dry; buy rust-resistant varieties; spray with ferbam[1] or zineb[1]; spray flowers with sulphur or benomyl[1].	**Annuals** Cleome Hollyhock Snapdragon	**Perennials** Aster Mallow
Leaves wilt and turn yellow; entire plant shuts down and dies.		*Wilt*	Remove infected plants and destroy; buy wilt-resistant varieties.	**Annuals** Aster Dahlia Snapdragon	

[1] = Inorganic treatment   * = Copyrighted brand name

4

Directory of
Popular Annuals

The plants selected for this directory cover a wide selection of annuals suited to a host of varied conditions. They can all be used successfully to provide seasonal color outdoors as annuals; there is enough variety listed here to allow the opportunity to make different planting choices each year. Names, descriptions, proper growth techniques, propagation, uses, and related species and varieties are all dealt with in depth. Color photos are included for each species that is profiled.

Whether you live in a suburban home with a large yard or in a condominium 14 stories above the ground with only a windy balcony to plant on, you will find annuals here that will work for you.

Many of the plants listed in the directory are grown everywhere—a relatively reliable guide to their success rate. Most plants can be found already started at garden centers. Others will have to be started from seed, either from mail-order catalogs that offer a wider selection or from seed packets found on racks locally. You will be able to familiarize yourself with enough annuals so that you can decide for yourself what will work best for you, depending on your location and the amount of time and effort you want to put into starting and maintaining an annuals garden.

Sweet Alyssum
Lobularia maritima

Alyssum flowers for months, even through the winter in milder climates. A member of the mustard family, alyssum is quite fragrant.

Description: Alyssum grows only a few inches high but spreads as much as a foot in diameter. The tiny flowers are closely packed around small racemes that grow upward as lower flowers fade. Although white is the most planted color, pink, lavender, and darker shades of violet are also available.

How to grow: Alyssum grows best in full sun in cool weather, but it will tolerate partial shade. The plants will survive light frosts. Space from 6 to 8 inches apart. Alyssum will reseed vigorously.

Propagation: Sow seeds outdoors as soon as the ground can be worked. Seeds germinate in 7 to 14 days at 65° to 70°F.

Uses: Alyssum is traditionally used for edging beds, borders, and as annual groundcover.

Related varieties: 'New Carpet of Snow' is the most planted, but the 'Wonderland' series consists of 'White,' 'Rosy-Red,' and 'Deep Purple.'

Bachelor's Button, Cornflower
Centaurea cyanus

The boutonniere flower is reputedly where this favorite got its name. And "cornflower blue" has frequently been used in the fashion trade to merchandise that particular shade.

Description: Bachelor's buttons grow 1 to 3 feet tall with innumerable round flowers held above the rather sparse, long and narrow gray-green leaves. The habit of growth is relatively loose.

How to grow: Full sun in average soil is good. For earliest bloom, sow seeds outdoors in the fall so they will start to grow before the first frost and bloom the next spring. Otherwise, sow seeds outdoors as early in the spring as the soil can be worked. Thin to 8 to 12 inches apart.

Propagation: To grow seedlings indoors, germinate at 65°F four weeks before planting out. Germination time is 7 to 14 days.

Uses: Bachelor's buttons lend themselves to informal planting, particularly with other annuals and perennials in beds and borders.

Related varieties: 'Blue Boy' grows to 2½ feet. 'Polka Dot Mixed' and 'Frosty Mixed' have white or pastel contrasts at petal tips.

Globe Amaranth
Gomphrena globosa

This tropical native has small, cloverlike flowers that will continually bloom throughout the whole summer season.

Description: Globe amaranth can grow up to two feet with newer, smaller varieties that are bushy dwarfs. The flowers are about one inch in diameter and have a somewhat papery texture. The basic color is violet, but many varieties exist.

How to grow: The only demand for good performance is sun. Plant in the garden after the last frost and space from 10 to 15 inches apart.

Propagation: Soak seeds in water for 3 to 4 days before sowing. Sow seeds in place in the garden after last frost. Seeds germinate in 14 to 21 days at 65° to 75°F.

Uses: The tall varieties are ideal for mid-border. Use dwarf varieties for edging beds, borders, or as a colorful ground cover.

Related species: *Gomphrena haageana* has yellow to orange, pine-cone shaped flowers.

Related varieties: 'Buddy' is a compact, purple-flowering variety, growing only 9 to 12 inches tall. 'Strawberry Fields' is bright red and grows to two feet with long stems. It is splendid for cutting.

Wax Begonia, Fibrous Begonia
Begonia semperflorens

The brightly colored bedding begonias are equally at home in full sun (except where temperatures stay above 90°F for days on end) or full but bright shade (where trees are pruned high). From first setting them out until laid low by frost, they'll be packed with white, pink, rose, or red blossoms. Virtually untouched by bugs or blight,

their only shortcoming is a relatively narrow color range.

Description: Uniformity is the trademark of most begonias—tight mounds of closely packed leaves covered with blossoms. All four flower colors are available with your choice of leaf color: chocolaty-red or shades of green. The deeper-colored or bronze-leaved varieties offer especially eye-catching contrast with flowers. There are also varieties with double flowers that resemble fat, little rosebuds and others with variegated foliage.

How to grow: Begonias perform well in rich, well-drained soil but the soil must be allowed to dry between waterings. They'll form tight, compact plants in full sun, with increasingly looser form and fewer flowers as you move them deeper into the shade. Most hybrids will grow

(continued on p. 92)

Wax Begonia, Fibrous Begonia

Begonia semperflorens

(continued from p. 91)
6 to 9 inches high and spread as wide.

Propagation: Most hybrids are grown from seed, but great patience is required. Dustlike seeds (two million per ounce) must be sown in December or January for large, husky plants by May. Germination temperature is 70° to 85°F and requires 14 to 21 days. Cuttings also root readily. A good way to start plants is on a sunny windowsill during winter.

Uses: Wax begonias lend themselves to large, formal plantings because of their uniform size and shapeliness. They're also suitable in front of summer annual borders and combine well with other cool-colored flowers in mixed plantings and containers.

Related varieties: The most popular, dark-leaved kinds are the 'Cocktail' series: 'Brandy,' 'Vodka,' 'Whiskey,' and 'Gin.' Good green-leaved varieties are found in the 'Olympia' and 'Prelude' series. 'Avalanche' begonias in pink or white are rangier, suited for containers and hanging baskets, where their arching growth habit is handsome.

Caladium

Caladium hortulanum

Caladiums are grown entirely for their brightly colored and wildly patterned foliage.

Description: Large, arrow-head-shaped leaves on long stems rise directly from the tuber buried in the ground below. Depending on conditions, each leaf can grow to 12 inches in length.

How to grow: Plant tubers directly in the ground after the soil has warmed, or start them early indoors in pots and plant them outside when the weather is warm. Caladiums thrive in high temperature and humidity. Outdoors, grow caladium in moist, rich soil, and protect them from intense sun. In the fall, dig tubers before frost, allowing them to gradually dry off. Store in a frost-free location.

Propagation: Multiply plants by cutting tubers in pieces, similar to potatoes, being sure each piece retains growing "eyes."

Uses: Caladiums are unsurpassed for foliage color in beds, borders, or window boxes. Grow in moist areas to reduce water needs.

Related varieties: 'Candidum' is white with green leaves and ribs; 'Pink Beauty' is pink with a green background; and 'Frieda Hemple' is solid red with a green border.

Blue Marguerite

Felicia amelloides

The blue marguerite's sky-blue color contrasts nicely with each flower's bright yellow center.

Description: Blue marguerite is erect in growth, from 1 to 2 feet tall. It has glossy, deep green leaves with flowers on relatively short stems in sky-blue to darker shades, centered with a yellow eye.

How to grow: Blue marguerite thrives in moist but well-drained soil, in full sun to partial shade. Truly hot weather causes their decline, making them best as a summer plant for maritime or mountain climates. Plant outside after all danger of frost has passed, spacing them 9 to 12 inches apart.

Propagation: Trailing forms are available only through cuttings; seed-grown plants are mostly upright. Sow seeds 6 to 8 weeks prior to planting out. Germination takes up to 30 days at 70°F.

Uses: Group them in beds and borders or use them in moist rock gardens.

Related species: *Felicia bergerana,* the 'kingfisher daisy,' grows to a height of about 8 inches—smaller than *F. amelloides*. It has longer and more narrow leaves and bright blue flowers with yellow centers.

Canna

Canna species

The parentage of these garden hybrids is very mixed; breeders have provided many sturdy and colorful kinds.

Description: Specimens grow from fleshy roots with erect stalks from which broad, long leaves emerge. Flower stalks rising in the center bear large flowers. Foliage may be green, bronze, or purplish in hue.

How to grow: Cannas need full sun and grow best in a deep, rich, moist, but well-drained soil. Plant roots directly into the ground after soil is warm and all danger of frost has passed. Use pieces of rootstock with 2 or 3 large eyes and plant two inches deep. Space 1½ to 2 feet apart.

Propagation: Few varieties are available by seed. Cut roots into pieces, each with 2 to 3 eyes, in the spring just prior to planting.

Uses: Use cannas in the center of island beds, at the sides or back of brightly colored borders, or near pools and ponds.

Related varieties: Tall varieties include: 'Yellow King Humbert,' yellow with scarlet flecks; 'The President,' bright crimson; and 'City of Portland,' a deep pink. Dwarf kinds growing to 2½ feet tall are available in several colors.

Cleome, Spider Flower
Cleome hasslerana

Exceedingly long stamens that extend well beyond the orchid-like flowers—somewhat resembling daddy longlegs spider—are what give the spider flower its name.

Description: Cleome flowers, with many opening at once, grow in airy racemes 6 to 8 inches in diameter. Flowers—white, pink, or lavender in color—perch atop stems that grow up to six-feet high.

How to grow: Cleome grows well in average soil located in full sun or minimal shade. It is very drought-tolerant, although it will look and grow better if it is watered well. Space plants 1 to 3 feet apart.

Propagation: Sow after the last frost when the ground is warm. Cleomes may also be started indoors 4 to 6 weeks earlier at a temperature of at least 70°F. Germination time is 10 to 14 days. In the garden, it reseeds prolifically.

Uses: Plant cleome for its height, to back up borders, in the center of island beds, or in any spot where its dramatic quality stands out.

Related varieties: 'Helen Campbell' is the most popular white variety. 'Rose Queen' is salmon-pink, and 'Ruby Queen' is rose-colored.

Cosmos
Cosmos bipinnatus

Cosmos is one of the fastest-growing annuals. Some varieties reach up to six feet by summer's end.

Description: Cosmos forms a lacy, open plant with flowers 3 to 4 inches in diameter. These "daisies" come in pink, red, white, and lavender with a contrasting yellow center.

How to grow: Cosmos grows best in full sun, but it will bloom acceptably in partial shade. Space at least 12 inches apart.

Propagation: Because it grows so fast, sow outdoors after danger of frost has passed. Barely cover seeds; they need light to germinate. Germination takes 3 to 7 days at 70° to 75°F.

Uses: Because of its height, cosmos should be planted at the back of borders and grouped against fences or other places as a covering.

Related species: *Cosmos sulphureus* is the source of the hot red and yellow colors of cosmos. Bloom is heavy from start until frost.

Related varieties: Most popular is the 'Sensation' series that comes in mixed colors. Separate colors of this series are also available.

Dahlia
Dahlia hybrids

From huge, dinner-plate-sized blooms down to midget pompons only two inches in diameter, dahlias show as much diversity as any summer flowering plant.

Description: Dahlias grow from 1 to 5 feet tall. Flowers come in every color except blue, and the form is varied: peonylike; anemone-flowered; singles; shaggy mops; formal, ball-shaped; and twisted, curled petals. The flowers are carried on long stems above the erect plants. The American Dahlia Society has classified dahlias by both type and size. There are 12 different flower types: single, anemone-flowered, collarette, peony-flowered, formal decorative, informal decorative, ball, pompon, incurved cactus, straight cactus, semi-cactus, and orchid-flowered.

How to grow: Dahlias are sun lovers and need air circulation around them. Soil should be fertile, high in organic matter, and moist but well-drained. Plant the tubers so that the eye is 2 to 3 inches below ground level. Do not plant container-grown dahlias any deeper than the level they were growing in their pot. Space tall varieties 12 to 18 inches apart, reducing the spacing for dwarf plants to as little as eight inches.

Propagation: Most of the large-flowered varieties are grown from tuberous roots available at garden centers or specialist growers. At the end of a summer's growing season, dig clumps of tubers and store in a cool but frost-free location until spring. Sow dahlia seeds 4 to 6 weeks prior to planting out at 70°F. Germination will take 5 to 14 days.

Uses: Taller varieties can be planted as a hedge with shorter flowers growing in front of them. Groups of three plants can be effective at the back of the border or in the center of large island beds. You can also feature compact varieties in the front of beds and borders.

Related varieties: There are hundreds of varieties; consult your garden center or a specialist grower. A few tuberous rooted varieties include 'Los Angeles,' a semi-cactus variety with deep red flowers and petals tipped in white; 'Canby Charm,' an informal decorative type with pink flowers that can reach a diameter of 12 inches; and 'Clown,' a golden-yellow variety with streaks of red in the petals. Seed-grown varieties are available as started plants or can be grown from seeds at home. 'Redskin,' a compact variety, grows up to 15 inches with bronze foliage—a remarkable contrast to the many different flower colors.

Dahlberg Daisy, Golden Fleece
Dyssodia tenuiloba

A charming little plant with sunny flowers, the Dahlberg daisy is now becoming widely available at garden centers.

Description: This species of daisy bears many golden-yellow, upright flowers measuring ½ inch in diameter. The long, narrow leaves are divided, giving a feathery appearance. Plants grow from 6 to 12 inches high, spreading as much as 18 inches.

How to grow: Dahlberg daisies grow well in full sun and well-drained, moderately fertile soil. However, they will also grow and bloom abundantly in poor soil and hot weather. Plant outdoors when the soil is warm and the danger of frost has passed. Space 6 to 12 inches apart.

Propagation: Sow seeds in place when the ground is warm. For earlier bloom, start seeds indoors 6 to 8 weeks prior to planting. Germination takes 8 to 12 days at 60° to 80°F.

Uses: Dahlberg daisy can be planted in rock gardens or in pockets among paving stones or patio blocks. It makes a superb edging for beds and borders and can be used as a ground cover plant for sunny areas. Its reseeding habit makes it ideal for naturalized gardens.

Dusty Miller
Senecio cineraria, Chrysanthemum cinerariaefolium

This name has been applied to a variety of similar, silvery plants including Artemisias, Centaureas, and Lychnis.

Description: *Chrysanthemum cinerariaefolium* grows 1 to 2½ feet tall with finely divided leaflets and white daisy flowers about 1½ inches in diameter. *Senecio cineraria* is a bushy subshrub that grows to 2½ feet tall with finely divided gray foliage.

How to grow: Preference for both plants is full sun and a rather ordinary, well-drained soil, although they will brighten lightly shaded areas, too. Plant in the garden when the soil has warmed and after danger of frost has passed. Space 8 to 10 inches apart.

Propagation: Germinate seeds of *Senecio cineraria* at 75° to 80°F and those of *Chrysanthemum cinerariaefolium* at 65° to 75°F. Germination will take 10 to 15 days. Sow seeds 12 to 14 weeks before planting out.

Uses: Excellent in containers, they're especially good to use as a bridge between two clashing colors

Related varieties: 'Silver Lace' has dissected, feathery leaves. 'Diamond' and 'Silverdust' develop finely divided silvery leaves.

Swan River Daisy
Brachycome iberidifolia

Quite variable in nature, flowers are blue, pink, white, and purple, each one centered with either yellow or black.

Description: The Swan River daisy forms a loose mound up to 18 inches tall with equal spread. A plant with numerous branches, it holds its 1½-inch flowers upright on slender stems.

How to grow: Brachycome needs full sun and a rich but well-drained soil. To encourage bushiness, young plants should be pinched once. Space plants nine inches apart in the garden.

Propagation: For early bloom, sow seeds indoors at 70°F six weeks prior to planting out after danger of frost has passed. Germination will take 10 to 18 days. Seeds may also be sown outdoors after the frost-free date. Cuttings will root in 15 days and are useful for multiplying good forms of brachycome.

Uses: Because of its mounding habit, brachycome is an ideal hanging basket or container plant. It also is useful for edging tall borders.

Related varieties: 'Purple Splendor' will give shades of blue to purple. For a range of all colors, plant 'Mixed Colors.'

Floss Flower
Ageratum houstonianum

These fluffy flowers in blue-lavender, white, and pink are favorites for window boxes and summer gardens.

Description: Ageratum is covered with fuzzy flowers about ½ inch in diameter on compact, mounding plants from 6 to 10 inches high. They will spread about 10 inches. Floss flower will bloom continuously from spring planting until fall.

How to grow: Grow in any well-drained soil in full sun or partial shade. Space 6 to 10 inches apart for solid color. Occasional deadheading will improve their performance.

Propagation: Start seeds indoors 6 to 8 weeks before planting. Seeds germinate in 5 to 8 days at 70°F.

Uses: Plant in the front of borders and beds. Most of the newer varieties form compact mounds that provide the scarce blue color so seldom found in annuals. Taller, older varieties make good cut flowers.

Related species: Golden ageratum, or *Lonas inodora*, has the same flower effect in bright yellow.

Related varieties: Several of the popular blue varieties are 'Adriatic,' 'Blue Danube,' and 'Blue Blazer.'

Gazania, Treasure Flower
Gazania ringens

This South African flower likes hot, dry summers. Gardeners treasure it for its daisylike flowers.

Description: Gazanias grow in rosette form with attractive notched leaves. Flowers rise 8 to 12 inches on short stems. They're white, pink, bronze, red, yellow, orange, and white.

How to grow: Gazanias prefer full sun and moderately fertile but well-drained soil. The only thing they don't like is heavy soil in hot, humid climates. Plant out as soon as the danger of frost has passed at 8 to 15 inches apart.

Propagation: Sow seeds outdoors after final frost or plant them indoors 4 to 6 weeks earlier. Seeds germinate in 15 to 20 days at 70°F. Cuttings taken in the summer root quickly.

Uses: Plant gazanias in the front of beds and borders. Use them as a ground cover in sunny, dry areas or in rock gardens.

Related varieties: The 'Daybreak' series blooms in 'Yellow,' 'Orange,' and 'Garden Sun,' combining yellow and orange. The 'Daybreak Mixture' includes pink and white colors.

Zonal Geranium
(*continued*)

Propagation: Cuttings root easily. Make cuttings 8 to 10 weeks prior to planting out for husky plants. Seed-grown varieties should be started 10 to 12 weeks prior to garden planting. Seeds germinate in 7 to 10 days at 70° to 75°F.

Uses: Zonal geraniums are among the best plants for formal beds. They can provide pockets of color in any sunny spot. Group three or more together for color impact in flower borders or along walks and pathways. They're classics in containers, all by themselves or mixed with other kinds of plants. Geraniums are also grown as standards—a single stem is trained to the desired height with a bushy canopy of flowers and leaves. Zonal geraniums will bloom through the winter in sunny windows.

Related varieties: There are many varieties available at garden centers in the spring. A few popular semi-doubles are 'Tango,' a bright orange-red with dark foliage; 'Forever Yours,' a vigorous red; 'Blues,' cherry blossom pink with unique rose and white markings near the center of petals; 'Schone Helene,' a 2-toned salmon; and 'Snowmass,' pure white. Seed-grown singles are generally found in series of many colors. Widely planted are 'Orbit,' 'Elite,' 'Ringo,' 'Bandit,' and 'Hollywood' varieties.

Zonal Geranium
Pelargonium x hortorum

Many gardeners consider zonal geraniums the epitome of summer flowers. Named for the dark, horseshoe-shaped color in the leaves of most varieties, these stalwart garden beauties are tender perennials that must be replanted each year except in the most favored climates. A majority of pelargonium species come from South Africa, but through hundreds of years of breeding, the parentage of today's varieties has been obscured.

Description: Zonal geraniums are upright bushes covered with red, pink, salmon, white, rose, cherry red, and bicolored flowers on long stems held above the plant. Flower clusters (or umbels) contain many individual flowers and give a burst of color. Plants from four-inch pots transplanted to the garden in spring will reach up to 18 inches high and wide by the end of summer.

How to grow: Zonal geraniums benefit from full sun and moderate-to-rich, well-drained, moist soil. Incorporate a slow-release fertilizer into the soil at planting time. Plant after all danger of frost has passed and the soil is warm. Space them 12 inches apart. The only other care requirement is deadheading spent blooms.
(*continued*)

Heliotrope, Cherry Pie
Heliotropium arborescens

Fragrance is one of the most alluring attributes of heliotrope. Flowers bloom in copious quantities of deep blue, violet, lavender, or white during the summer.

Description: Heliotrope has long, gray-green leaves with deep veins; reaching a height of one foot with an equal spread is reasonable. Many tiny flowers are clustered in the large heads carried well above the foliage.

How to grow: Any good garden soil with medium fertility in full sun will grow good heliotropes. Normally, plants are started early indoors (from seeds or cuttings) and transplanted outdoors when danger of frost has passed and the ground is warm. Depending on the size of transplants, space from 8 to 15 inches apart.

Propagation: Sow seeds 10 to 12 weeks before planting out. Seeds germinate in 7 to 21 days at 70° to 85°F. Root cuttings in four-inch pots in February in order to have husky plants for May planting.

Uses: Tuck heliotropes into rock gardens, or grow them in the front of borders.

Impatiens, Busy Lizzie, Patience

Impatiens wallerana

Impatiens flower in almost all colors. Their tidy mounding habit makes them ideal low-maintenance plants.

Description: Breeders have developed a variety of compact, self-branching plants whose flowers are borne above the foliage. Flowers are white, pink, rose, orange, scarlet, burgundy, and violet, with many variants. Foliage is deep, glossy green or bronze in color. Most specimens grow 12 to 15 inches high in dappled shade.

Propagation: Sow seeds 10 to 12 weeks before the last frost date. Germination takes 10 to 20 days at 75°F. Use a sterile soil mix, because young impatiens seedlings are subject to damping off. A fungicide is recommended. Cuttings root in 10 to 14 days.

How to grow: Impatiens will grow in any average soil. In cool or coastal areas, impatiens will grow and bloom well if their roots are kept well-watered. In deep shade, bloom diminishes.

Uses: Impatiens can be used in beds, borders, planting strips, and containers. They are beautiful in hanging baskets and planters.

Lobelia

Lobelia erinus

Few flowers have the intense blue provided by certain varieties of lobelia.

Description: These lobelias have small, round leaves and flowers up to ½ inch in diameter. Some varieties are compact and mound to six inches; others are definite trailers.

How to grow: Lobelia grows best in cool areas. Space 4 to 6 inches apart in the garden or in containers.

Propagation: Seeds are tiny and should be started indoors 10 to 12 weeks before planting outdoors. Seeds germinate in 20 days at 70° to 80°F. Seedling growth is slow, and the early stages should be watched carefully to prevent damping off.

Uses: Use the mounding forms for edgings, as pockets in rock gardens, or in the front of taller plantings beside walks and pathways. The trailing varieties are among the best for containers of all kinds.

Related varieties: Mounding forms include: 'Crystal Palace,' deep blue-flowers and bronze foliage; 'Cambridge Blue,' sky-blue flowers; and 'Rosamund,' cherry-red. Some trailers include: 'Sapphire,' deep blue with white eyes; 'Blue Cascade,' light blue; and 'White Cascade.'

Lantana

Lantana hybrida

These shrubby plants are abundantly covered through the summer with brightly colored blossoms. The garden varieties bear white, yellow, gold, orange, and red flowers; usually the older flowers in each cluster are a different color than the younger ones.

Description: Lantanas are woody shrubs with large, rough leaves. They grow about three feet tall and equally wide over a summer's growth. When protected against frost, they can grow to 15 feet or more in height over a period of years.

How to grow: Lantanas need full sun and hot weather—and actually poor soil—to give their best performance. They are frost-sensitive, so plant outdoors after the ground has warmed thoroughly. Space the plants about 18 inches apart.

Propagation: Take cuttings in February for spring planting.

Uses: Lantanas are most often used in containers. They grow well in sunny window boxes, hanging baskets, or patio planters.

Related species: *Lantana montevidensis* is a widely grown, pink-lavender flowering species. Its growth is more trailing.

French Marigold, American Marigold

Tagetes patula, Tagetes erecta

These all-American plants come in such an array of bright colors over a long season that they're a mainstay of gardeners everywhere.

Description: American marigolds can be tall plants, growing up to 36 inches high, although breeding has produced shorter heights. They have large, fully double flowers in yellow, gold, and orange. French marigolds are bushier and more compact with smaller flowers. Triploids, a cross between French and American marigolds, resemble French marigolds but have larger flowers.

How to grow: Marigolds grow best in full sun with moist, well-drained soil, although they will tolerate drier conditions. Plant them outdoors as soon as all danger of frost has passed. Space French marigolds 6 to 10 inches apart; Americans 10 to 18 inches apart.

Propagation: Seeds may be sown in place. Seeds germinate in 5 to 7 days at 65° to 75°F.

Uses: Grow taller ones to the center or rear of beds and borders, or as planting pockets in full sun, or in containers.

Melampodium

Melampodium paludosum

Large, bright green leaves have many yellow, daisylike flowers peering forth all summer long. *Melampodium paludosum* is one of 36 species in this genus.

Description: Melampodium will form a vigorous, bushy plant 10 to 15 inches high, and about as wide, in the garden. The flowers are small, up to one inch in diameter.

How to grow: Melampodium needs full sun. An average-to-rich, moist but well-drained soil is satisfactory. Plants should not be allowed to dry out. Plant outdoors as soon as all danger of frost has passed and the ground is warm. Space 10 to 15 inches apart.

Propagation: Sow seeds indoors 7 to 10 weeks prior to planting outdoors. Seeds germinate in 7 to 10 days at 65°F.

Uses: Plant melampodium where you want some contrast between flowers and foliage. Melampodium can be used as a sunny ground cover or be planted in rock gardens in front of flower borders.

Related varieties: 'Medaillon' is the most planted variety. It grows up to 20 inches tall, and as wide, and is covered with small, golden-yellow flowers all summer.

Nasturtium

Tropaeolum majus

Nearly every kid who's been near a garden has grown a nasturtium. And today's salad-conscious adult has certainly enjoyed the peppery tang of nasturtium leaves and flowers among their greens.

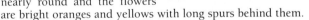

Description: Nasturtiums are vigorous and can grow as either vinelike or compact bushy plants. The leaves are nearly round and the flowers are bright oranges and yellows with long spurs behind them.

How to grow: Nasturtiums need full sun in a dry, sandy, well-drained soil. They're at their best in regions with cool, dry summers, although they will grow elsewhere, too. Sow seeds outdoors in the ground after the last frost. Depending on variety, space them 8 to 12 inches apart.

Propagation: Sow seeds where they will grow; germination takes 7 to 12 days at 65°F. Do not cover the seeds; they need light to germinate.

Uses: Dwarf varieties are good for flower borders, beds and edging paths and walks. Vining varieties can be tied to fences or posts and trailed from window boxes, hanging baskets, or other containers.

Related varieties: 'Dwarf Double Jewel,' in separate colors and a mix, has light yellow, gold, orange, rose, and crimson flowers.

Nicotiana, Flowering Tobacco

Nicotiana alata grandiflora

Related to the tobacco plants of commerce, flowering tobacco has been bred for its ornamental value.

Description: A low rosette of large, flat leaves supports the tall flowering stems covered with many star-shaped flowers. Flower colors include white, pink, maroon, lavender, green, red, and yellow. The plants can grow up to three feet tall.

How to grow: Nicotiana grows best in fertile, humus-rich, moist, well-drained soil in partial shade, or full sun in cooler areas. They are tough plants that will tolerate high temperatures. Transplant to the garden when all danger of frost has passed, spacing 8 to 12 inches apart.

Propagation: Seeds may be sown in place, thinning the seedlings to the right spacing. Elsewhere, start the plants indoors 6 to 8 weeks prior to planting out. Seeds germinate in 10 to 20 days at 70°F. Don't cover seeds; they need light to germinate.

Uses: Nicotiana is a plant that can give much-needed height to beds and borders. Group them in clusters for more impact.

Nierembergia, Cup Flower

Nierembergia hippomanica violacae

The common name of "Cup Flower," although rarely used, refers to the shape of the flower, which is somewhat like an open-faced bowl.

Description: Nierembergia has attractive, thin, narrow leaves topped at the ends with bluish or purple flowers. The plants develop outward rather than upward, up to six inches high, and will spread a foot.

How to grow: Grow nierembergia in full sun and well-drained soil with adequate moisture. Medium fertility is adequate to grow them well. Transplant to the garden when all danger of frost has passed. For full coverage, plant them 5 to 6 inches apart.

Propagation: Sow seeds indoors 10 to 12 weeks prior to planting in the garden after the last frost. Seeds germinate in 14 to 21 days at 70° to 75°F.

Uses: Grow nierembergia as a flowering ground cover in full sun, massed in large patches or beds. It's an ideal edging plant for beds and borders, traveling along paths and walkways with ease.

Pansy
Viola x wittrockiana

Pansies are the ultimate in cool season color, blooming until weather turns torrid. They are related to violets.

Description: Pansies produce flowers continuously as they grow. Flowers range from two inches in diameter up to giants of five inches or more. Some have clear colors, but many have the unique faces that are so appealing.

How to grow: In mild winter areas, plant as soon as the weather cools in late summer. Even areas with short freezes can enjoy winter pansies; once the weather warms, they'll start opening blossoms. Elsewhere, enjoy them for a short season in the spring. Space 6 to 9 inches apart.

Propagation: Start seeds 6 to 8 weeks prior to planting out. They will germinate in 10 to 15 days at 68°F.

Uses: Pansies are suitable for the front of borders and beds, in small groups among other flowers, and in containers.

Related species: Several varieties of violas, which are derived from *Viola cornuta* and *Viola tricolor,* include 'Helen Mount,' which is often called 'Johnny Jump Up' for its yellow and violet-faced flower.

Portulaca, Moss Rose
Portulaca grandiflora

Portulaca's profusion of sunny flower colors combined with its toughness make it a natural for difficult garden sites. It will do even better under less difficult conditions.

Description: Moss roses grow nearly prostrate—a mat of fleshy leaves with stems topped by flowers. Newer varieties are available in a myriad of jew-ellike colors—yellow, gold, orange, crimson, pink, lavender, purple, and white.

How to grow: Full sun, sandy soil, and good drainage are musts for portulaca. Since they are frost-tender, they should not be planted outdoors until the danger of frost has passed. Space them 1 to 2 feet apart.

Propagation: Sow in place as soon as danger of frost has passed and the soil is warm. For earlier bloom, start indoors 4 to 6 weeks ahead. Seeds germinate in 10 to 15 days at 70° to 80°F.

Uses: Reserve your problem areas for portulaca. They are notoriously good container plants that do not languish if you forget to water them one day.

Petunia
Petunia x hybrida

A plant that has long held the eye of breeders, petunias have flowers with charming varia-tions—open bells, crisped, curled, waved, and doubled-up into fluffy balls. The enormous color range even includes a yellow variety.

Description: Garden petunias are divided into two types: multifloras and grandifloras. Each has single and double forms, with grandiflora petunias being larger (although new hybrids have blurred this distinction).

How to grow: Well-drained soil in full sun suits petunias best. They grow well in cool temperatures and will stand a few degrees of frost if plants are well-hardened before planting. Space petunias 12 inches apart. To promote more branching and increased bloom, shear plants back halfway in midsummer.

Propagation: Start seeds indoors 10 to 12 weeks prior to planting outdoors. Seeds germinate in 10 to 12 days at 70° to 75°F.

Uses: Beds, borders, walkways, paths, containers—all will accommodate an abundance of petunias. Some varieties are especially recommended for containers, since they mound up and billow over the edges.

Rose Mallow
Lavatera trimestris

Lavatera is related to both hibiscus and hollyhock.

Description: Rose mallow grows to 3 to 5 feet by the end of summer. It branches vigorously to form a sturdy bush. The flowers, borne in leaf axils, are 3 to 4 inches in diameter.

How to grow: Grow rose mallow in full sun and average, well-drained soil. Plant outdoors as soon as the ground can be worked in the spring. Space 1 to 1½ feet apart.

Propagation: Sow directly in the garden where the plants will stay; it is difficult to successfully transplant seedlings. For earlier bloom, sow indoors 6 to 8 weeks prior to outdoor planting. Seeds germinate in 14 to 21 days at 70°F.

Uses: Lavatera can be used along pathways or walks or grow a row of them from the middle to the rear of a border bed, depending on border height. The pink and white colors also mix well with other flower colors. Lavatera makes good cut flowers.

Related varieties: 'Mont Blanc' has pure-white flowers; 'Mont Rose' is rose-pink; and 'Silver Cup' has large, pink flowers.

Salpiglossis, Painted Tongue

Salpiglossis sinuata

A kaleidoscope of color, each flower is dipped in shadings of color and strong veins. Related to petunias, salpiglossis has the same, open-faced, trumpetlike flowers.

Description: Salpiglossis is an upright growing species, reaching a height of three feet in the garden. Flowers are about 2½ inches in diameter. The colors are cream, lemon-yellow, gold, orange, brown, red, scarlet, violet, and near blue. Most of them are overlaid with veins and other patterns of color.

How to grow: Salpiglossis grows best where summers are moderate, in full sun, and fertile, well-drained soil. They must have a continuous supply of moisture. Transplant them outdoors in the spring as soon as all danger of frost has passed.

Propagation: Sow seeds indoors eight weeks prior to planting out. This will allow good-sized plants for putting into the garden after the danger of frost has passed. Seeds germinate in 15 to 20 days at 70° to 75°F.

Uses: Salpiglossis are ideal for the center of beds or borders as long as other plants cover their somewhat untidy feet.

Salvia, Scarlet Sage

(continued)

Uses: Salvia provides some of the purest reds and scarlets in the garden world, and their vertical growth makes them superb accents in the garden. Plant them as spots of color against other colors. They're a classic combination with blue and white for patriotic plantings. Their ability to bloom well in light shade makes them especially useful with pastel colors that tend to fade in the sun. They also make good container plants.

Related species: *Salvia farinacea* is a perennial in milder climates that is now widely used as an annual throughout the country. It's common name is "mealycup sage" for the grayish bloom on its stems and foliage. It grows 18 to 24 inches tall and produces either blue or white flowers. 'Victoria' is the most popular blue; its counterpart is 'Victoria White.' *Salvia patens*, gentian sage, is named for its rich indigo-blue flowers that have a long blooming season.

Related varieties: 'Carabiniere' grows to 12 inches and, in addition to red, has separate colors of coral-shrimp pink, orange, blue-violet, and creamy white. 'Red Pillar' is taller and blooms somewhat later. The tallest reds, 'America' and 'Bonfire,' will grow to two feet in the garden.

Salvia, Scarlet Sage

Salvia splendens

Salvias are best known for their spiky color that is dependable in any climate and adaptable to full sun or partial shade with equal ease. Salvia comes in brilliant red, creamy white, rose-colored, and purplish variants.

Description: Depending upon variety, salvia will grow from eight inches to three feet tall. The spikes of flowers are composed of bright bracts with flowers in the center of each. They are either the same color or contrasting.

How to grow: Salvia is a good dual-purpose plant that will perform dutifully in full sun or partial shade. It needs average soil and continuous moisture to perform its best. Transplant seedlings to the garden after danger of frost has passed. Depending on variety, space from 8 to 12 inches apart.

Propagation: Although seeds can be sown directly in the garden when the soil is warm, sowing indoors in advance will bring earlier flowering. Sow the seeds 6 to 8 weeks before the final frost. The seeds germinate in 12 to 15 days at 70° to 75°F.

(continued)

Sanvitalia, Creeping Zinnia

Sanvitalia procumbens

Although not a zinnia, sanvitalia has enough resemblance to one to fit its common name of "creeping zinnia." Golden-yellow flowers bloom nonstop all summer until frost.

Description: The plant is a creeper, reaching to 12 inches in diameter with flowers above topping out at six inches. The flowers aren't large, but they're so abundant that they nearly obscure the foliage.

How to grow: Sanvitalia prefers full sun but will adapt to partial shade with less flowering. It is tolerant of most garden conditions. Plant outdoors when all danger of frost has passed and the soil is warm. Space plants 4 to 6 inches apart.

Propagation: Sow seeds in place when ground has warmed. For earlier bloom, start indoors 4 to 6 weeks before outdoor planting. Seeds germinate in 10 to 15 days at 70°F.

Uses: Use it as an edging for the front of borders, along sidewalks and paths, and in rock gardens. Sanvitalia trails well from containers.

Related varieties: 'Mandarin Orange' brings a new color to sanvitalia.

Sapphire Flower
Browallia speciosa, viscosa

Sapphire flowers bloom heavily from early spring to fall frost, and year-round in sunny windows or greenhouses. They're at their best in cool or coastal gardens, but with partial shade or an eastern exposure they will consistently grow well elsewhere.

Description: B. speciosa varieties grow in a loose mound to 18 inches high and as wide, their lax habit allowing them to trail. The most-planted variety of B. viscosa ('Sapphire') is a compact, rather stiff plant that doesn't trail.

How to grow: Plant in rich, well-drained soil but keep moist. Plant large varieties 10 inches apart and dwarf ones six inches apart. Browallia is a good shade plant, although with a looser habit and sparser flowers.

Propagation: Start seeds indoors 6 to 8 weeks prior to planting out after the last frost. At temperatures of 70° to 75°F, they'll take 14 to 21 days to germinate.

Uses: Sapphire flowers are grown in beds, borders, or rock gardens. Compact plants make good edges for a tall border. They are also excellent container plants.

Sunflower
Helianthus annuus

Whether giants of the garden at 15 feet tall or barely topping one foot, these natives of North America come in a variety of colors and forms.

Description: Typically growing from 10 to 15 feet tall, sunflowers have coarse leaves and flower heads up to one foot or more in diameter. Although they started out as yellow flowers with brown or purple centers, there are now many variations.

How to grow: Sunflowers prefer full sun and will grow in any soil. They're tolerant of heat and drought. Plant the tall varieties 12 to 18 inches apart, dwarf ones at 9- to 12-inch spacings.

Propagation: Sow seeds outdoors after final frost. Seeds germinate in 10 to 20 days at 70° to 85°F.

Uses: The dwarf kinds can be used in beds and borders, while the taller varieties are best at the back of the border. The smaller-flowering varieties can also be used as cut flowers.

Related varieties: 'Piccolo' grows to four feet and bears rather graceful, four-inch, semi-double, gold flowers centered in black. 'Sunspot' has 8- to 12-inch blooms on plants only 18 to 24 inches high.

Snapdragon
Antirrhinum majus

Children love snapdragons because they can snap open the flowers like puppets. Snapdragons endure cool weather and are widely planted for winter color in mild-winter areas.

Description: Snapdragons uniformly bear a whorl of flowers atop slender stalks. The best known are ones with snappable flowers, but new kinds have open-faced flowers including double forms. Colors include white, yellow, burgundy, red, pink, orange, and bronze.

How to grow: Plant in rich, well-drained soil with plenty of organic matter. Grow in full sun. Space tall varieties 12 inches apart, small varieties six inches apart. Pinch tips of young plants to encourage branching. For cool season bloom in Zones 9 and 10, plant snapdragons in September.

Propagation: Germination takes an average of 8 days at 70°F. For early bloom, sow seeds indoors 6 to 8 weeks before setting outdoors after last frost.

Uses: Use the tall varieties for the back of the floral border and for cut flowers. Short varieties are good in borders and as edgings.

Sweet Pea
Lathyrus odoratus

In cool maritime or mountain climates, sweet peas will bring forth their beauty all summer. In Zones 9 and 10, they're best in cool seasons like winter and early spring.

Description: Sweet peas are vining plants that climb vigorously—6 to 8 feet over fences and other supports. The flowers are pink, white, red, lavender, purple, and near blue.

How to grow: In mild winter areas, sow seeds outdoors in the fall. Elsewhere, plant as soon as ground can be worked. Sweet peas need full sun and a deep, rich soil. The shortest varieties need no support.

Propagation: Nick seed coats with a knife and soak seeds overnight in water. Before planting, treat with a culture of nitrogen-fixing bacteria available at garden stores. Seeds will germinate in 10 to 14 days at 55° to 65°F.

Uses: Grow them against fences, over trellises, arches, and pergolas. The dwarf varieties can be planted in a border.

Related varieties: 'Early Mammoth Mixed' has many colors. 'Bijou' is a variety with a bushy habit, growing up to 12 inches with a number of colors.

Torenia, Wishbone Flower

Torenia fournieri

Torenia is a colorful plant that thrives in shade and hot, humid weather.

Description: Torenia forms a compact mound about one foot high with many branches. Leaves are oval or heart-shaped. The flowers look a bit like open-faced snapdragons with prominent markings on the petals. The most predominant color has been blue, but new varieties are pink, rose, light blue, and white.

How to grow: Torenias grow best in rich, moist, well-drained soil. They thrive during summer in partial shade. They like high humidity and won't tolerate being dry. Plant outdoors after all danger of frost has passed, spacing plants 6 to 8 inches apart.

Propagation: Sow seeds 10 to 12 weeks prior to outdoor planting. Germination takes 10 to 15 days at 70°F.

Uses: Plant Torenia in groups of three or more in woodland bowers; grow clumps along paths or walkways. Because it grows evenly, it's a good candidate for formal beds in sun or partial shade.

Related species: *Torenia concolor* is a tender trailing perennial.

Vinca, Madagascar Periwinkle

Catharanthus roseus

These tropical plants stand up well to heat and humidity. Researchers are currently developing new varieties with additional colors beyond the familiar white, pink, and rose.

Description: Vinca flowers are round, 1 to 2 inches in diameter, and borne at the tips of branches or shoots that bear glossy, green leaves. The flowers of many varieties also have a contrasting eye in the center of the bloom.

How to grow: Vinca is at its best in hot conditions—full sun, heat, and high humidity. Plant at 8 to 12 inches apart, after the soil has warmed.

Propagation: Sow seeds 12 weeks prior to setting out after last frost. Germination takes 14 to 21 days at a temperature above 70°F. Maintain warm temperatures after germination and don't overwater.

Uses: Vinca is good for massing and edging, and exceptional as a container plant. It is extremely heat tolerant.

Related varieties: Popular varieties include 'Blanche,' pure white; and 'Pinkie,' a rosy pink. 'Pacifica Red' is the deepest red-rose available.

Verbena

Verbena x hybrida

Verbenas are garden treasures in areas where few other plants will grow. Some varieties trail; others form mounds of color.

Description: The trailing varieties may reach 18 inches in diameter, while the mounding types will grow to about one foot high and wide. The flowers bloom in clusters.

How to grow: Verbenas prefer well-drained, sandy soil with good fertility. Plant after all danger of frost has passed. Space plants 12 (upright types) to 18 (trailing types) inches apart.

Propagation: Verbenas are slow in the early stages. Sow seeds 12 to 14 weeks prior to planting in the garden. Germination takes 3 to 4 weeks at 75° to 80°F.

Uses: The trailing types are ideal for rock gardens, trailing over walls, and as edgings for garden beds and borders. Use mounding types in beds and borders. Verbena also trails nicely from containers.

Related varieties: 'Blaze' is a red variety; 'Crystal,' a white; and 'Delight,' a salmon-pink. These are all trailers. Mounding verbenas include the 'Romance' and 'Sandy' series and 'Trinidad'—a fluorescent-rose color.

Zinnia

Zinnia elegans

Zinnias are among the favorite American garden flowers, loved for their variety of colors.

Description: Zinnias can be grouped into three classes: tall (to 2½ feet), intermediate (to 20 inches), and dwarf (to 12 inches). Flowers come in almost every color except blue.

How to grow: Zinnias need full sun and rich, fertile soil. They grow best in hot, dry climates after the final frost, when the soil is warm. Depending on the size of the variety, space 6 to 12 inches apart. Powdery mildew can be a problem in humid locations.

Propagation: Zinnias grow fast, and early bloom can be achieved in most climates by sowing seeds directly into the soil. Seeds germinate in 5 to 7 days at 70° to 75°F.

Uses: Dwarf and intermediate varieties can be used in beds and borders or in container plantings. Taller varieties should be moved to the back of the border or the cutting garden.

Related varieties: The tall variety includes 'Zenith' hybrids that come in many separate colors and a mix. The dwarf variety includes 'Peter Pan' hybrids that have large flowers on short stems.

Master Gardener Q & A

Commonly Asked Questions

Q: I have several large patio containers of trees and shrubs growing with mixed annuals. How do I over-winter these containers?

A: Remove the annuals from the containers at the end of the season. Move the containers to a location protected from the warming sun and winter wind. Insulate the soil with mulch—compost, bark, or leaves—and make sure the containers receive adequate water during dry spells. Try planting some spring flowering bulbs in place of the annuals to enjoy some early season color.

Q: I have trouble growing flowers in my shade garden. Are there any colorful shade-tolerant plants that I can use?

A: Aside from using perennials with some bloom, and contrasting color and texture, a few annuals will thrive in the shade given proper moisture and nutrients. The most shade-tolerant annuals that add color all season are coleus (grown for colorful foliage), wax begonias, and impatiens, which are available in a host of colors. Depending on the depth of shade, still other annuals, such as ageratum, sapphire flower, caladiums, and sweet alyssum—may be successful.

Q: When can I safely plant annuals in the spring?

A: From your local Extension Office, find out the date of your area's average last frost. After that date, planting should be safe; but remember, this date is an average and you can expect a later frost some years. When you purchase annuals, condition them to the sunlight, wind, and night temperature for several days before planting them in the garden. Be prepared to protect them from a late-season freeze.

Q: My hanging baskets of annuals look great each spring when I purchase them. By midsummer they look dried up and have few blooms. How can I keep them fresh and full of flowers?

A: Follow three basic principles when growing flowering baskets—water, fertilize, and groom. The soil mass in a basket is very small—it heats up and dries out quickly—so daily watering may be needed. Fertilize the plant with a liquid balanced fertilizer every two weeks. And groom your plant often. Deadhead and pinch back leggy growth to promote heavier flowering and branching.

Q: What should be done this fall to prepare a bed of annuals for next spring?

A: When this year's plants have died from frost, cut them to the ground and, to prevent this year's pests from over-wintering, remove all debris from the area. Have your soil tested now—add lime if necessary but wait until spring to fertilize. Cultivate organic matter into the soil and apply a fresh layer of mulch to prevent winter weeds from germinating. Your bed should be ready for spring planting.

Q: Is it possible to save any of my annuals through the winter for next year's plantings?

A: Several types of annuals overwinter well in the house. Coleus, geraniums, impatiens, and wax begonias hold nicely as houseplants. Dig up the plant with as much of its root system intact as possible and pot it, using quality potting soil. Cut the plant back by 40 to 50 percent, leaving some foliage on the plant. In the house, provide the plants with as much light as possible, keeping the soil slightly moist.

Q: I'd like to grow annuals for cutting and arranging. What types make the best cut flowers and where should I plant them?

A: Look for varieties with tall stems in the colors you'd like to use for arranging. Many species of annuals are available in varieties that have different characteristics. Some will be short and bushy for edging and massing, while others will be tall—excellent for cutting. It is a good idea to grow them in the back of the border or design a bed especially for cutting. A row or more in a sunny vegetable garden, for example, serves as an ideal place to grow cut flowers.

Q: What is the best way to stake my tall and floppy annuals?

A: Use materials that will be unobtrusive in the garden. Natural brush and twigs blend in well with garden plants; green bamboo stakes are available at garden centers. It is best to set up the stakes during planting time so the roots are not damaged during installation. Tie the plants loosely with string, plastic wrap, or even leaves of tall ornamental grasses. Avoid wire ties, as they easily cut flower stems.

Q: Which annuals require the least amount of maintenance time?

A: Choose varieties that will not require deadheading or much additional irrigation. Some annuals drop their flowers naturally while others put energy into seed production, and must be groomed for continual bloom. Ageratum, alyssum, begonias, dusty miller, impatiens, and vinca are a few self-cleaning annuals. Ageratum, marigolds, ornamental peppers, portulaca, and vinca are among the drought-tolerant species. Prepare your soil well with organic matter (such as wood chips, leaves, or compost) to increase the intervals between waterings and to save maintenance time.

Q: It seems that the only bedding plants available are short varieties suited for the front of the border. What can I do to get some height for the back of the border?

A: A greater selection of varieties is available through mail-order seed catalogs. Some companies sell a large selection of starter plants as well as seeds, but you may enjoy starting your own seedlings. Start small-seeded varieties on a sunny windowsill several weeks before planting outside. Many varieties can be sown directly in the garden.

Q: Do you have any suggestions to help encourage children to enjoy gardening?

A: Success is the best motivator. Encourage children to have a garden space of their own, but work with them to ensure success. Grow plants from large seeds, or use transplants for immediate color. Grow varieties like morning glories and gourds—quick growing vines which produce abundant flower or fruit—and colorful zinnias, or balsam. Encourage the child to collect seeds to save for next season. Most of all, go out and enjoy the garden together!

Zinnias are perfect for introducing a child to gardening.

Perennials

1

How to Plan for Lasting Color

Perennials are plants that survive winter outdoors to produce new growth and flowers each summer. Unlike annuals, which can flower continuously for several months, most perennials only bloom for two to three weeks. Therefore, it's necessary to plan your garden carefully in order to have color in perennial beds during selected periods. By carefully working out a plan in advance on paper, you can be assured of a colorful show all season long.

It would be a mistake to place emphasis exclusively on perennial flowers. There is much beauty in the textures and subtle colors of perennial foliage as well. Spreading silver-gray mats of cerastium; bold hosta clumps in various shades of blue-green, green and white, and gold; fine-laced fern fronds—the list of attractive foliage goes on and on. Those who grow perennials tend to be as aware of (and enthusiastic about) foliage as they are about flowers!

Whether you use just a few perennials in bold masses among shrubs or under trees, mix them in with annuals, or specialize in the many varieties of one particular kind, the weekend gardener will especially appreciate that perennials provide dependable beauty year after year.

Choosing the Right Colors

There are several aspects of color that need to be considered when planning perennial plantings. The primary source of color is, of course, from flowers. But another equally important consideration is the color provided by existing backgrounds: fences, house walls, flowering shrubs, or the blossoms in neighboring gardens. If, for example, the background is painted white, white flowers planted against it will become virtually invisible. If the background contains bright red flowers, you may not want the vivid contrast that purple blooms would add. If the area is backed by dark woods or evergreens, you should keep in mind that dark shades of blue and purple will disappear and whites, yellows, silver-grays, and yellow-greens will stand out.

In addition to such physical considerations, there are also emotional ones: color can be mood setting. Red, yellow, and orange shades are bright, warm, and cheering. On the other hand, blues, silvers, and whites are calming and cooling—they can be soothing during the heat of summer. A nostalgic, romantic look can be achieved by using pale pastels. A modern, upbeat style results when pure bright colors are mixed. Think about the mood and atmosphere you'd like to create in each area of your garden; it may differ from one location to another and even from one season to the next.

If you feel uncertain about color, you may want to use proven combinations with the help of a color wheel. There are three basic winning combinations. The first is monochromatic, which combines all of the various shades, tints, and tones of a single color. The second is complementary, and includes all of the variations of two colors exactly opposite each other on the color wheel. The last is analogous—those variations of three colors that are found adjacent to one another on the color wheel. These are not the only possible combinations, but they are the easiest to use and the most certain to succeed.

Two final hints on color: White flowers will blend easily with any other colors you select; and varying the intensity of different flower colors in your design will often help add vitality and interest to the planting.

Although you'll want to plan the colors for your garden with care, inevitably some of your choices will not work out as happily as you had envisioned. Don't be too worried about getting it all exactly right in advance. You can always move or remove those plants that do not blend well. Part of the fun in gardening is to make adjustments and changes from season to season.

🖎 *Proper color selection can mean the difference between a drab perennial garden and a vibrant one.*

Full Color Wheel

A color wheel can be a helpful tool in choosing flower colors that blend well together. All of the shades, tints, and tones—as well as the pure color of any spoke on the color wheel—will automatically combine well.

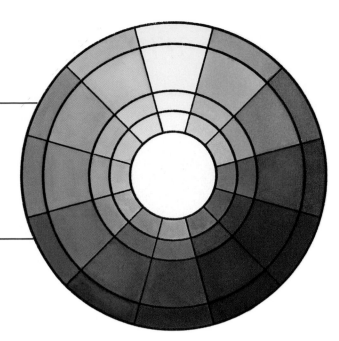

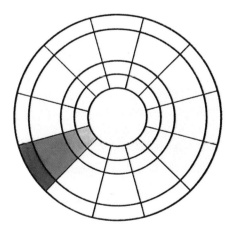

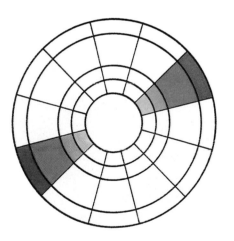

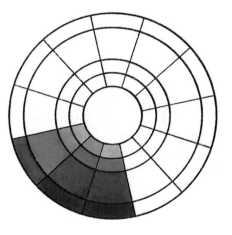

Monochromatic Colors

A monochromatic design is one in which all of the flower colors are in a single color line. The only variety will be in their range—from dark, to intense, to pastel shades of that one color (e.g., from navy blue, to bright blue, to baby blue).

Complementary Colors

Using two colors opposite each other on the color wheel will produce a complementary color scheme. Starting again with blue, this would blend all of the clear blues with all of the clear oranges.

Analogous Colors

Analogous designs include flowers of any of the hues in any three spokes that are side-by-side on the color wheel—for example: all the blue shades, plus all of the blue-violet shades, and all of the violet shades.

Form and Texture

Plant form and texture are especially important aspects of perennials because your plants will not be in bloom for a good part of the growing season. In fact, in the case of some perennials, form and texture are all that matters. Fern clumps take us from the early spring unfolding of their fiddleheads, through the fully open filigree of their fronds, and on to their golden autumn color. Flowers are not utilized for this effect at all. Many hostas, stonecrops, and ornamental grasses are also better known for their foliage effects than for their flowers.

An extra bonus to be savored and utilized in the landscape is a plant that has lovely blossoms as well as an attractive growth habit. The flowers of perennials vary in form and texture: the huge, airy clouds of baby's breath; the tall, handsome spires of delphinium and foxtail lilies; the round pompons of chrysanthemums and peonies; and the graceful arches of bleeding heart (each bloom perfectly heart-shaped).

Among perennials, there are some outstandingly handsome examples of foliage and form. Peonies have a rugged, bold leaf cluster that turns to wonderful shades of pink or bronze in the autumn; hostas provide dramatic low clumps that can be used alone or combined with other plants; the gray-green globe thistle foliage makes a handsome bush; and the tall, slender Japanese and Siberian iris foliage provide a wonderful spiky contrast to round-leaved neighbors.

Fortunately, many perennials offer this added bonus of interesting texture and/or form to the garden. In many instances, they also offer a color contrast as well. Use plants with these bonuses wherever possible, although it doesn't mean you should completely bypass those that only have attractive blooms to their credit. Instead, intermix outstanding stars with duller plants for added interest. Repeat forms and textures throughout your garden for a solid, unified design. You'll produce a complete planting, which is interesting throughout the growing season—whether in bloom or not.

Dainty goldentufts mingle with irises. Smaller-flowering species can often complement plants with larger displays.

The Varied Forms of Perennials

The form, or shape, of perennial plants is important to consider when designing a garden. By selecting plants with a balance of varying forms, the garden will be more interesting to look at. Ground-hugging mats; tall, spiked growth; as well as arching and rounded plants provide a visual variety you'll enjoy even when the plants aren't in bloom.

Ground-hugging

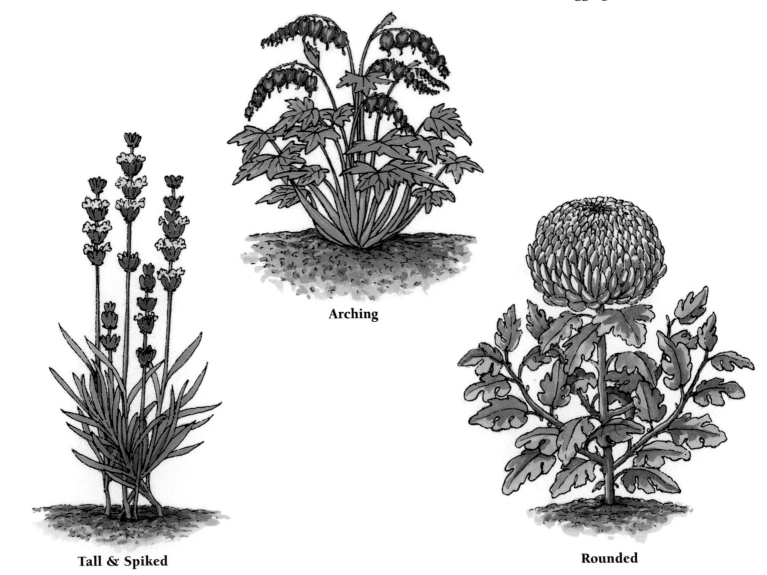

Arching

Tall & Spiked

Rounded

Textures of Perennials

A variety of textures adds to a garden's beauty. Placing plants with feathery foliage or flowers next to ones that have coarse, bold characteristics will produce a dramatic-looking garden. It's helpful to pretest how plants will look together by placing potted samples side by side.

Feathery

Coarse & Bold

Patterned Foliage and Flowers
Some plants add interest with patterned foliage or flowers; stripes, spots, or splotches of color all provide variety to the basic forms. Some flowers are two-toned, with outer petals of one color and inner petals of another. Other plants have lower petals of one shade and upper petals of another shade (e.g., the iris).

Striped

Splotched

Two-toned

Spotted

Variegated

Beauty in the Shade Garden

Even under the best circumstances, a shade garden cannot compete with a sunny garden for bright colors. In fact, most shade-tolerant plants offer soft, subtle hues: whites, pinks, pale blues, and yellows rather than blazing oranges and reds. On the other hand, these subtle colors, often lost in the sunny garden, really stand out in a shady one. Nothing beats pale hues for adding color to a shade garden, and pure white is the brightest color of all in the shade. Look for these pale shades in the perennials you select.

Foliage can also add color to the shade garden. White and yellow striped and marbled leaves, or silvery-mottled ones, can brighten even the shadiest spots. Leaf colors are much more durable than those of flowers, lasting through the entire growing season. Variegated shade-tolerant plants can make an excellent long-term solution to overbearing shade. Finally, the shade garden, as subtle as it may be during spring and summer, often turns surprisingly colorful in fall when autumn leaves far outshine the best flowers the mixed border can produce.

Truly beautiful shade gardens often rely more on attractive combinations and contrasts of foliage texture and plant forms than their flowers. Light and airy fern fronds stand out from heavy, oblong hosta leaves, which in their turn can be highlighted by the small leaves and prostrate growth patterns of ground covers. Subtle differences in the shades of foliage green become more distinct when there are few flowers to steal the show. Nature provides a vast and pleasing array of foliage colors: blue-greens, apple-greens, dark greens, and more.

Shade gardens can be planted just as formally as any other garden, but a more natural look is usually preferable. Both Oriental gardens (with their sparse appearance, meandering paths, and small pools) and English gardens (with their overflowing beds of mixed plants) make ideal styles for shade gardens. If your shade garden is already at least partially forested, however, consider establishing a wild garden.

You can easily establish a wild garden by planting hardy yet decorative shade-tolerant plants among the trees in an informal pattern. This technique is known as naturalizing. The goal is to introduce or reintroduce plants into the landscape that will be capable of growing and spreading under existing conditions with a minimal amount of help from you. The plants you introduce will depend on several factors—notably your local climate—but look for perennials that are capable of taking care of themselves. Consider both native wildflowers that may once have grown there and nonnative varieties of equal ornamental appeal. Avoid plants that are invasive.

Shade gardens often require quite a bit of effort to establish, but a relatively small amount of upkeep. For example, with sunlight already at a premium, most weeds don't stand a chance. Established

Balloon flowers, with their distinct shape and rich hues, are an example of perennials that thrive in shade gardens.

shade plants and ground covers take what is left of the light, leaving nothing for would-be competitors.

Fall leaves often integrate perfectly into a shade garden. Leave them where they fall, and they'll supply a natural mulch that regenerates and enriches the soil while helping to suppress weeds. Large leaves could smother growth, so they should be chopped up into small pieces (run a lawn mower over them or rent a chipper) before being spread among the shade garden plants.

Shade gardens with heavy root competition will require special help. Such beds will dry out quicker than open, sunny beds. Unless you are prepared to irrigate regularly, plant selection is extremely important. Choose varieties that can survive periodic drought. When you do water, water deeply. Remember you're watering for two: the trees that cause the shade and the plants that grow beneath the tree boughs. If you let nature take its course, the shallow-rooted understory plants will be the first to suffer during a drought. If temperatures and drought become too severe, the tops of established perennials may die to the ground and go dormant. This process is natural for perennial plant survival; the plant will come back as usual next season.

SHADE-TOLERANT PERENNIALS

anemones (*Anemone* sp.)
astilbe (*Astilbe* sp.)
balloon flower (*Platycodon grandiflorus*)
bellflower (*Campanula* sp.)
bergamot (*Monarda* sp.)
bergenia (*Bergenia* sp.)
bishop's hood (*Astrophytum* sp.)
bleeding heart (*Dicentra* sp.)
bowman's root (*Gillenia* sp.)
bugleweed (*Ajuga* sp.)
Siberian bugloss (*Brunnera* sp.)
creeping buttercup (*Ranunculua repens*)
cardinal flower (*Lobelia cardinalis*)
chameleon plant (*Houttuynia* sp.)
black cohosh (*Cimicifuga* sp.)
columbine (*Aquilegia* sp.)
coralbell (*Heuchera* sp.)
crane's bill (*Geranium* sp.)
daylily (*Hemerocallis* sp.)
dichondra (*Dichondra* sp.)
foxglove (*Digitalis* sp.)
globeflower (*Trollius* sp.)
goat's beard (*Arunucus* sp.)
goldenstar (*Chrysogonum* sp.)

goutweed (*Aegopodium* sp.)
hosta (*Hosta* sp.)
ladybells (*Adenophora* sp.)
leopard's bane (*Doronicum* sp.)
ligularia (*Ligularia* sp.)
toad lily (*Tricyrtis* sp.)
lily-of-the-valley (*Convallaria* sp.)
liriope (*Liriope* sp.)
gooseneck loosestrife (*Lysimachia clethroides*)
lungwort (*Pulmonaria* sp.)
dead nettle (*Lamium* sp.)
pachysandra (*Pachysandra* sp.)
periwinkle (*Vinca* sp.)
plume poppy (*Macleaya* sp.)
primrose (*Primula* sp.)
rodgersia (*Rodgersia* sp.)
Christmas rose (*Helleborus* sp.)
meadow rue (*Thalictrum* sp.)
self-heal (*Prunella* sp.)
speedwell (*Veronica* sp.)
spiderwort (*Tradescantia* sp.)
turtlehead (*Chelone* sp.)
yellow waxbell (*Kirengeshoma* sp.)
violet (*Viola* sp.)

SHADE-TOLERANT BULBS

crocus (*Crocus* sp.)
glory-of-the-snow (*Chionodoxa* sp.)
meadow saffron (*Colchicum* sp.)

narcissus (*Narcissus* sp.)
Siberian squill (*Scilla siberica*)
snowdrop (*Galanthus* sp.)

Sequence of Bloom

Because individual perennials have their own limited season of bloom, it's important to know when you can expect each of them to flower. If you want color throughout the entire growing season, you'll need to plan on a succession of bloom provided by different species. With some proper planning, it's possible to do this entirely with perennials, even though perennials don't have to stand alone. To obtain summer-long bloom, it's feasible to intermix annuals with perennials—the annuals will provide additional flower color from midsummer to late summer. Also, remember that perennial and annual bulbs offer additional summer color possibilities. Most varied and beautiful are the many hardy lilies that provide an outstanding display of different colors and forms throughout the summer.

Summer isn't the only season when bulbs add beauty to the landscape. All of the spring-flowering bulbs—tulips, daffodils, flowering onions, crocuses, scillas, snowdrops, hyacinths, anemones, etc.—are certainly well-known, popular, and easily grown perennial additions to most gardens.

Plant the bulbs so the flower stems will be taller than the adjacent plants—this way, their lovely display will be fully visible. As the flower stems and leaves die back, they'll disappear below the level of adjacent plant foliage and be hidden from view.

When developing your garden plan, avoid clumping all of the plants that bloom at the same time in one part of the garden. Make sure you to have a balance of early, midseason, and late bloomers mixed throughout the planting area. Observe your plantings throughout the seasons and note where color needs improved balance. Plant large blocks—three or more plants—of just a few varieties per bloom period. You'll feel as though the entire garden is in bloom, although it's the balanced masses of color that attract attention. Note how the garden changes—both in color scheme and balance—from week to week. A yellow and white spring garden might transform into orange and purple by July.

At first, the idea of intermixing and underplanting may sound too complex. Don't become discouraged. Although it's difficult to plant a well-balanced perennial garden by simply digging holes in the ground and poking plants into them, the job becomes fairly simple if you take the time to draw up a plan on paper in advance. This lets you detect any problems and change them before you ever buy or plant anything. There will probably still be some changes to be made from year to year as you discover new plants you'd like to add, existing plants that you decide to abandon and replace because they never seem to prosper, and others that you feel would look better if moved to a different location.

🌿 *By choosing plants with successive bloom dates, you can keep your garden flowering from early spring to late fall.*

2

Getting Your Garden Off to a Good Start

Unlike beds for annuals or vegetables, perennial plant beds are not dug up and replanted every year. Once perennials are planted, there will be no need to do more than routine weeding, feeding, cultivating, and mulching for several years. Eventually, though, many perennials and bulbs would benefit from being lifted from the soil and divided to make several new plants.

Strong, healthy plants are better able to survive such difficulties as drought, insect infestations, and diseases. Learn how and when to do these simple maintenance tasks that will ensure success with perennials. This will almost certainly result in less work in the long run. Included in this chapter is information about how to properly handle pregrown, potted, and bare-root plants. The hints in these sections will help you to reduce plant loss during the critical transplanting stages. You'll find suggestions about how to maintain perennial bulbs and how to keep your perennials strong and flowering for many years.

Study the information contained here before laying out and tilling your perennial planting areas or purchasing any plants. You'll find the time spent in advance preparation will save much future effort.

Transplanting from Pots

Many garden shops and nurseries offer an extensive variety of perennials planted in containers. Whereas in the past there were just a few mail-order specialists from whom the more unusual perennials could be purchased, it's now possible to obtain what you want locally. This allows you to select the individual plants you prefer and to see their condition before you buy.

Potted perennials are offered in a number of sizes from small plants in three- to four-inch pots to mature plants in large metal or plastic containers. The small plants are usually only a few months old. In most instances, these will not produce blooms the first season. Those in large containers are often in bloom at the time of purchase and can be expected to quickly become established in their new sites. Smaller plants usually cost less than larger ones; when small plants are priced high, it's because they're rare or exceedingly slow or difficult to propagate. Container plants should be planted outdoors as promptly as possible after purchase. The longer they're kept in containers, the more likely they are to dry out and become pot-bound. If you must hold plants for a long time prior to planting, place them where they'll be under light shade and be sure to water them. When you're ready to plant container-grown plants, thoroughly moisten the soil before knocking them out of the pot. Plunge the container into a pail of water to above the pot's rim for a few minutes. Snap off any roots sticking out of the pot bottom. The plant should slide out into your hand. If it doesn't, cut the pot open and peel it off, avoiding damage to the roots as much as is reasonably possible.

Loosen and remove any excess soil from around the roots. Most soilless mixes will fall away on their own. If the mix adheres to the roots, take away only as much as comes off easily with your fingers. Soilless mixes dry faster than garden soil, so you want to eliminate what you can without disturbing the root ball.

When selecting potted plants, look for signs of healthy growth and proper care. Weak plants rarely survive transplanting.

Always place the plant in the ground at the same depth as it was in the pot and provide a water-holding area by forming a soil dam a few inches away from the stem. Transplant in the evening or on a cloudy day to keep the sun from burning tender roots. Otherwise, provide shade for three to four days by setting an overturned box or a newspaper cone over each plant. Tuck a two-inch mulch layer around the plants and deep water as needed the first growing season.

Transplanting Potted Plants

1 Submerge potted plants in water before transplanting. To avoid damage to the plant top and to help keep the root ball intact, spread your hand over the top of the pot with stems and leaves poking out between your fingers. Then turn the pot upside down and gently tap its rim against something solid to slide the plant from the container.

2 The roots need to spread out after planting, rather than continuing to grow in a tight mass. If they resist loosening with your fingers, cut up into the sides of the root ball in several places with a sharp knife or scissors, then shake the roots loose a bit more with your fingers before planting.

3 The plant hole should be somewhat larger in diameter than the root ball and deep enough to allow you to plant at the same depth as the plant was growing in the container. Fan out the loosened roots over a small soil mound in the center of the hole to encourage spreading root growth.

4 Firm soil around the plant stem and roots. Create a soil dam around the plant and fill it with water. The soaking water will help settle the soil and remove any remaining air pockets around the roots—air pockets can cause delicate feeder roots to dry out and die. Apply mulch around the crown and under trailing foliage.

Setting Bare-Root Plants

🌿 *Delicate oriental poppies are often purchased in bare-root form.*

had an hour or so to take up water. Most will revitalize. Report any that don't show signs of new growth after three weeks, explaining the dry condition upon arrival. Plant supply houses are so experienced in packing bare-root plants that there is seldom a problem. When there is, it's usually because the shipment was somehow delayed in transit.

Ideally, bare-root plants should be planted immediately after arrival. If that's impossible, unpack them right away and place their roots in a container of water (do not submerge the tops). The sooner they're planted, the less energy they lose. If you must delay planting, pot the plants in containers and grow them as potted plants until you're ready to plant them in the ground.

Most perennials are best transplanted in the spring or, as a second choice, in the fall. Bearded irises, oriental poppies, and peonies usually fare better if moved only in the fall.

Place bare-root plants at the same depth as in the nursery—look for the soil line on the stem as a guide. However, those that arrive as dormant roots have no stems or top growth as indicators.

These are the depths at which to plant the following types: oriental poppy—top of root two to three inches below soil surface; peony—lay root flat with top of clump one inch beneath soil surface; bearded iris—lay flat with top of clump right at, or slightly above, the soil surface. Specific planting instructions will usually accompany your shipment.

The term "bare-root" is self-explanatory: There is no soil around the plant roots when you unpack the plant, although there is often a bit of moist excelsior packing. Plants sent by mail order are often packed bare-root. You can also occasionally find perennials in garden centers that are packed this way.

This technique of packing works perfectly well and is in no way harmful to the plants, as long as the roots have remained moist in transit. If you find the roots are bone dry when you receive your shipment, there is some cause for concern. If this happens, thoroughly soak the plant roots immediately, then plant them outdoors after they've

When planting bare-root plants, don't just dig a small hole and jam the roots into it. Thorough preparation at planting is a guaranteed timesaver. Make the hole large enough so you can carefully spread the roots out in all directions. Take care to prepare the soil well—your perennials will want to remain undisturbed for many years. Add organic matter and improve drainage as necessary. Mound the soil slightly so it will settle to the original grade of the garden. Aftercare is the same as for container-grown plants from this stage onward.

Planting Bare-Root Plants

1 Unpack bare-root plants as soon as they arrive, planting them as soon as possible. Keep the roots moist and protect them from the wind and sun—they don't have any soil around them to help protect their feeder roots from drying out! Trim any extra long or damaged roots with sharp scissors before planting.

2 Set the plant in the hole so the soil line on the plant is at the same level as it was in the nursery. Spread out the roots evenly to help encourage well-distributed root growth.

3 Fill in the soil firmly around the roots, creating a dam around each plant. Fill the dam with water, and mulch the bed. If plants have begun to sprout, provide shade to the new transplant for one day with a newspaper cone or similar shading.

Coping with Shade

Many shade gardens are naturally cool and moist. They are usually surrounded by deep-rooted trees and copious amounts of natural mulch from fallen leaves. Their soils are normally rich, deep, and easy to dig. These are the easiest shade spots in which to garden, as shade plants thrive under such conditions. In such places, plantings can be made directly into the ground with little special preparation.

Other shade gardens are also cool, but dry rather than moist. They are filled with shallow-rooted trees and shrubs that soak up every drop of rain. The soil is often poor and hard-baked, depleted of nutrients by gluttonous roots. These gardens present quite a challenge for the gardener. Digging can be very difficult. When you carefully cut away sections of root-clogged soil and replace it with good humus-rich earth to nurture a special plant, the invasive roots of nearby trees and shrubs are soon back.

Perhaps the greatest disappointment to the owner of a shady yard is that lawns are difficult to grow. Most lawns will grow quickly at first, needing frequent mowing, but they are sparse and subject to dieback. These lawns generally require regular overseeding to maintain even a semblance of thickness. Some gardeners believe that fertilizing or watering abundantly will help, but to no avail. The only way to get a reasonably healthy lawn in a shady spot is to use lawn seed mixes designed for that purpose. These mixes contain a larger percentage of shade-tolerant grass species than regular lawn grasses. But even with special lawn seed mixes, results are often mediocre in truly shady spots. Lawns and shade simply don't mix.

It is often because of poor lawns that many people stumble upon the concept of shade gardens. They replace part of the lawn first with one plant, then another, and soon find their yard looking better than ever even though little green grass is left.

If you insist on a low-growing carpet of greenery in a yard where lawns do poorly, consider shade-tolerant ground covers. They make nice, even carpets in various tones of green, and should require little maintenance. This allows the gardener to develop healthy, low-maintenance beds that will persist for many years.

Actually, a shady garden requires little maintenance once it has established itself. The undergrowth of naturally shady sites is composed of numerous perennials—suited specifically for either moist or dry conditions. Plant selection is critical, since plants that require moist shade will quickly die out in a dry, shady garden. Many perennials are natural choices for shade gardens.

It is sometimes possible, although rare, to increase the amount of light in a shady garden. If overhead foliage is dense, you may be able to remove a few overhanging branches and bring in more dappled sunlight.

Small areas surrounded by buildings or fences get little sunlight. Shade-tolerant plants may be your only option.

How to Beat Root Competition in a Shade Garden

1 There are three basic ways to beat root competition in a shade garden. However, remember to keep the health and well-being of the trees as a priority; don't disturb too much too fast. One way is to dig down into the soil and insert a bottomless container to keep the roots out. Fill the space inside the barrier with good soil.

2 Another method is to plant in containers. Pots, trays, and flower boxes set on top of the soil will stymie even the most invasive roots. This is often an ideal way to introduce annuals into the shade garden.

3 The final method is to install raised beds, filling each bed with at least 12 inches of top-quality soil. Limit the amount of area covered by such beds as the new soil level will suffocate the trees if the majority of a tree's roots becomes completely covered.

Bulb Maintenance

Once planted in a permanent spot, hardy bulbs require little care. Water new plantings throughout the fall until the ground freezes to stimulate good root growth. In spring, as bulbs begin to bloom, work bulb fertilizer into the soil at their bases. This will supply nutrition for the development of healthy bulbs and abundant blooms the following year. Let the foliage of bulbs die down naturally; bulbs need their leaves to absorb energy. Leaves should only be removed and composted once they begin to yellow naturally (generally in early summer for spring- and fall-flowering bulbs and fall for summer-flowering ones).

Most bulb plantings are permanent, so little care is needed during the summer months, when the spring-flowering bulbs are dormant. But be careful not to dig them up accidentally while their leaves are absent. When space is needed for other plantings, hardy bulbs can be carefully lifted after blooming, with roots and leaves intact, and planted elsewhere. After several years of growth, the bulbs naturally multiply. They tend to become overcrowded and their flowering diminishes. When this happens, lift the bulbs just when their leaves begin to fade in early summer. Separate the clumps into single bulbs and replant them as soon as you are able. It is possible to hold the bulbs until fall planting by letting the bulbs dry in the sun for a few days, then removing the faded leaves. Store in a dry, warm spot out of sunlight (a tool shed is ideal) until fall planting time.

Resistance to cold winter weather is rarely a problem for hardy bulbs. Planted deep beneath the ground, they are capable of surviving and even thriving in extreme conditions. On the other hand, permanent bulb plantings, especially fresh ones, are subject to frost heaving, which can thrust the bulbs out of the ground. For that reason, cover recently planted areas with a three-inch layer of mulch consisting of organic material—such as shredded bark, leaves, or evergreen branches—once the ground freezes. Mulching is most important in areas where snow cover is lacking, particularly in Zone 4 or colder (see the Zone Map on pages 44-45). Naturalized bulbs rarely need mulching. Those planted in wooded areas receive an abundant supply of natural mulch from fallen leaves; those planted in lawns or meadows have sod to protect them from heaving.

Summer flowering bulbs, such as lilies, require different care than other hardy bulbs since they grow throughout the summer and never really go entirely dormant. They should be lifted only in late fall and then immediately replanted, taking care that their tender bulbs never dry out. In any case, lilies are generally best lifted only when severely overcrowded because they resent any disturbance.

🌷 *Hardy bulbs are very attractive and require little in the way of maintenance, making them ideal choices for the weekend gardener.*

Dividing Perennials

Perennials—especially those that thrive and spread abundantly—need to be dug up and divided every few years. This provides the opportunity to keep the plant within bounds and to remove older, less vital portions. A natural by-product of this plant division is additional plants, which can be replanted in other parts of your own yard or shared with other gardeners.

Perennials can be divided by taking pieces away from their outer edges—separating them from the main plant by cutting through the crown with a knife or a sharp-bladed spade. It's best to lift the entire plant from the ground, and pull or cut apart the pieces. Discard the older, center portion and replace the clump with a fresh, healthy section.

Some plants divide easily. They're loosely interwoven and can be separated into chunks simply by pulling them apart with your hands. Others are so tightly held together that it becomes a definite challenge to break them up. Fortunately, the tough ones are also very hardy and will survive even if you ultimately have to resort to using a meat cleaver! Japanese irises, lupines, and gas plants fall into this latter category.

The primary concerns here are to keep as many of the roots intact as possible, and to have some roots and some foliage in each division. Trim back excess top foliage to balance the loss of feeder roots that takes place when the plants are dug up and torn apart. Avoid the impulse to get as many separate clumps as possible. Larger clumps will thrive, while small divisions are likely to struggle and grow slowly.

Except for the earliest spring bloomers, the best time to divide most perennials is spring. Divide the early-spring bloomers right after they've finished blossoming. In warm climates, fall is a good time to divide perennials, as their roots will become reestablished during the mild winter. There are a few plants—peonies, irises, and oriental poppies—that, even though they bloom in early summer, do better if they're divided after they've finished flowering.

Always plant the new divisions at the same depth as they were growing before lifting. Firm the soil around each new plant and water well to help settle the soil closely

When a perennial looks overgrown, it is time to divide it. Take special care to avoid harming the delicate root systems.

around the roots. The addition of enough water-soluble fertilizer to make a weak feeding solution during this watering will help get the new plants off to a good start. If nature doesn't provide adequate water during the first several weeks after division, be sure to deep water as needed.

When dividing plants that have large fleshy roots, such as dahlias and bearded iris, look for growth tips or buds. Then use a sharp knife to carefully cut the cluster apart, making sure there is at least one bud with each division. Let the divisions air dry for a half hour or so after cutting before replanting them—this will give the wounds some time to seal over, thus reducing the possibility of rot or infection.

Division of Perennial Clumps by Hand

The simplest way to divide loosely woven perennial clumps is by pulling them apart with your hands. Following natural divisions, divide them into several large clumps rather than into many very small ones. This will provide fewer plants, but they'll be more vital and sure to produce flowers the first season after division.

Using Spading Forks to Divide Perennial Clumps

It's usually possible to pry heavy clumps apart by pushing two spading forks into the clump. Some are so tenacious, however, that they must be hacked into chunks with a heavy knife, cleaver, or hatchet. Don't be afraid of doing the plant any harm—those that are this tough won't be fazed by such treatment!

Dividing Rhizomes

Some perennials have large, fleshy underground stems called rhizomes. Bearded irises are one example. To divide these types, dig up the entire clump and shake off the soil. Using a sharp knife, cleanly cut them into smaller clumps containing three or more buds. Replant the new portions at the same depth as before dividing.

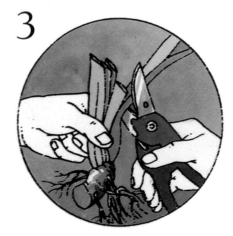

Landscaping with Perennials

Because of the permanence of perennials, it pays to give advance consideration to where to plant them and which ones to use. You'll do some shifting and adjustment as you see the plantings develop, but you'll want to keep this to a minimum. Poor planning costs time—it's certainly easier to make changes on paper!

By this point, you've analyzed your site. You know what type of soil you have to work with; you know the exposures of the beds and living areas; and you know you want to plant perennials—but where do you go from here?

If you have difficulty envisioning how an area might look when planted, create a three-dimensional mock-up. Poke sticks or pieces of leafy brush into the ground where you want bushes and trees, and mark out flower beds and patio areas with stakes linked together by twine or a garden hose. Sit in the patio area and look out at the make-believe landscape. Study it from wherever you'll view it. Move the markers around until they produce the best possible arrangement. Install a more permanent label in each location until the planting is executed.

In this chapter, you'll find information on how to use what you've learned about your property to plan perennial plantings for your custom garden.

Putting a Garden on Paper

🔖 *All your planning and preparation will be rewarded when your garden blooms into a magnificent array of color and texture.*

Planning a perennial flower garden for a succession of bloom all season long is a fairly complex undertaking. There are so many details that must be considered: light and soil preferences, the size and height of plants, the color and form of blooms, the texture of the foliage, and the growth habits of the plants are all important. And then there are those plants that can be planted under and between others to give two seasons of bloom in the same space: spring bulbs under summer- and fall-blooming plants, and summer lilies under plants that flower in spring or fall. Initially, the thought of laying out such a plan can be daunting, but if taken one step at a time, it becomes less overwhelming.

The first step is to make a list of your plant favorites. Research the characteristics of each plant on the list to learn what size they'll grow to, when they will bloom, what colors they come in, what kind of soil and light they prefer, and any other important information. This will help you to select the best plant from your list for each spot you've marked in the yard.

Sketch the layout on a piece of paper and note your choices. For flower beds, lay out detailed plans of exactly which plants you will be using, how many, and where they will go. The more natural the layout, the easier it will be to maintain. Use plants that will be allowed to grow into each other. The more dense the planting becomes, the less opportunity weeds have to invade. You can include ornamental grasses in your plan so that a limited number of weeds will look at home in the bed. A weekend gardener doesn't want to feel bogged down by painstakingly weeding beds.

Plan locations of the basic year-round perennials as we've done in our sample layout (see page 129). Then take a piece of tracing paper and lay it over the basic planting plan. Mark those areas where bulbs can be interplanted and choose suitable varieties. Finally, make up "proof sheets" identifying which portions of the garden will be colorful during each segment of the growing season. Check to see whether or not it's well balanced. If not, make switches and changes as necessary. Double check to be certain that no tall plants are in front of shorter ones, that there are no colors that are likely to clash, and that no shade lovers have been placed in a sunny bed (or vice versa). Inevitably, there will be a need for a few changes and substitutions as your garden grows, but by carefully studying your advanced plan you can at least avoid the obvious mistakes.

From these plans you can then determine how many of each kind of plant you will need. Armed with this information, will be ready to make your purchases and begin your planting.

How to Plan a Garden

1 Mark the locations for each kind of plant you want in the border using a list of your favorites as a reference. Keep in mind that tall plants should be at the back and low ones in the front, the colors and blooming seasons should balance throughout the garden, and a mixture of foliage colors and textures will add interest to areas not in bloom. Select plants suitable for the amount of light and moisture available.

Colors

Pink = P
Blue = B
White = W

Favorites

Bleeding heart: P, W	Pansy: B, W
Candytuft: W	Peony: P, B, W
Delphinium: B, W	Phlox: P, W
Foxglove: B, W	Speedwell: B
Japanese iris: B, W	Tulip: P, B, W
Madonna lily: W	

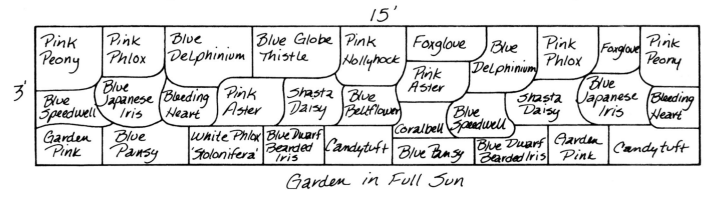

Garden in Full Sun

2 Once all of the garden is laid out, place a sheet of tracing paper over the plan and mark those areas in which a double season of bloom is possible—either by underplanting with spring flowering bulbs or summer flowering lilies, or by intermixing plants that die back early in the season with others that will expand and cover the same space after they are finished for the year.

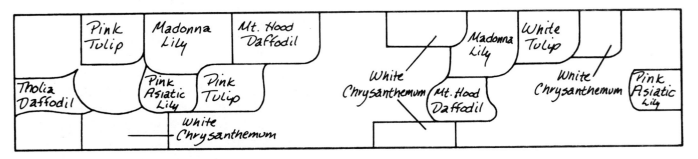

Bulbs and Mums Overplanting Overlay

3 Using the basic plan and the overlay as a guide, create a separate "proof" sheet on tracing paper for each portion of the flowering season: spring, early summer, late summer, and fall. Do this by marking each section of the garden that will be in flower and what colors they will be during that season. Study these to see what changes are needed to improve the balance of color through the entire growing season.

Colors
Pink = P
Blue = B
White = W

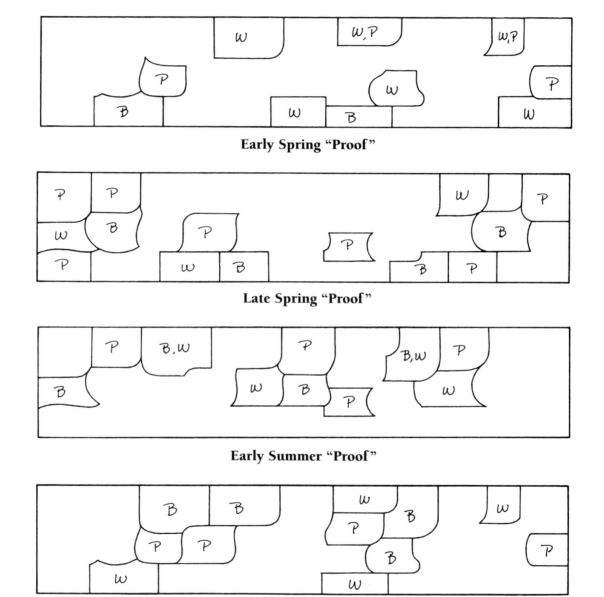

Early Spring "Proof"

Late Spring "Proof"

Early Summer "Proof"

Late Summer "Proof"

Entrance Gardens, Borders, and Island Beds

🌿 *This entrance garden is bold, colorful, and eye-catching.*

The approach for laying out such plantings is similar to that shown for our side border, but there are some additional points that must be considered. For example, the unique aspect of an entrance garden is that it will be viewed briefly. This is an area people are likely to move through quickly rather than linger in or sit and view for an extended period. Therefore, it must be planted simply and for immediate impact. This is not the place for subtle combinations and rare species; it's where a bold, eye-catching display is needed.

This doesn't necessarily mean that it must be bright or garish. Repeated or massed groups of white or pastel flowers can be effective, too. Even an all-foliage display can be dramatic when well chosen. Plants with strong perfumes are also more likely to be enjoyed in this situation where more subtle scents might go unnoticed. Sometimes these strong perfumes, which can be overpowering adjacent to an outdoor sitting area where they're constantly being inhaled, are ideal for short-term enjoyment.

In contrast to entrance gardens, flower plantings (such as borders) that will be enjoyed at leisure, either while sitting among them outdoors or viewing them from inside, may be more low-key in their design. They should invite the eye to keep coming back for another look to perhaps discover additional aspects that weren't obvious at first. Here, of course, the plantings will be more interesting if there are contrasts of flowers, foliage textures, and colors.

Island beds—plantings that are centrally placed and viewed from all sides—require a different design approach than side beds. In order to be effective from every direction, it's necessary to lay them out so that the tallest plants are located in the middle of the bed rather than at the rear. It is therefore necessary to have many more plants of low and intermediate heights in these plantings than tall ones.

Flower beds come in all sizes and outlines. Choose a layout that best suits the surrounding garden, your house style, and your personal preferences.

The border layout we used as an example in the preceding section is a simple rectangular one suitable for use in front of a fence, a hedge, the side of a building, or a row of flowering shrubs. But this is not the only setting and these are not the only proportions suitable for your perennial plantings.

Because they're not demanding, perennials are ideally suited for use as often as possible in entrance gardens, as well as in borders and island beds.

Eye-Catching Entrance Gardens

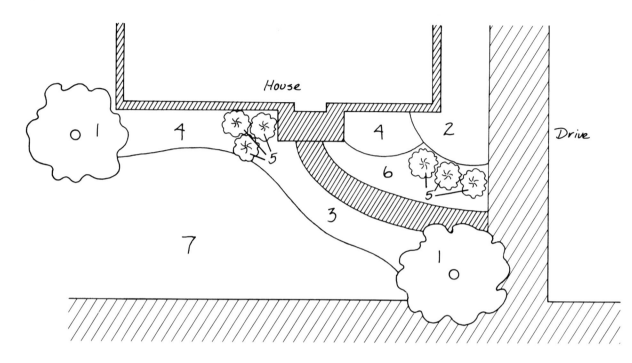

Entrance gardens should be simple yet eye-catching in layout. Otherwise, they may not be noticed during the brief moments they're viewed.

Note: The following lists are to be used for making a selection of one variety for each area. Entries should be kept simple for best results and greatest impact.

1. Attractive specimen shrub or small tree:
Golden arborvitae (columnar variety)
Cutleaf red maple
Redbud
Silverbell

2. Broadleaf evergreens:
Boxwood
Ilex
Pieris
Rhododendron

3. Low, neat-growing perennials:
Candytuft
Hosta
Lavender
Lily turf
Stonecrop

4. Medium-height perennials or flowering shrubs:
Azaleas
Daylilies
Peonies
Roses

5. Dramatic grass clumps:
Fountain grass
Maiden grass
Variegated molinia

6. Second choice from group #3

7. Lawn

Corner Beds & Side Borders

Borders come in a wide variety of sizes and shapes. Their outline and plant content depends on the surrounding landscape, the land contours, and your own personal tastes.

■ = Tall

□ = Intermediate

■ = Low

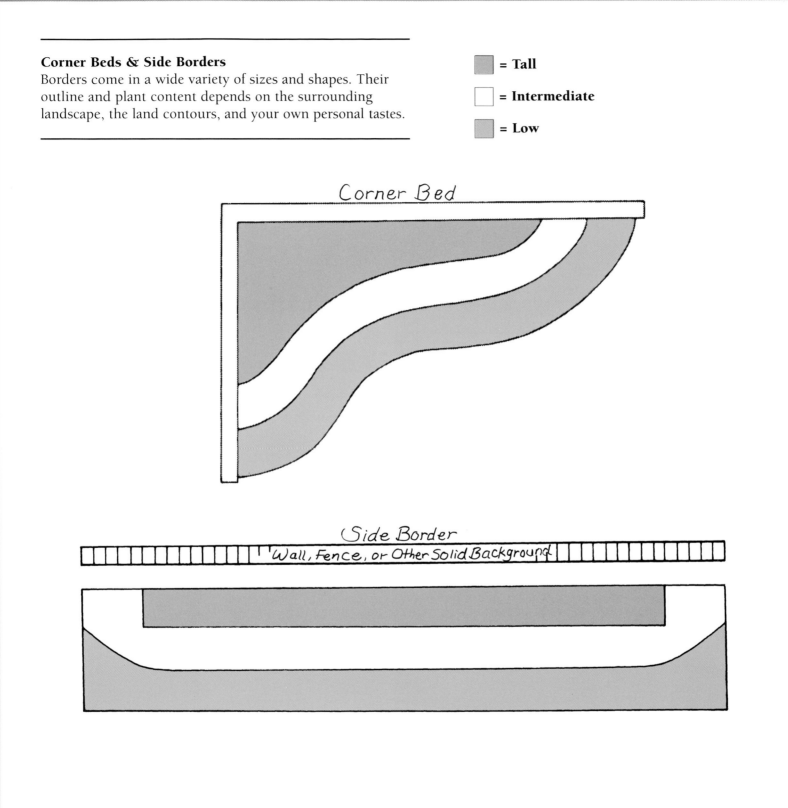

Corner Bed

Side Border

Wall, Fence, or Other Solid Background

Planning an Island Bed

Island beds are surrounded on all sides by lawn or paving, so they are seen from every direction. It becomes a challenge to have them looking nice from all sides. Planning the layout of an island bed differs from a side border because the tallest flowers are clustered in the center of it, rather than arranged along the back edge.

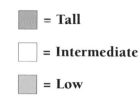

▨ = Tall

☐ = Intermediate

▨ = Low

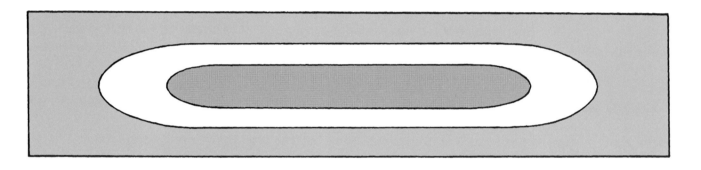

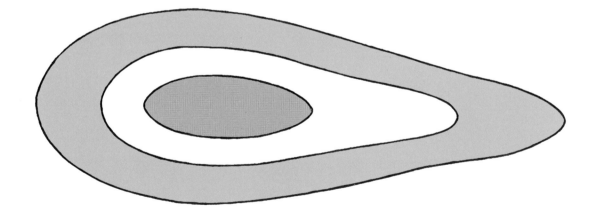

Planning the Bulb Garden

The use of bulbs in the landscape is one of the easiest ways to achieve successive bloom and still keep a low-maintenance planting. Most bulbs are easy to grow and have a long life. Even planting time fits into the gardener's schedule, since most bulbs are planted after the annuals have died from frost and the general growing season is over.

Bulbs are classified according to their flowering season: late-winter and spring flowering, summer flowering, and fall flowering. Within each seasonal group, there are early, midseason, and late bloomers. Among spring-flowering bulbs, for example, late-winter flowering bulbs (such as snowdrops and iris reticulata) are followed by early spring bulbs (such as Dutch crocus and Siberian squill). By mid to late spring, narcissus and tulips are blooming, which are finally followed by very late season bulbs (such as alliums). Within each bulb category, there are further divisions. Tulips, for example, are available in early, mid-season, and late varieties. In the same way, among the summer bloomers, there are early, midseason, and late lilies. In fact, a bulb garden composed of only lilies can bloom right through the summer if care is taken in selecting the right varieties.

Just about any soil is acceptable, although a generous addition of organic matter to poor soils is wise. The only thing bulbs will not tolerate is waterlogged soil. If your chosen site stays moist or wet for long periods, consider planting bulbs in raised beds so they get the drainage they need.

Most hardy bulbs (lilies are a notable exception) lose their leaves in early summer, so it is important to plan ahead to fill in the gaps. Clusters of annuals and perennials, for example, can be interplanted among groups of bulbs. Ground covers and bulbs make an even better marriage: Bulbs will grow right through the ground cover, bloom, then disappear from sight until the following year. Choose an open, shallow-rooted ground cover to minimize competition with the bulbs.

Bulbs look best planted in groups or straight rows rather than scattered randomly through the garden. Clusters of at least three to five large bulbs such as lilies; seven to ten medium-sized bulbs such as tulips, or hyacinths; and 12 or more small bulbs such as crocuses or Siberian squills are fine. Leave some space between each cluster of bulbs to interplant ground covers, annuals, or perennials that will help cover up the foliage of the bulbs as they begin to fade.

Bulbs are particularly well-suited for most naturalized plantings. Varieties should be chosen to suit the present conditions and planted permanently so they seem to have always been part of the landscape. Formal plantings are not recommended for naturalized gardens. In fact, one fairly common planting method is to toss bulbs into the air and plant them where they fall.

Bulbs are nature's season extenders, blooming when other plants are still dormant or have already faded.

What is a Bulb?

Gardeners tend to refer to any plant with an underground storage organ as a bulb, but there are actually many different categories.

True Bulbs

True bulbs are made up of modified leaves that are attached to a flat basal plate and surround the following season's bud. Many true bulbs, such as tulips and narcissus, are surrounded by a papery outer tunic. In others, such as lilies and fritillarias, the bulb is covered by fleshy scales.

Corms

Corms look like bulbs on the outside, including the flat basal plate and the papery tunic. But when they are cut open, they have a solid starchy interior stem. Crocuses are an example of typical corms.

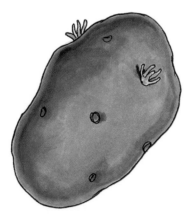

Tubers

Tubers are modified stems with starchy interiors but no basal plate or tunic. Both roots and shoots sprout from the same growth buds, called "eyes". The potato is a typical tuber. Tuberous roots appear similar to tubers, but are actually swollen roots. Dahlias produce tuberous roots.

Rhizomes

Rhizomes are thickened underground stems. They grow in a horizontal direction, sprouting new sections as they spread. The bearded iris (*Iris germanica*) is a typical rhizome.

Soil Level

2"

4"

6"

8"

10"

Planting

Plant hardy bulbs in early fall and tender bulbs in late spring. Prepare a planting hole several inches deeper than the recommended planting depth and mix organic matter into the soil. Add bone meal or bulb fertilizer, and enough soil to bring the hole to the proper planting depth. Set the bulb and fill with fresh soil.

Naturalizing Bulbs

Some species of bulbs are particularly well suited for naturalizing in the garden. Choose varieties that will multiply on their own, to create a natural effect. Plant in drifts to create an established-looking stand. Narcissus is commonly naturalized under deciduous trees, since the trees allow plenty of light in the spring when the bulbs are in leaf.

Perennials and Bulbs in Containers

In most instances, perennials and bulbs are best grown directly in the ground. However, there are occasions when it's desirable to grow them in containers as potted plants.

Container plants can be the answer for soilless locations such as an apartment balcony, a deck, or a patio. Use perennials and seasonal bulbs in containers throughout your living areas—at the main entrance, on patios and decks, or in dark corners of your landscape that need brightening up. Choose perennials that look beautiful both while they're in bloom as well as when they are not. When the garden soil is so poor that it's nearly impossible to successfully grow plants in it, container plantings can be the solution.

In order for plants to prosper in containers, a primary rule is that the plants must have regular watering and feeding. Be certain the pots have adequate drainage capability. Containers need repotting when they show signs of becoming rootbound. An easy way to check is by knocking the plant out of the pot every six months to see how jammed with roots it has become—when they're solidly matted, it's time to shift into a slightly larger pot, or to divide the plant into several pieces and repot.

Raising container-grown perennials allows you to have those varieties that are not winter hardy in your climate. By growing them in containers, it's possible to easily move them into the house or a special shelter over the winter, then back into the garden in the spring. For those plants that are half-hardy or require only slightly milder winters than those you have, it's possible to place them on an unheated enclosed porch or other similar location where daylight sun can reach them, but they're not subjected to extremely low temperatures. If prolonged sub-zero temperatures persist, a small space heater on a low setting will provide enough heat to prevent damage.

Finally, it's fun to grow perennials and bulbs as indoor plants, forcing them to bloom out-of-season, providing attractive displays within your home. After all, most houseplants are, in fact, perennials that are tropical and therefore not hardy enough for growing outdoors in most parts of the country. To force bulbs and perennials, you

🌺 *A container garden is very versatile. On a whim, you can rearrange your plants or change them altogether.*

must trick them into blooming—get the plants to react as though it is their natural bloom season. Where winters are long enough, keep potted perennials and bulbs outside to allow at least eight weeks of winter dormancy. Then, bring them inside, giving them plenty of sunlight, water, and heat until they bloom. Typical spring bulbs will bloom in about three to four weeks. Some gardeners enjoy the novelty of growing various perennial bulbs in containers for winter bloom: tulips, daffodils, hyacinths, amaryllises, crocuses, narcissi, and lilies are among the most popular choices.

MIXED CONTAINERS

A succession of bloom is possible by using a mix of plants in a container. Early-blooming crocus and pansies may be followed later by tulips. As tulip foliage begins to die, later perennials—maybe thread-leaf coreopsis and hybrid lilies (grown from bulbs)—show summer color. Using containers of perennials is a fun way to bring accent into an otherwise nondescript space.

Gardening in Containers

Good drainage is essential for successful container growing. Cover the drainage holes to keep in soil. Pieces of broken pottery, fine screening, or a coffee filter may be used. If additional drainage is needed, add a layer of small stones, perlite, or coarse sand in the bottom of the container. If the container is located where dripping water would do damage, place a drip tray under the container to catch excess water.

How to Care for Container-Grown Plants

Perennials in containers must receive special care over winter in cold climates. Keep them in the house or a greenhouse if they are tropical varieties. Those that withstand freezing can be kept in an unheated area such as an enclosed porch and will only require some heating during prolonged, extreme cold spells. Watering should be cut back severely during this dormant period.

4

Directory of Popular Perennials

Perennials are certainly versatile plants. They can grow in good soil and poor soil; some flourish in full sun and others are quite content with deep shade. The sizes and shapes nature provides them with are so diverse that any gardener can select perennials to suit his or her garden location and conditions.

The following encyclopedia was designed in order to help gardeners in all regions of the United States make the best perennial selections possible. Botanical and common names, compatible USDA zones, descriptions, ease of care, how-to-grow techniques, propagation, uses, and related species and varieties are all dealt with in detail. Photos are included for each entry. Listed here are some of the especially hardy and low-maintenance varieties of proven perennials.

The adaptability of perennials truly makes them all-purpose plants. If perennials are carefully selected and planted, the weekend gardener will be well on the way to enjoying many years of interest from the many colors, forms, and textures of perennials. And if you like what you've created, you have the satisfaction of knowing that with a little bit of work your garden can flourish year after year.

Japanese Anemone

Anemone species

Zone: USDA 5b

This specimen's genus comes from the Greek word for "wind." Many of the plants in this family are called wind flowers.

Description: The Japanese anemone's strong-stemmed, showy flowers have five or more petal-like sepals that enclose numerous golden stamens with compound, attractive leaves. Mature clumps can reach a height of five feet.

Ease of care: Easy

How to grow: The anemone needs fertile, moist soil with plenty of organic matter mixed in as the roots (or rhizomes) resent heavy clay and wet earth. They enjoy full sun in northern gardens but will easily adjust to partial shade. Anemones need partial shade in southern gardens. In areas that have severe winters with little snow cover, plants should be mulched in late fall. Protect flowers from early frosts in colder areas of the country.

Propagation: By division in early spring or by root division

Uses: Anemones are especially beautiful when grown in large clumps.

Astilbe, Garden Spiraea

Astilbe species

Zone: USDA 3

Beautiful plants for the garden, the astilbes available to gardeners today are usually the result of hybridization and are listed as *Astilbe* x *Arendsii* in garden books and nursery catalogs.

Description: Astilbes are lovely plants both for their dark green, fernlike foliage and their long panicles (or spikes) of flowers that resemble feathery plumes. Depending on the type, they can bloom from spring until the end of August.

Ease of care: Easy

How to grow: Astilbes do well in full sun but are best with partial shade, especially in the southern parts of the country. Soil should be moist with plenty of organic matter mixed in.

Propagation: By division

Uses: The larger varieties work well in the garden border as specimen plants. Colors include white, pink, red, rose, and lilac. Heights vary from 12 to 40 inches. They also make an effective ground cover.

Stoke's Aster

Stokesia laevis

Zone: USDA 5b

Stoke's aster, a native American wildflower that looks similar to a China aster, was originally found from South Carolina to Florida and Louisiana.

Description: Leaves are alternate and spiny-toothed toward the base, with the upper leaves clasping the stem. Fluffy blue to lavender flowers are 2 to 5 inches across on well-branched, 1 to 2 foot stems.

Ease of care: Easy

How to grow: Stokesias need full sun and good, well-drained soil. New plants take a year or two to settle in before maximum bloom. They should be mulched in areas with bad winters and little snow cover. Remove spent blooms for flowers to continue blooming until September.

Propagation: By seed or by division in spring

Uses: Stokesias are excellent decorative flowers for the front of the bed or border. They are good cut flowers, and the seedpods can be used in dried arrangements.

Balloon Flower

Platycodon grandiflorus

Zone: USDA 4

A one-species genus, balloon flowers are so named because the unopened flowers look like small hot-air balloons.

Description: Balloon flowers are clump-forming perennials with alternate leaves of light green on stems that usually grow between 1½ and 3 feet tall. They bear 2- to 3-inch balloon-shaped buds that open to bell-shaped flowers with five points.

Ease of care: Easy

How to grow: Balloon flowers like moist, well-drained soil in full sun or partial shade. They prefer places with cool summers. Plan the plant's position carefully as it is not until late spring that the first signs of life appear.

Propagation: By division in midspring or by seed

Uses: Blooming for most of the summer, balloon flowers are attractive in borders, with the smaller types growing best along garden edges.

Related varieties: 'Album' bears white flowers; 'Mariesii' has blue flowers on 12- to 16-inch stems; and 'Shell Pink' bears soft-pink flowers.

Basket-of-Gold, Goldentuft

Aurinia saxatilis

Zone: USDA 4

Once included in the *Alyssum* genus, these charming flowers of spring now belong to the mustard family.

Description: Attractive, low gray foliage growing in dense mats gives support to clusters of golden-yellow, four-petaled flowers floating 6 to 12 inches above the plants.

Ease of care: Easy

How to grow: Aurinias need only well-drained, average soil in full sun. Plants will easily rot in damp locations and resent high humidity. They can be sheared after blooming.

Propagation: By cuttings or by seed

Uses: Aurinias are quite happy growing in the spaces between stone walks, carpeting a rock garden, or growing in pockets in stone walls where their flowers become tumbling falls of gold.

Related varieties: 'Mountain Gold' has silvery, evergreen leaves and fragrant, bright yellow flowers. 'Citrina' bears lemon-yellow flowers.

Bergamot, Bee-Balm, Oswego-Tea

Monarda didyma

Zone: USDA 4

These are stunning, native American plants that have been garden favorites for decades.

Description: Sturdy, square stems growing to four feet tall have simple leaves. They are topped by crowns studded with lipped, usually bright red, pink, purple, or white flowers blooming from summer into fall.

Ease of care: Easy

How to grow: At ease in almost any soil, bergamots prefer a slightly moist spot with full sun; they become somewhat floppy when grown in the shade. These plants are vigorous spreaders, so excess plants should be removed from time to time.

Propagation: By seed or by division in early spring

Uses: Useful for the wild garden in moist soil or by the waterside, they are also beautiful in beds or borders because of their long season of bright bloom. The flowers are beloved by hummingbirds and butterflies.

Bellflower

Campanula species

Zone: USDA 4

The botanical name is from the Latin word for "bell" and refers to the shape of the flowers.

Description: Bellflowers are usually various shades of blue or white and bloom from late spring into early summer.

Ease of care: Easy

How to grow: Bellflowers need a good, moist, but well-drained soil with plenty of organic matter mixed in. In the North, plants will tolerate full sun as long as the soil is not dry, but elsewhere a spot in semi-shade is preferred.

Propagation: By division or by seed

Uses: Plants are beautiful in the border, useful in the rock garden, and fine for the shade or wild garden.

Related species: *Campanula carpatica* blooms at a height of 10 inches with solitary blue flowers. It is effective as an edging or tumbling over a small rock cliff. *Campanula glomerata,* or the clustered bellflower, usually bears a dozen blossoms in tight clusters at the top of a 14-inch stem. *Campanula persicifolia,* or peach bells, bears white or blue flowers on stems up to three feet high and prefers moist soil.

Heartleaf Bergenia

Bergenia cordifolia

Zone: USDA 3

Bergenias trace their origins from Siberia and Mongolia. As such they are perfectly happy in low temperatures when covered with snow.

Description: Thick, rounded evergreen leaves, often one foot long, grow from a single crown and are edged with red in cold weather. Flowers are pink with waxy petals, which bloom in drooping clusters.

Ease of care: Easy

How to grow: These plants prefer light shade and good, moist soil with plenty of organic matter.

Propagation: By division or by seed

Uses: Excellent as an edging in the border or planted in groups on slopes, bergenias are also a fine addition to the rock garden.

Related species: The winter begonia, *Bergenia ciliata,* develops large, rounded leaves that are densely hairy on both sides. *Bergenia purpurascens* has dark green leaves that turn beetroot-red in winter.

Related varieties: 'Evening Bells' has bright red winter foliage and rose-pink flowers; 'Silverlight' bears blush-white flowers.

Bishop's Hat, Barrenwort

Epimedium species

Zone: USDA 4-5 (depending on species)

Distinctive foliage and delicate flowers make epimediums a wonderful perennial addition to any garden.

Description: Epimediums have sturdy, heart-shaped leaves with a toothed edge on wiry stems that closely resemble a jester's hat or, in some species, a bishop's miter or biretta. They bloom in April and May.

Ease of care: Easy

How to grow: Epimediums like good, well-drained, somewhat moist garden soil in open shade, although they will tolerate some sun. They do well under tree canopies.

Propagation: By division or by seed

Uses: Classified by most nurseries as a rock garden ground cover, epimediums are also excellent for the edge of a border.

Related species: *Epimedium grandiflora* grows about one foot high with white flowers tinged with pink at the tips of the spurs.

Bleeding Heart

Dicentra species

Zone: USDA 4

These heart-shaped pendant flowers with spurs at the base have attractive foliage until midsummer.

Description: Bleeding hearts display clusters of rose, pink, or white flowers on arching sprays of fernlike foliage.

Ease of care: Easy

How to grow: Bleeding hearts need open or partial shade with an evenly moist, slightly acidic soil. Plenty of peat moss must be used when planting, while pine needles or pine bark are good for mulching.

Propagation: By division in early spring or by seed; roots are fleshy and sold by the number of eyes present on plant starts.

Uses: This plant is a lovely sight when planted in a shady bed or woodland border.

Related species: *Dicentra eximia*, or the fringed bleeding heart, will bloom until frost if given protection from the heat. *Dicentra formosa* is a rose-colored species and usually is about 18 inches high. *Dicentra spectabilis* is the a garden favorite with deep pink flowers blooming from May to June on 24-inch stems.

Blazingstar, Gayfeather

Liatris species

Zone: USDA 4

Blazingstars are good garden plants native to North America.

Description: Simple, linear leaves on usually stout stems grow in clumps from thick rootstocks. Flower heads are set along tall spikes and bear fluffy disk flowers resembling feathery staffs.

Ease of care: Easy

How to grow: Blazingstars need good, well-drained soil in full sun to succeed. Wet, winter soil will usually kill the plants. The taller varieties sometimes require staking. They are especially valuable as cut flowers.

Propagation: By division of older plants in spring or by seed

Uses: Clumps of blazingstars are perfect for the bed and border.

Related species: *Liatris pycnostachya*, the cattail or Kansas gayfeather, grows up to five feet, and bears spikes of purple flowers. *Liatris scariosa*, or the button snake-root, bears purple or white fluffy disk flowers on spikes from three to six feet tall.

Bluestar, Blue-Dogbane, Blue-Star-of-Texas

Amsonia tabernaemontana

Zone: USDA 4b

Bluestars are native wildflowers found in wooded areas and on river banks from New Jersey to Tennessee to Texas.

Description: Blooming in May and June, bluestars have five petals and are a lovely pale blue color. After flowering has terminated, the upright stems with narrow leaves are still attractive. In the fall, the foliage turns a beautiful butterscotch-yellow.

Ease of care: Easy

How to grow: Plants should be established in any reasonably fertile garden soil. They grow between 2 and 3 feet tall and are somewhat tolerant of dry soil. Blossoms are better when given full sun, but bluestars will tolerate just a bit of shade. They will self-sow, with seedlings becoming bushy clumps in a few years.

Propagation: By division in the early spring

Uses: Bluestars belong in any wild garden and in beds or borders.

Boltonia

Boltonia asteroides

Zone: USDA 4

Boltonias are native American wildflowers found in poor or damp soil as far north as Manitoba, Canada; then south to Florida, and west to Texas.

Description: Plants resemble asters with sturdy stems, narrow leaves, and dozens of white flowers in clusters. Blooming from late summer into fall, a well-situated boltonia will be covered with bloom.

Ease of care: Easy

How to grow: Boltonias prefer average garden soil in full sun. Like many wildflowers, they will be larger in moist, fertile soil.

Propagation: By division in spring or fall

Uses: Since boltonias grow 5 to 8 feet high, they are best at the rear of the garden. A line of these plants will become a flowering hedge of great charm. They can be used with ornamental grasses or mixed with fall asters.

Related varieties: 'Snowbank' is an excellent, four-foot selection of the species. 'Pink Beauty' has soft pink flowers.

Butterfly Weed, Milkweed

Asclepias tuberosa

Zone: USDA 4a

Butterfly weed is a native American wildflower that is at home in both the wild garden and the perennial border.

Description: Blooming from late spring into summer, the individual orange-shaded flowers are striking in their beauty. The plants bear thin leaves and are most attractive when in flower.

Ease of care: Easy

How to grow: Butterfly weed tolerates a wide variety of soil types, but performs best in an average garden setting with full sun and good drainage. Once a butterfly weed develops a good root system, it becomes a long-lived, drought-resistant plant.

Propagation: By division in early spring or by seed

Uses: Butterfly weed does well in meadows and in wild gardens. The flowers can be cut for fresh bouquets.

Related species: The swamp milkweed, *Asclepias incarnata*, has pinkish flowers on 2- to 4-foot stems and will do well in wet situations.

Siberian Bugloss

Brunnera macrophylla

Zone: USDA 4

From western Siberia, these plants are perennial forget-me-nots, named in honor of Swiss botanist Samuel Brunner. Some catalogs still call this species *Anchusa myosotidiflora*.

Description: Showy blue flowers about ¼-inch across bloom in clusters during spring. The leaves are large and heart-shaped on slightly hairy stems. Plants can reach two feet in height but usually remain at 18 inches.

Ease of care: Easy

How to grow: Brunneras prefer a deep, moist soil with an abundance of organic matter, in full sun (only in the North) or partial shade. They will, however, do reasonably well in a dry spot if they have shade.

Propagation: By division or by seed

Uses: They are lovely in the front of a border but are exceptionally attractive when naturalized at the border of a wooded area or in a wild garden along a stream or by a pool. After blooming, the large leaves make an effective ground cover.

Chrysanthemum

Chrysanthemum species

Zone: USDA 4 to 6

Chrysanthemums are members of the daisy clan, numbering more than 200 species of ornamental plants.

Description: Leaves are typically divided, highly aromatic, and sometimes develop basal rosettes. Stems are strong and flowers are showy.

Ease of care: Easy to moderately difficult

How to grow: Chrysanthemums prefer well-drained, evenly moist soil in full sun. The majority of chrysanthemums are late-blooming, short-day plants with flowers initiated by decreasing day length. They benefit from frequent pinching, which promotes bushy growth.

Propagation: By cuttings, by division, or by seed

Uses: Garden mums (*Chrysanthemum* x *morifolium*) come in a number of flower styles and colors. Mums can be purchased as rooted cuttings from nursery suppliers to be set out in spring.

Related species: *Chrysanthemum* x *superbum*, or the shasta daisy, produces four-inch flowers on 1- to 3-foot stems. *Chrysanthemum nipponicum*, the Nippon daisy, bears white flowers on two-foot woody stems.

Columbine

Aquilegia species

Zone: USDA 4

Columbines are beloved by hummingbirds, are perfect for cut flowers, and have a long season of bloom.

Description: Single or bicolored flowers float on top of a cluster of compound leaves. Flowers come in red, yellow, blue, white, or a combination.

Ease of care: Easy

How to grow: Columbines are easy to grow, adapting to almost any reasonably fertile, well-drained garden soil. They will do well in full sun or partial shade.

Propagation: By seed

Uses: Columbines are excellent in beds and borders.

Related species: *Aquilegia caerulea* is the Colorado columbine, with sky-blue blossoms and white centers on wiry stems growing to two feet. *Aquilegia canadensis* is the wild Eastern columbine, with graceful flowers having long, red spurs and yellow faces on 1- to 2-foot stems.

Related varieties: The hybrid types vary between 1 to 3 feet in height and are available in many varieties and colors. Among the best are the 'Music' hybrids.

Coralbell, Alumroot

Heuchera sanguinea

Zone: USDA 4

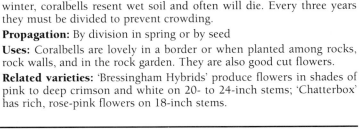

Coralbells are American wildflowers originally from New Mexico and Arizona.

Description: Coralbells have mounds of basal leaves that are rounded and lobed, rising from a thick rootstock. The flowers are tiny bells on 1- to 2-foot slender stems blooming from spring into summer.

Ease of care: Easy

How to grow: In areas of hot summers, these plants like a bit of shade, but usually they prefer as much sun as possible. Plant them in good, well-drained garden soil with a high humus content and kept moist. In winter, coralbells resent wet soil and often will die. Every three years they must be divided to prevent crowding.

Propagation: By division in spring or by seed

Uses: Coralbells are lovely in a border or when planted among rocks, rock walls, and in the rock garden. They are also good cut flowers.

Related varieties: 'Bressingham Hybrids' produce flowers in shades of pink to deep crimson and white on 20- to 24-inch stems; 'Chatterbox' has rich, rose-pink flowers on 18-inch stems.

Purple Coneflower

Echinacea purpurea

Zone: USDA 3

This lovely American native was once found naturally from Ohio to Iowa and south to Louisiana and Georgia.

Description: Prickly, cone-shaped heads of bronze-brown are surrounded by rose-purple petals (really ray flowers) on stout stalks from 2 to 4 feet high. Leaves are alternate, simple, and coarse.

Ease of care: Easy

How to grow: Coneflowers will take almost any well-drained garden soil in full sun. If soil is too good, the flowers must often be staked.

Propagation: By division in spring or by seed

Uses: Coneflowers are beautiful plants for the back of a small garden border and they are a welcome addition to a wildflower garden.

Related species: *Echinacea pallida* is a similar wildflower species from the Midwest with thinner and more graceful petals.

Related varieties: 'White Lustre' and 'White Swan' are two varieties with white flowers; 'Bright Star' bears maroon flowers; and 'Magnus' has rosy purple petals with a dark disk.

Coreopsis

Coreopsis species

Zone: USDA 4

Coreopsis is a Greek word for "buglike." This referred to the shape of this plant's seeds, which were thought to look like ticks.

Description: Small daisies in shades of yellow and orange grow on wiry stems up to three feet high. Leaves vary from simple, oval shapes in basal rosettes to fernlike foliage.

Ease of care: Easy

How to grow: Coreopsis are happy in almost any well-drained garden soil in full sun. They are drought-resistant and an outstanding choice for hot, difficult places.

Propagation: By division in spring or by seed.

Uses: Excellent for the wild garden and in the formal border, these flowers are prized for cutting. The smaller types are also good for edging plants. Coreopsis are well suited for patio containers and hanging baskets.

Related species: *Coreopsis grandiflora* 'Sunray' bears double, golden-yellow flowers on two-foot stems.

Crane's-Bill
Geranium species
Zone: USDA 4

Crane's-bill is named after the female part of the flower that resembles a crane's beak. *Geranium* is the genus; these plants are not to be confused with the common summer or florist's geranium that is really a *Pelargonium*.

Description: Crane's-bill is usually a low-growing plant with lobed or deeply cut leaves on forked stems. It bears five-petaled flowers in great profusion blooming from spring to summer.

Ease of care: Easy

How to grow: Garden geraniums need good, well-drained garden soil in full sun or light shade in areas of hot summers.

Propagation: By division or by seed

Uses: In a border or a rock garden, crane's-bills are lovely plants. They make excellent ground cover and are striking when grown along a wall, letting the stems and flowers tumble over the edge.

Related species: *Geranium cinereum* is a low-growing plant usually reaching about eight inches in height with one-inch pink flowers.

Gaura
Gaura Lindheimeri
Zone: USDA 6

There are a number of gauras that are native American wild-flowers; however, this particular species is the best for the garden. Found naturally from Louisiana to Texas and south to Mexico, the white flowers will slowly fade to pink as they age.

Description: Gaura has alternate, lance-shaped leaves up to three inches long on stout stems. It blooms with one-inch, white, four-petaled flowers that persist throughout the summer. Stems can reach to six feet.

Ease of care: Easy

How to grow: Gauras need full sun in good, deep, well-drained garden soil because the tap root is very long. They are both drought- and heat-resistant.

Propagation: By division in spring or by seed

Uses: Perfect for both a dry garden and a wild garden, gauras are also very attractive in a formal border. In northern climates, they bloom late in the season and are charming when planted with aster and ornamental grasses.

Daylily
Hemerocallis species
Zone: USDA 3

Each flower of the daylily opens, matures, and withers in 24 hours or less. There are over 30,000 varieties of daylilies.

Description: Daylilies have fleshy roots with mostly basal, sword-shaped leaves that can grow up to two feet long with tall, multi-branched stalks, each containing many six-petaled lilylike flowers.

Ease of care: Easy

How to grow: Daylilies are carefree, wanting only good, well-drained garden soil in full sun. They benefit from partial shade in the South.

Propagation: By division in spring or fall

Uses: By mixing varieties, a succession of bloom is possible from spring to late fall. Use daylilies in borders, or in small groups mixed in the shrub border. Daylillies also make a good erosion control cover on a bank.

Related varieties: 'Bertie Ferris' has midseason blossoms of deeply ruffled persimmon on 15-inch stems; 'Catherine Woodberry' has pale, orchid-pink flowers on 30-inch stems; 'Hyperion' is a fragrant lemon lily blooming midseason on 42-inch stems.

Goat's Beard, Wild Spirea
Aruncus dioicus
Zone: USDA 4

Goat's beard has been revered for years; the genus was named by Pliny, a Roman naturalist.

Description: Plants can grow as high as six feet and look like a bush. Then in early autumn, the plants come into bloom, producing many showy plumes of tiny, white flowers. The plants bring color to the garden after the usual spring show has passed.

Ease of care: Easy

How to grow: Goat's beard is easy to grow as long as light shade and moist soil are provided. It grows well in moist bottomland and should never lack for water during the summer.

Propagation: By division in the spring or by seed

Uses: Plant goat's beard in the rear of the border in the light shade of high trees. A waterside garden is also a good choice, especially when the plants have a tree-filled background.

Related species: *Aruncus aethusifolius* is a dwarf variety that makes a 6- to 8-inch mound of feathery leaves and one-foot spires of white, plume-like blossoms.

Ornamental Grasses

***Gramineae* family**

Zone: USDA 3-5

Ornamental grasses are a distinct family of plants unsurpassed for the perennial garden. Many of the seed heads of grasses are beautiful and help to extend the garden season through winter.

Description: The stems, or culms, of true grasses are round and hollow, and stem sections are joined by solid nodes. Roots grow deep into the ground, making the plants drought tolerant. Flowers are usually feathery or plumelike and feature an awn, or a barbed appendage, that is often quite long.

Ease of care: Easy

How to grow: Most grasses prefer well-drained soil in full sun. There are exceptions; some tolerate wet soil, and some accept shade. The only chore connected with growing perennial grasses is the annual pruning of the dead stems and leaves before new growth begins to emerge.

Propagation: By division in spring

Uses: Large types make beautiful specimen plants and screens. Some lower-growing varieties make excellent ground covers. Adding interest to the perennial border, the fine textures of grasses helps to blend and unify contrasting plantings. Grasses blend nicely with foundation plantings.

Related species: Many species of grasses are suitable for garden use. Some of the most popular types are listed here. *Calamagrostis acutiflora stricta,* or feather reed grass, reaches five to seven feet and tolerates wet soils. Reed grass blooms late in spring, showing its seedheads through the following winter. *Helictrotrichon sempervirens,* or blue oat grass, is valuable for its blue color and the form of the leaves. It grows to two feet. With its red leaves, *Imperata cylindrica rubra,* or Japanese blood grass, makes a fine ground cover. *Miscanthus sinensis* 'Gracillimus,' or maiden grass, forms a fountain of thin, arching leaves. In the fall, tall seedheads are formed that open into plumes persisting well into winter. *Miscanthus* 'Zebrinus,' or Zebra grass, looks like a tropical plant that has adapted to the North. Reaching a height of eight feet, the arching leaves are dashed with horizontal bands of a light and creamy golden-brown that only appears as the summer heats up. Massive clumps are formed over the years. Other varieties of *Miscanthus* develop into bold specimens with graceful winter plumage. *Pennisetum alopecuroides,* or fountain grass, produces leafy fountains about three feet high and blossoms on arching stalks.

Hosta, Plantain Lily

***Hosta* species**

Zone: USDA 3

Next to daylilies, the most-common garden perennial plants are hostas.

Description: Large clumps of basal leaves with pronounced veining and smooth or wavy edges distinguish hostas. Leaf colors come in various shades of green, often with many variegations. Lilylike flowers on tall stems (or scapes) in white and many shades of blue bloom from late spring to late summer.

Ease of care: Easy

How to grow: Hostas do best in good, well-drained, moist garden soil with plenty of humus. They require some sun to partial shade to deep shade, depending on the species and variety.

Propagation: By division or by seed (some species)

Uses: Hostas are the backbone of the shade garden. The smaller types are excellent in the border or as ground cover. The larger varieties become elegant specimen plants forming gigantic clumps of leaves over the years. They are also excellent in pots.

False Indigo, Wild Indigo

Baptisia australis

Zone: USDA 3

A beautiful plant in leaf, in flower, and after going to seed, false indigo was originally planted to produce a blue dye for early American colonists.

Description: This large plant grows to four feet in height. The blue-green, compound leaves on stout stems are attractive all summer; and the dark blue, pealike flowers that eventually become blackened pods are very showy.

Ease of care: Easy

How to grow: Baptisia needs well-drained soil in full sun, but will accept some partial shade. Being a member of the legume family, baptisia will do well in poor soil. The root systems of older plants become so extensive that they are difficult to move.

Propagation: By division or by seed

Uses: One baptisia will in time cover an area several feet in diameter with gracefully arching foliage. These plants are excellent for a meadow garden, a wild garden, or planted along the edge of the woods.

Iris

Iris species

Zone: USDA 3 and above

This large genus contains more than 200 species in the northern hemisphere and is most abundant in Asia. The plants are responsible for a marvelous array of flowers plus, in many cases, fine foliage. The blue flags, *Iris versicolor* or *I. prismatica,* are lovely wildflowers from the Northeast, appearing in ditches and boggy areas along country roads.

Description: Irises usually have basal leaves in two ranks—linear to sword-shaped—often resembling a fan, arising from a thick rootstock (or rhizome) or, in some species, from a bulb. They bloom in shades of pink, blue, lilac, purple to brown, yellow, orange, almost black, and white. There are no true reds.

Ease of care: Easy

How to grow: Most irises need sunlight. Except for those like the water flag (*Iris Pseudacorus*), which delights in a watery spot, or the Japanese iris (*I. ensata*), which thrives in a humus-rich, moist soil, most irises also prefer a good, well-drained garden soil.

Propagation: By division in the fall or by seed.

Uses: Even though the bloom period is short, a bed of irises is ideal for a flower garden. There are irises for the poolside and the pool, the wild or woodland garden, the early spring bulb bed, and the rock garden.

Related species: *Iris germanica* (tall bearded iris), hardy to USDA 4, usually comes to mind when people think of irises. The flowers come in a multitude of color combinations and sizes, with hundreds of new varieties introduced every year. It is usually spring blooming, but some bloom again in fall. *Iris cristata* (crested iris), hardy in USDA 5, prefers partial shade and a humus-rich soil and blooms in early spring. It is lavender-blue with a two-inch yellow crest across a six-inch stem. *Iris ensata* (Japanese iris) is hardy in USDA 6. Blossoms are often more than six inches wide on stiff, tall stems, blooming in June and resembling layers of colored linen waving in the wind. *Iris Pseudacorus* (yellow flag) is a beautiful plant for the bog or at the edge of a pond or pool. The flowers, blooming from May to June, are yellow on 40-inch stems. *Iris sibirica* (Siberian iris), hardy in USDA 4, has beautiful 3- to 4-inch flowers on 30-inch stems and great foliage—the swordlike leaves stand erect and eventually form a large clump.

Lady's Mantle

Alchemilla species

Zone: USDA 3b

Lady's mantles are attractive plants usually grown for both their foliage and their unusual chartreuse flowers.

Description: The plants grow between 8 and 14 inches high, with lobed leaves of gray-green that bear silky hairs.

Ease of care: Easy

How to grow: Lady's mantles are easy to grow in average garden soil where summers are cool and moist, preferring some protection from hot sun in midsummer. In warmer parts of the country, they need a moist, fertile soil and light shade. As the summer progresses, the plants become larger and have a tendency to flop about.

Propagation: By division in spring

Uses: The flowers appear in clusters in early summer, standing well above the leaves, and last for several weeks. They are excellent when cut. These plants can be used in the front of the garden border or along the edge of a low wall where the leaves are easy to see.

Related species: *Alchemilla alpina,* alpine lady's mantle, grows about eight inches high; *Alchemilla erythropoda* grows about six inches high.

Lavender

Lavandula angustifolia

Zone: USDA 6

These are species of aromatic herbs originally hailing from the Mediterranean. The genus name, meaning "to wash," alludes to the ancient custom of scenting bath water with oil of lavender or a few lavender flowers.

Description: Plants tend to be shrubby, usually with square stems and narrow, evergreen leaves that are white and woolly when young. Flower spikes are terminal clusters of lavender or dark purple flowers, blooming in late June and bearing a pleasing scent.

Ease of care: Easy

How to grow: Lavender plants want full sun and well-drained, sandy soil—preferably non-acidic. In areas where there is no snow cover, the plants should be mulched. In colder areas, prune back the dead wood in the spring.

Propagation: By soft cuttings in spring or by seed

Uses: Lavender is perfect as a low hedge and in clumps next to rocks. It is also suitable in front of stone walls that face away from the wind.

Ligularia

Ligularia species

Zone: USDA 4 to 6

This plant's name comes from the Latin word *ligula*, which means "little tongue," referring to the tonguelike shape of the large petal on each of the ray flowers.

Description: Basal leaves on stout stems are either round or kidney-shaped. They bear tall spires with yellow or orange flower heads.

Ease of care: Easy

How to grow: Ligularias do best in partial shade and good, humus-rich garden soil that is kept evenly moist. Since the roots form large clumps, plenty of space should be allowed between plants.

Propagation: By division in spring or by seed

Uses: Ligularias are great in the back of shady beds, along borders, in bogs, or planted at the edge of water gardens.

Related species: *Ligularia dentata* varieties 'Orange Queen' and 'Othello' each has leaves up to one foot wide. The first is green throughout with flowers of a deeper orange, while the second has leaves that are green on top and purple underneath.

Peony

Paeonia species

Zone: USDA 5

Not only are the peony flowers beautiful, the plants themselves are especially attractive.

Description: Most herbaceous peonies are shrubby plants with thick roots and large, compound, glossy green leaves on reddish stems. They bear large, many petaled, showy flowers.

Ease of care: Easy

How to grow: Autumn planting is best; the peony prefers full sun and good, well-drained, moisture-retentive soil rich with humus. Plant with the "eyes" or growing points to the top about 1½ inches below the soil surface. Mulch the first year to protect from severe cold.

Propagation: By division of the roots

Uses: As specimen plants, in beds or borders, and even in the cutting garden, peonies can be an important part of any garden.

Related species: *Paeonia Mlokosewitschii*, or the Caucasian peony, bears yellow flowers about five inches across. *Paeonia suffruticosa*, the Japanese tree peony, is actually a bush, usually reaching a height of five feet and a spread of six feet.

Lungwort, Jerusalem Sage

Pulmonaria officinalis

Zone: USDA 4

Lungworts, one of the first flowers of spring, are exceptional plants for both their blossoms and foliage.

Description: Lungworts have simple basal leaves growing to one foot long, which are spotted with silver-white splotches. Terminal coiled clusters of five-lobed flowers, which in many species open as pink and then fade with age to blue, bloom in the spring.

Ease of care: Easy

How to grow: While lungworts will persist in poor soil, they do best when planted in a good, moist garden soil in partial to full shade.

Propagation: By division in fall or by seed

Uses: Lungworts are excellent plants for the shade garden, the wild garden, and even as ground covers on banks under the shadow of trees and bushes.

Related species: *Pulmonaria angustifolia* 'Azurea' is a European plant that bears brilliant blue flowers. 'Janet Fisk' has silver on its foliage.

Garden Phlox

Phlox paniculata

Zone: USDA 3

Phlox are popular plants—easy to grow, great for color, and marvelous for cutting.

Description: Phlox are clump-forming perennials with strong stems that bear simple, lance-shaped leaves. These stems are topped with clusters of fragrant, showy, five-petaled flowers arising from a narrow tube.

Ease of care: Easy

How to grow: Garden phlox need good, well-drained soil in full sun or light shade, and plenty of water during the summer. Plants are often prone to powdery mildew. Keep individual plants 18 inches apart to promote air circulation. Divide plants every three years to keep them vigorous.

Propagation: By division or by seed

Uses: Phlox can be bunched by color or mixed. The taller types work best at the rear of the border.

Related varieties: The Symons-Jeune strain of phlox was developed both for strength of stems and resistance to fungus (a major problem, as most of the phlox are susceptible).

Poppy

Papaver orientale

Zone: USDA 4

Papaver is the ancient Latin name for the flowers of this plant and is thought to refer to the sound made in chewing the seeds.

Description: The poppy's basal leaves are covered with hairs. Graceful stalks grow to four feet and bear single or double flowers with petals of crepe-paper-like texture surrounding many stamens.

Ease of care: Easy

How to grow: Poppies are undemanding, wanting only good, well-drained soil in full sun. Drainage is especially important in the winter as water will rot the roots. Place the crown three inches below the soil surface and mulch the first winter to prevent heaving.

Propagation: By division in the fall or by seed

Uses: Use poppies in beds or borders in combination with other perennials or in single groupings.

Related species: *Meconopsis cambrica,* or the Welsh poppy, has four-petaled, orange or yellow flowers that close at night.

Russian Sage

Perovskia species

Zone: USDA 4

A plant of great charm, originally from Afghanistan and West Pakistan, Russian sage is aromatic in addition to being beautiful. The genus is named in honor of a provincial Russian governor, V. A. Perovski.

Description: A subshrub with a woody base produces gray-white stems up to four feet tall, bearing small, oval, aromatic leaves with gray-white hairs on the undersides. Sprays of small $\frac{1}{4}$-inch, violet-blue flowers appear in late July and August.

Ease of care: Easy

How to grow: Well-drained soil and a spot in full sun are the requirements for these plants. They are not at all fussy. Cut any branches that remain after winter to the ground in early spring.

Propagation: By cuttings

Uses: As a specimen, as a hedge, or planted in a mass, these late-flowering plants will always elicit comments from garden visitors. Also, the flowers are excellent when cut.

Christmas Rose, Lenten Rose, Hellebore

Helleborus species

Zone: USDA 4 to 5

The genus is an ancient Greek name for the plant.

Description: Deeply divided, usually evergreen leaves grow from a thick rootstock, producing flowers with thick petals (really sepals) appearing in late fall, winter, or early spring.

Ease of care: Easy

How to grow: Hellebores require a good, deep, well-drained soil with plenty of humus and partial shade. When temperatures fall below 15°F, blooming is usually put off until the weather warms. At low temperatures, some protection is needed.

Propagation: By division or by seed

Uses: The foliage makes an excellent ground cover. Flowers are good for cutting, and the plants can be grown in pots or in a greenhouse.

Related species: *Helleborus niger,* or the true Christmas rose, bears white or pinkish-green flowers.

Salvia, Meadow Sage

Salvia x superba

Zone: USDA 4

Several types and colors of perennial salvias are available to the gardener.

Description: *Salvia x superba* is a sterile hybrid found only in cultivation. It has gray-green, paired leaves covered with tiny hairs underneath on square stems growing up to three feet high. They bear spikes, or bracts, of violet-purple flowers that contain smaller, true flowers.

Ease of care: Easy

How to grow: Salvias need full sun and a good garden soil with excellent drainage.

Propagation: By division or by cuttings

Uses: Use salvias in drifts—the effect will be one of many flower spikes.

Related species: *Salvia azurea,* or the blue salvia, is a native American plant reaching five feet in height and bearing deep blue flowers. 'Grandiflora' is a variety of the species that has larger flowers.

Related varieties: 'Blue Queen' has deep violet flowers through June.

Speedwell

Veronica spicata

Zone: USDA 4

Speedwell is a plant of the roadside with pretty flowers that "speed you well." In Ireland, a bit of the plant was pinned onto clothes to keep the traveler from accidents.

Description: Plants have simple, oblong, two-inch leaves on strong stems. They grow to 18 inches, bearing densely branching spikes of delicate, blue or pink flowers that bloom in summer.

Ease of care: Easy

How to grow: Speedwells will succeed in any good, well-drained garden soil in full sun or partial shade. Plants will not usually survive in overly wet soils in winter.

Propagation: By division or by seed

Uses: The taller varieties are beautiful in both bed and border as well as in the rock garden. They are good cut flowers.

Related species: *Veronica latifolia* 'Crater Lake Blue,' bears flowers of a deep blue on 18-inch stems. *Veronica prostrata* is a mat-forming type with deep blue flowers on four-inch stems.

Globe Thistle

Echinops Ritro

Zone: USDA 4

Globe thistles are large and stalwart plants that produce attractive balls of small, individual flowers.

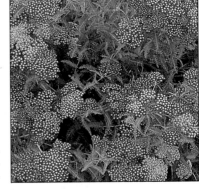

Description: Globe thistles are 1½-inch balls of metallic-blue blossoms atop stout, ribbed stems that grow 3 to 7 feet tall. The spiny-edged leaves are white and woolly underneath.

Ease of care: Easy

How to grow: Globe thistles are not fussy as to soil and do well in full sun or open shade. Once established, they are very drought-resistant.

Propagation: By division in the spring or by seed

Uses: The larger species are impressive when used in background plantings or when grown as specimen plants. The smaller types are attractive in a bed, border, or wild garden.

Related species: *Echinops sphaerocephalus* is a species that is much taller, sometimes reaching seven feet and best used where a strong statement is needed.

Related varieties: 'Taplow Blue' has a more intense blue color in the flowers.

Stonecrop

Sedum spectabile

Zone: USDA 4

There are perhaps 600 species of these succulent herbs found mostly in the North Temperate Zone.

Description: Sedums have strong stems with succulent, alternate leaves. Terminal clusters of small, star-shaped flowers have five petals.

Ease of care: Easy

How to grow: Sedums thrive with full sun and well-drained garden soil, although they are able to withstand drought and do amazingly well in poor soils.

Propagation: By cuttings or by division

Uses: Excellent in the bed or border, stonecrop is a long-lived, low maintenance perennial. It is especially effective in large masses.

Related varieties: Probably one of the most popular perennials in the garden world today is *Sedum* 'Autumn Joy.' They are always attractive: whether in tight buds of a light blue-green atop two-foot stems; rosy pink in early bloom; in late bloom as the flowers turn mahogany; or a russet-brown during the winter. *S. spectabile* 'Brilliant' opens its pink flowers a month ahead of 'Autumn Joy.'

Yarrow

Achillea species

Zone: USDA 3b

The botanical name refers to *Achilles*, the legendary Greek hero, who is said to have used a species to heal wounds.

Description: Yarrow will grow between 1 and 3 feet high, blooming from June until frost. Flowers are small and arranged in flat heads on top of stout stems. The foliage is finely cut and resembles a fern.

Ease of care: Easy

How to grow: Yarrows are tolerant of drought and suitable for any garden soil that has good drainage. Plants revel in full sun, although they will tolerate a small amount of shade.

Propagation: By division in spring or fall

Uses: Yarrow are excellent in garden borders and mass plantings.

Related species: The wildflower *Achillea Millefolium* is suited for the meadow or wild garden; the cultivar *Achillea*, 'Crimson Beauty,' bears rose-red flowers on two-foot stems; *Achillea Ptarmica*, 'The Pearl,' blooms with small, round, white flowers like its namesake on 3- to 4-foot stems.

Master Gardener Q & A

Commonly Asked Questions

Q: It's late winter and I've not yet planted the spring-flowering bulbs purchased last fall. Can they still be planted?

A: Spring flowering bulbs need the winter to establish new root systems and to finish development to bloom. If the bulbs are not spongy—an indication of a dying bulb—you should still be able to grow the bulbs; just don't expect flowering the first year. Care for the plants with fertilizer and regular waterings. If the plant is able to build back its strength, it will probably flower the following season.

Q: It's mid-winter and my bulbs and some perennials are beginning to emerge. Should I cover the plants to protect them from the elements?

A: Bulbs and perennials usually begin their growth at the right time, and are prepared for additional cold weather. Remove a bit of the mulch from around the plant. This will cool the soil and slow some of the growth. Just allow the plants to grow naturally and they'll bloom when the time is right.

Q: When is the best time to dig and separate bulbs?

A: The foliage of most spring bulbs will naturally turn yellow about six weeks after flowering. This is a good indication that the plant has produced and stored enough energy to survive and bloom next season. When leaves have begun to turn yellow, dig deeply to remove the entire clump. Gently shake the soil from the bulbs and break individual bulbs from the clump. Immediately replant the bulbs.

Q: After several years in a sunny location and well-drained soil, my peony hasn't bloomed. What's wrong?

A: Your plant is probably planted too deeply. Dig the plant in early fall and inspect the roots for any unusual damage. Adjust the pH to between 5.5 to 6.5. Replant so that the crown—the part where the buds form—is one to two inches below the soil surface. Water deeply and apply mulch so the plant can reestablish itself.

Q: When do I divide clumping perennials such as coralbells and Japanese iris?

A: Most perennials divide easily in fall, if done early enough for the roots to establish themselves several weeks before the ground freezes. Late blooming types can be divided in spring, providing there is ample rain or irrigation to encourage rapid rejuvenation of the root systems. Expect a reduction of flowering until the plants become reestablished in their new positions.

Q: What is the difference between inexpensive perennials grown from seed and the more expensive ones grown from divisions?

A: Some perennials are easily grown from seed, and produce flowers within a year or two. However, named cultivars—plants with specific desired characteristics—may only be reproduced through cuttings or by division from the parent plant, which displays the unique features. Because it takes longer to produce quantities of plants by division than by seed, production of these cultivars is usually more expensive.

Master Gardener Q & A

Commonly Asked Questions

Q: How can I keep spreading perennials like Monarda from invading my more timid plants?

A: Control invasive perennials by forming a barrier around the parent plant. The barrier needs to be set in the ground deep enough to prevent the rhizomes from growing beneath it. Use a large black nursery container with its bottom cut out; sink it in the ground to about ½ inch higher than soil level. Plant in the center of the pot and disguise the rim with a light layer of mulch.

Q: Most of the perennials have finished blooming, and I'd like to clean up the garden. How far down can I cut the plants?

A: It's important to leave the crown of the plant undisturbed so the basal leaves can continue to grow and produce food for the plant's winter survival. Cut flowering stalks to about four inches. The remaining stubble will identify the plants' locations so that you won't disturb them during bulb planting or winter gardening.

Q: What is the best method of fertilizing a perennial border of many different types of plants?

A: If the soil is properly prepared with organic matter, and the bed is mulched, only an annual application of complete fertilizer is needed. In early spring, when the plants actively begin growth, sprinkle fertilizer on the soil. Apply by hand to avoid fertilizer settling on the leaves. Use the directions on the bag to calculate the amount to apply.

Q: Why do some of my "full sun" selections of perennials burn up in my southern garden?

A: Garden books categorize light requirements of perennials according to the average light intensity of North American gardens. Plants that need full sun in New England may need protection from the hot afternoon sun in Georgia. Use references to guide your planning, but the best advice comes from experimenting with different species under various light conditions. Also, the use of mulch will aid in keeping soil temperatures lower.

Once a perennial border has established itself, little fertilization should be required to keep it thriving.

Trees, Shrubs & Vines

1

Getting Started with Woody Plants

Woody plants—that is, trees, shrubs, and woody vines—form the background of your home's landscape. Without them, beds and borders would seem to float on a sea of grass. Woody plants define the landscape, indicating its limits and breaking it up into separate parts. It would be as hard to imagine a landscape without trees, shrubs, and vines as it would be to imagine a living room without walls or a ceiling. Woody plants are essential elements in a garden's design.

Many other plants are seasonal. They grow in spring, bloom through summer, and then disappear in fall and winter. But wood, by its nature, is permanent. Even woody plants that lose their leaves are still visible during the winter months, their stark trunks and craggy branches continuing to define the landscape.

From spring's earliest flush of green to the colorful bark and graceful silhouettes of the winter landscape, woody plants bring life and movement to the garden all year long. Trees, shrubs, and vines tend to dominate the areas where they grow. They outcompete weeds, resist drought, and are generally able to recover readily from even severe insect attacks and other pests. As a result, woody plants require far less care than any other plant group. Once well-established, in fact, most of them literally take care of themselves.

Woody Plants in the Landscape

Woody plants are a permanent, year-long presence in the landscape. This permanence helps determine their major uses. It might help to consider the landscape as if it were a living room. The floor would be formed by low-growing plants and ground-hugging constructions, like lawns and ground covers, patios, and pavement. They form the base of any landscape. But what about the rest of the landscape, the walls and ceiling? That's where trees, shrubs, and climbing plants enter into the picture.

Shrubs and vines, as well as related constructions such as fences, form the walls of the room. They help define its boundaries, separating your yard space from your neighbor's and one garden area from another. This is most obvious when plants are grown as a hedge, but even informal plantings of shrubs will help to define the boundaries between various areas.

Shrubs can also offer a screen for privacy, or they can block unsightly views. If the goal of the screen is to block an undesirable view, evergreens—either conifers or broad-leaf varieties—are the plants of choice, since their cover is permanent. Taller shrubs can also be used as windbreaks or to create a bit of shade in an overly sunny spot.

Vines are used much like shrubs, except they must be grown on some sort of support, such as a fence or trellis. A hedge may need many years to grow high enough to block a view, but you can create the same effect in a year or two by planting a vining specimen at the base of a fence. Vines are also useful in places where space is lacking. Most cling so closely to their support that they take up only inches of horizontal space.

After the "floor" and "walls" have been taken care of, the outdoor living room now needs a ceiling. Although the sky can serve as a ceiling, it can be too much of a good thing. Trees block out a portion of the sky, defining the sky's borders in much the same way a picture frame helps define a work of art. Trees also contribute structure to the garden. Their trunks and branches act as posts and beams to bring the sky down to a more human scale.

Trees have other uses as well. No other characteristic of trees is as obvious in the landscape as the shade they provide. Using their ability to filter sunlight and to cool the air, leaves are able to reduce the temperature by up to 10 degrees on a hot summer day. So every garden should have at least one shady nook. Some trees are known as "shade trees." These types are usually taller trees with a broad crown. Smaller trees can also provide plentiful shade, although you may need to remove some of the lower branches to allow for sitting space under the tree.

The colorful fall foliage of trees, shrubs, and vines can beautify and add a sense of privacy to your home or yard.

Defining Woody Plants

Woody plants come in all shapes and sizes, from tall and upright to low and creeping. Aside from producing wood, these plants have one thing in common: persistent stems, meaning the stems survive from one year to the next. This distinguishes woody plants from herbaceous (nonwoody) plants like perennials, which die back to the ground each year. Although many woody plants lose their leaves in the winter or dry season, the stems survive and produce new leaves the following year. Trees, shrubs, and most vines are woody plants, but the boundaries between each group are not always clear.

One common definition of a tree is a perennial plant that bears only one single woody stem (the trunk) at ground level. Size is not a determining factor in this definition. Shrubs have several stems rising from ground level. Shrubs are also usually smaller. There are many obvious exceptions, such as trees with multiple trunks that can be very hard to distinguish from tall shrubs. These definitions, however, do help to distinguish between the two groups.

Humans also influence plant growth by pruning and other practices. For example, a gardener may prune off all the secondary stems of a shrub, leaving only one main trunk, thus creating a "standard" (tree-form shrub). A gardener may also repeatedly cut back young trees, forcing them to branch at their base, turning them into shrubs. Subshrubs are plants with woody stems, yet they die back at least partway to their roots each year. Some true shrubs, such as butterfly bush, will behave as subshrubs in cold or extreme climates.

Vines can be separated into three main categories: woody vines, which have permanent above-ground stems; perennial vines, which die back to the ground each winter and then sprout again in spring; and annual vines, which start anew from seed each year. A woody vine can be considered a shrub that needs some sort of support to grow well. Some woody vines (including many types of clematis) die back to the ground each year, just as subshrubs do, especially under harsh climatic conditions. Only woody vines are covered in this section.

Trees, shrubs, and woody vines are classified as either deciduous or evergreen. Deciduous woody plants usually lose most or all of their leaves by winter. Many deciduous plants have attractive fall colors. Evergreen plants remain clothed in foliage throughout the year. They do lose their leaves, but gradually rather than all at once; they are never completely barren.

The term "evergreen" is often mistakenly thought to pertain strictly to conifers (cone-bearing plants). This is not the case. There are broad-leaved evergreens, including boxwoods and most rhododendrons, and deciduous conifers, such as larches and bald cypress. In many plant catalogs, woody plants are divided into three categories according to their foliage: deciduous, broad-leaved evergreens, and needled evergreens.

🌿 *Radiant azaleas bloom under the light of a beech tree.*

Chapter
2

Checking Out
All the Options

Trees, shrubs, and vines make up a vital part of the
landscape, yet many people purchase them with no more
thought than deciding what to eat for dinner that night.
They go to the nursery, pick out a plant that looks
interesting, and plant it where they think it will look
good. Never for an instant do they consider its needs or
its eventual size or shape. With annuals, that's not such a
big mistake. If annuals do poorly or look awful in the spot
where you planted them, you can always try something else
next year. Woody plants don't offer the same option. Trees,
shrubs, and vines are comparatively expensive, and they are permanent
or nearly so. You can't just dig them up and move them with ease. You should
know how each woody plant will behave under present conditions before you
make your purchase.

In this chapter you'll learn the different uses for trees, shrubs, and vines so
you won't make mistakes when planning your landscape. How can you get the
most out of your woody plants? Which are best for fall color, winter contrast,
spring flowers, and summer shade? Which are well-adapted to your conditions
and which should be avoided? These are just some of the questions to
consider in selecting trees, shrubs, and vines for your landscape.

Designing with Trees, Shrubs, and Vines

Designing your landscape is much like decorating your home, but you need to plan even more carefully. After all, you can always move the sofa or change the picture on the wall until you get just the right effect. However, you can rarely move a tree, shrub, or vine once it is established. The most effective landscape design always comes from thoughtful planning. Before you fill your car with trees and shrubs from the nursery, plan your landscape on paper.

Start by mapping out your yard. Graph paper is perfect for planning. It takes much of the difficulty out of measurement (each square can be a precise measurement, say 1 foot by 1 foot) and makes drawing straight lines a snap. It also makes it is easier to lay out the plants for installation, as the yard can be marked off to match the grid of the paper. Draw in the permanent structures first: the house, the garage, the sidewalk, the driveway, and anything else you will not be moving or changing in a major way. Include such features as windows in your house, which help determine special views you'll want to enhance. Draw these in pen. Next consider any plants or secondary constructions (fences, garden walls, lightpoles, and the like) that are already in place and not likely to change. These can be either penciled in or inked in, depending on how sure you are that they really will stay the same. Also include any easements or utilities that you must keep clear, such as water and sewer hookups, and underground power and gas lines. Remember to add utilitarian constructions such as telephone poles, tool sheds, and fire hydrants that you may want to make less visible, as well as any features of your neighbor's yard that you want to either continue to enjoy or hide from sight. Don't include anything you intend to remove. You now have the base on which to develop your plan.

The next step is to start testing your landscape ideas. Pencil in a few shrubs or trees (or cut out their forms in paper and paste them in place). If the initial results look good on paper, try putting more plants elsewhere. Any time something you add doesn't please you, just erase it and start again. Consider your family's needs both now and in the future; the plantings should mesh with these

🌿 *Decorative vines, like this purple clematis, can be trained to climb up fences and trellises, creating living walls of bright color.*

requirements. For example, if you have young children and intend to install an above-ground pool to keep them busy for the summer, don't plan to plant tall trees nearby because their shade simply won't be welcome.

Once you have your plan, it is time to start shopping for plants—but again, only on paper. At this point, look for shapes, forms, and heights rather than specific species. Try to visualize the height of the plants you want, and the space they'll take up. Include some variety in your plan but don't hesitate to use the same plant in different places or in mass plantings. The pattern thus created will help unify the landscape. Plantings of totally disparate trees, shrubs, and vines will look like a hodgepodge collection. Consider contrast and balance, texture and color, scale and form. If you have large trees on your lot, remember that the scale of your plantings will have to be much larger than in a yard with no trees or only young ones. Large trees tend to dwarf other plants unless the other plants are also large. To easily determine if your plan is well-balanced, use color in your plan to distinguish between various types of plants. You'll want to be able to tell your evergreen trees apart from your deciduous or flowering trees, and so on.

Planning on Paper

Use graph paper to develop a scale drawing of your house and yard. Ink in permanent structures, then pencil in those features that you are considering planting. Make ample notes to help you better organize your thoughts. When you've developed a plan that seems to meet all your needs, you can begin to look for the proper species to plant. Pencil in potential plantings until you have a design that suits your needs.

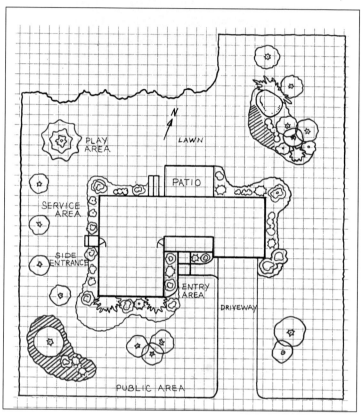

Accent Plants

An accent plant usually stands out from the other plants surrounding it because of an unusual feature. An unusual form, a brilliant display of color, or an oddly shaped plant may attract attention. Don't overdo accent plants or they lose their effectiveness. They are designed to draw the eye, and the eye can't look in several directions at once. Use no more than one accent plant in each major part of the garden.

Putting Woody Plants to Good Use

🌱 *Flowering rhododendron shrubs line this backyard walkway. Woody plants define and accent the features of your property.*

Many woody plants are well-suited to serve as garden accents. The features that woody plants can offer may be a special shape or texture or foliage of a contrasting color. It could simply be a plant that would be quite ordinary in other circumstances but stands out because it is different from the surrounding plants.

Shade trees need to be carefully placed, or they will quickly crowd each other out. Check their eventual width and plant them so they will barely touch at maturity. Try planting shade trees about 20 feet from the house on the southwest or west sides. They can make convenient air conditioners, lowering the indoor temperature by as much as 20 degrees Fahrenheit. Deciduous shade trees have the advantage of blocking excess summer sun, but during the winter, when their leaves fall, they let in much needed light.

Flowering trees are smaller than shade trees and are not as likely to overpower the landscape. They make excellent accents when planted singly, and this is often their best use on small lots. For larger areas, you can try mass plantings or repeating them to define a straight or curved line. Many flowering trees offer all-season interest, with showy spring flowers, green or bronze summer foliage, colorful leaves in the fall, and bright fruit or attractive bark in the winter.

Shrubs are easy to incorporate into the landscape as long as their eventual height and width are taken into account. Shrubs can be planted singly as accent plants, or together in borders to form a background for other garden plants. When used as hedges, shrubs can be planted much closer together than they would normally be.

Houses can best be integrated into the surrounding land through foundation plantings. Plant shrubs and vines, possibly even small trees, near the walls of the building. Do not place foundation plants too close together or too close to the walls. Find out their full diameter at maturity and space them appropriately. Low-growing and spreading shrubs are ideal subjects for foundation plantings. Taller shrubs, especially conical or columnar ones, can be planted at the corners of the building or between windows. Do not plant tall shrubs in front of windows.

Climbing plants are ideal for landscaping because their eventual height and width are limited by the structures on which they grow. Unless climbing plants "escape" by reaching into nearby trees or other structures (and they can always be pruned if they do), they'll remain within bounds. Be careful about planting clinging vines—such as English ivy—up against the house itself. If the mortar is weak, the vine can damage the house's structure. (Scrape at the mortar with a key: If it resists, there will be no danger of damage.) Just in case, consider training vines up trellises set about a foot away from the house.

The Size and Shape of Woody Plants

Woody plants, as opposed to herbaceous plants, build on their growth of previous years, becoming bigger and bigger with time. There is a limit, of course—a small shrub will never become a tall tree—but most woody plants will continue to increase in size throughout their lives. Growth is modest, however, once they attain their full size.

The "full size" of any woody plant is a highly variable point. A tree growing in ideal conditions will become much larger than the same species growing in a spot for which it is poorly adapted. In general, trees and shrubs grown in full sun will be much broader and fuller, yet often not as tall. If the same species has to compete with other trees and shrubs (for instance, in a forest), it will often grow beyond its "maximum" height but have a narrow growth habit with fewer branches. Size and breadth are also dependant on the space available. Because of restricted root growth, a shrub in a container may reach only a fraction of its natural size.

Vines differ from other woody plants in that they adapt to the size of their support. A climbing plant may have the potential to reach 50 feet in height, but if it is growing on an eight-foot trellis, it won't get much higher than the trellis.

The ultimate size and shape of trees and shrubs can be controlled by pruning. Often, the plants in a moderate-size hedge would actually grow to become trees, but their small growth can be maintained indefinitely by judicious trimming.

For these and other reasons, the sizes given are only approximate. If a tree is said to eventually attain a height of 60 feet, that is what it can be expected to reach in average growing conditions.

Some trees and shrubs are fast-growing. They can put on several feet of new growth a year. Fast-growers are ideal when quick results are desired. Most fast-growing woody plants, however, are also short-lived. You may be better off planting fast-growing trees and shrubs to quickly give your landscape the proper volume. At the same time, you can plant slower-growing but longer-lived plants that will one day comprise the backbone of your landscape after the short-lived plants are removed.

Trees and shrubs can be divided into groups based on different growth habits. Many trees and shrubs may have one growth habit when young and another when mature. Vines can be divided according to the way in which they climb and the kind of support they need. However, all vines can also be grown as ground covers. Just plant them in an open space with no objects to climb, and they will spread nicely. As soon as the vine finds a likely support, it will climb it.

🦢 *From subtle shades of green to dazzling purples, yellows, or reds, a remarkable variety of woody plants are available to satisfy nearly any need of the weekend gardener.*

Selecting for Hardiness

The term "hardiness" is considered by most gardeners to apply to cold hardiness, which is the ability of a plant to adapt to a given degree of cold. But the subject is actually much more complex than that. Many supposedly "hardy" trees and shrubs from the Pacific Northwest, for example, do poorly in the Midwest and Northeast. This is not because of the cold, but rather because of the hot, dry summers. Plants adapted to cold conditions often will not grow well in the South. These plants need cold temperatures to signal a time of dormancy or a time to flower.

Local nurseries or botanical gardens are good sources for information concerning cold hardiness as well as whether a given plant will do well under local conditions. Always ask before you buy. It can be frustrating to plant a sapling believing it will become a large shade tree only to discover it barely grows under local conditions.

Woody plants are far more susceptible to temperature change than perennials since they don't die back to the ground. Instead, their branches and buds are exposed to winter's coldest temperatures. It is important to choose woody plants that are adapted to your climatic zone.

There are several different hardiness zone maps, but the one most used in North America was created by the United States Department of Agriculture (USDA). See pages 44–45 for the current USDA map.

Most North American garden plants have been classified according to their adaptability to cold and have been assigned a particular hardiness zone based on the coldest temperatures at which the plants can be expected to do well. For example, the silk tree (*Albizia julibrissin*) is considered hardy to Zone 6. It will do well in that zone and in zones with higher numbers, such as Zone 7 or Zone 8, but not in Zone 5b, which is colder.

🖎 *The brilliantly colored panicles of crape myrtle can brighten spaces in warmer climates, but it will not flower and could get tip blight if grown in colder areas.*

Remember that hardiness classifications are indications only. It is not always necessary to follow them to the letter. For example, if you can offer good snow cover, excellent growing conditions, and protection from dominant winds, you might be able to grow a plant a half zone, or even a full zone, beyond its normal classification.

Within a species, individual plants may be hardier than the average. These extra-hardy plants are often used to breed even hardier plants. The USDA, for example, has been working on developing hardier varieties of crape myrtle, holly, camellia, and many others. Cuttings or seeds taken from plants already growing beyond their normal range often yield hardier plants and are well worth experimentation if one of your favorite plants doesn't normally grow in your area. Specialist nurseries can offer clones of trees, shrubs, and vines adapted to colder climates.

3

Caring for Woody Plants

Learning about woody plants and their needs and taking into account the conditions in your yard are just the first steps in growing trees, shrubs, and vines. You also need to know how to plant them and how to care for them once they are in the ground.

Planting a tree, shrub, or vine properly is one of the most important steps in growing it. How well a woody plant does in the first few years depends directly on the way it was handled as it was placed in the ground. If the plant gets off to a poor start, it may never recover enough to become a useful element of your landscape. The initial care and extra effort you take in preparing soil, planting, and tending the needs of the plant until it becomes more self-sufficient will almost guarantee that your woody plant will have a long, healthy existence.

Once planted and established in its location, a woody plant needs little care: much less than most other plants. However, if you want your plant to give its best performance, you do have to meet its needs. Careful mulching, feeding, and pruning will ensure that your tree, shrub, or vine will always look its best.

Planting and Transplanting

Even if you're experienced at planting woody plants, it is worth reviewing planting techniques. Studies have shown that some former methods were not helpful, notably planting depth and soil improvement.

The new rule in planting trees and shrubs is to dig a hole three times as wide as the root ball but no deeper. This is a major change compared with previous recommendations, which promoted deep digging before planting. The theory behind the new method is that roots should be resting on solid ground so they can support the plant's weight. Loose soil beneath the root ball causes it to sink too deeply into the ground, burying the crown of the plant. Don't improve the soil by adding amendments unless you are planning to improve a large area. A small bowl of improved soil may restrict root growth from outreaching areas of original soil. Instead, loosen the earth on the side of the hole as well. The goal is to produce a wide but shallow space with loose soil into which the roots can grow for many years to come.

Set the plant in the hole so that the soil line (a distinct mark at the base of the stem showing the point where the plant was originally covered in soil) is slightly above its previous level. In sandy soils, the plant can be placed level with its original mark. Do not plant too deeply.

Most nurseries offer trees, shrubs, and vines in three basic forms: bare-root, balled-and-burlapped, and in containers. Each form has its own requirements at planting time. Balled-and-burlapped and bare-root plants should be planted as soon after purchase as possible.

Top pruning is unnecessary unless there are competing leaders; prune to remove all but one. Damaged branches or ones that cross or grow at awkward angles should also be removed.

Shrubs and young trees can easily be transplanted from one part of the garden to another as long as care is taken to remove as large a root ball and undisturbed soil as possible. The general rule is to dig up one foot diameter of root mass for every inch of trunk, with the measurement starting six inches above the soil level. Transplanting is best done in early spring or in fall, when the plants are dormant. If you are unable to transplant immediately (within the next few hours), make sure the root ball is covered with an old blanket or similar cover and watered thoroughly. The roots must never be allowed to dry or burn in the sun.

During their first year of growth, newly planted trees, shrubs, and vines need to be watered more regularly than established plants. Always water thoroughly, soaking the ground entirely, then let the soil nearly dry before watering again. A ring of raised soil around the plant will act as a catch basin for rainfall and irrigation.

Young trees (such as this eastern white pine) can be planted in their burlap bag after all ties are removed.

Fertilizing and Mulching

Like all living organisms, woody plants need various nutrients and minerals, but unlike animals they do not need to be "fed" on a regular basis. They draw from the sun's rays, the air that surrounds them, and the soil in which they grow. In most cases, a single annual fertilization is sufficient, starting the year after planting. Fertilizer is best applied in spring or early summer. Avoid fertilizing woody plants in late summer or fall. They have to harden off at that time of year, and a late application of fertilizer may stimulate rapid, weak growth that will not overwinter well.

Nurseries offer a wide variety of fertilizers, including some specifically designed for woody plants. Choose a slow-release fertilizer, that will ensure that your plant's needs are met over a long period of time rather than all at once. Most organic fertilizers naturally liberate minerals slowly, making them excellent choices.

Fertilizer should be applied evenly throughout the area covered by the plant's root system. The root system often stretches beyond the spread of the plant's branches, especially on established plants. As a rule of thumb, calculate that the roots reach at least a foot beyond the plant's branches.

Granular fertilizers are easy to apply either by hand or by spreader. Carefully follow the directions on the package; you can apply less fertilizer than recommended, but never more. Water thoroughly after application to carry the fertilizer to root level. In the case of large trees, especially those that have to compete with grass for minerals, professional arborists often drill into the ground beneath and around the tree's canopy and fill the holes with fertilizer. This ensures that the fertilizer reaches the tree's roots rather than being used by the grass above. Specially conceived fertilizer stakes do much the same and can be applied by punching them into the soil with a hammer.

In the wild, most woody plants grow with a deep layer of fallen leaves covering their soil and roots. This layer keeps the soil from overheating in summer or alternately freezing and thawing too rapidly in winter. It also keeps the soil from drying out too much and reduces or prevents the growth of weeds. The leaves also keep grasses in check, so woody plants in natural settings almost never have to compete with grasses. For these reasons, it is well worth your time to cover the soil at the base of woody plants with an organic mulch.

Many materials can be used as a mulch: chopped autumn leaves, wood chips, bark nuggets, garden compost, and the like. Any fresh materials, such as sawdust, manure, or grass clippings, should be allowed to compost for several months before use. If used fresh, the breakdown process would deplete essential nutrients from the surrounding soil.

🌫 *Mulch protects woody plants from severe weather. Keep mulch moist to prevent it from becoming a fire hazard.*

Applying Fertilizer

Fertilizer should be broadcast a foot from the base of the plant to a foot or so beyond the spread of the outer branches. Apply fertilizer just prior to the plant's active growth period. Record the type and amount of fertilizer applied to keep as a handy reference until adjustments must be made to compensate for annual growth.

Applying Mulch

Apply mulch over the entire root area of the plant. Although a few inches of mulch is sufficient, the plant will probably be healthier the larger the area covered by mulch. Mulch is biodegradable; it will break down while feeding the plant so additional mulch will need to be spread. Keep the base of the trunk clear from mulch to prevent insect and disease attack.

Maintaining Your Trees, Shrubs, and Vines

🌸 *Once established, woody plants need surprisingly little maintenance to keep them healthy and beautiful.*

Woody plants are considerably easier to maintain than most landscape plants (such as annuals and perennials). In fact, once established, most need little care at all, especially if they are planted in fertile soil and their root zone is protected by mulch. Beyond an occasional pruning and fertilization, watering as needed, and replacing the mulch at their base, woody plants should thrive with little care on your part. But there are a few special pointers applicable to specific cases that may help you obtain better performance from your plants.

Woody plants need water less frequently than other ornamental plants because of their deep roots. When woody plants do need water, however, they require greater quantities of it all at once. To water them efficiently, set the sprinkler or irrigation system at a relatively low pressure but leave it on for a longer period of time. As a result, the tree or shrub receives roughly the same amount of water as other plants, but slowly, soaking the root zone to a greater depth. Superficial waterings, such as those for lawns, do more harm than good to woody plants.

Exposure of woody plants to cold winter winds can cause problems due to desiccation, even among plants that are fully hardy. The damage is most evident in conifers and broad-leaf evergreens, which can turn brown by spring, especially on the side most exposed to harsh winter winds. Damage to deciduous plants may be obvious only when they green up in spring. Leaf or flower bud damage can be seen by the dieback in different areas.

This damage is most easily prevented by making sure the plant does not lack water. If rain is lacking, keep watering throughout the autumn even though the plants appear dormant. If there is a mid-winter thaw, make sure the plant is well hydrated. This will help keep the flower and leaf buds supplied with moisture.

Early-spring blooming plants risk damage from late frost. If this occurs, soak the plant from top to bottom overnight with a sprinkler. Moving water rarely freezes.

As a weekend gardener, you are wise to choose varieties of woody materials that have proven hardy in your area, but gardeners have an interest in trying the unusual. Woody plants of marginal hardiness or those grown beyond their normal hardiness zone will require special winter protection. Surround them with burlap or snow fencing (or a combination of both) to filter winds and help collect snow. Fill enclosures with straw or oak leaves packed around the stems. You can also use the branches of conifers to cover them, especially on sides exposed to dominant winds. Vines can be taken down from their trellis, tied together, laid on the ground, and covered with a thick mulch of leaves.

A mature tree that serves a function—such as providing shade or framing a view—is invaluable. Once structural damage from ice or wind occurs, or it is discovered that internal rot exists from disease or insect infestations, corrective action deserves serious consideration. Because a mature tree is impossible to replace, a professional arborist should be called to evaluate the situation. The weekend gardener may not have the time, the tools, or the knowledge to correct major damage. The arborist will be able to advise whether the tree can be saved or if removal is inevitable.

Any tree extending much beyond the height of surrounding trees will be subject to lightning damage, especially if it is the only tall object in the vicinity. Damage can range from scarcely noticeable to severe, killing the tree outright. Since a large tree not only has considerable value but is also impossible to replace, you may want to consider protecting it with a lightning rod. Consult an arborist for recommendations and installation.

Winter Protection

Marginally hardy plants should be protected from drying winter winds. Prepare the plant for winter by watering it deeply and supplying it with several inches of mulch. Broad-leaf evergreens are most susceptible to drying winds. Their leaves continue to lose moisture on sunny winter days; if the soil is frozen, roots cannot take up water and the leaves will dry and turn brown.

Watering

Woody plants need approximately one inch of water a week, less if their roots are covered in mulch or the soil is very heavy. Water slowly and deeply so less frequent waterings are needed.

4

Keeping Ahead of the Challenges

Trees, shrubs, and vines are generally easy to grow and maintenance free. In the best of all worlds, it would be nice to say, "Just plant them and let them grow!" Unfortunately, that isn't always possible. Occasionally things do go wrong. They may be the result of mistakes you yourself have made, but more often they result from accidents or natural phenomena beyond your control. A lawn mower damages a trunk, a hungry insect moves in, or you wake up one morning to find your favorite shrub is white with mildew. These are all things that can occur, and you should be prepared for them.

Some damage to trees, shrubs, and vines can be prevented as long as you are aware of the potential problems. Other damage may occur despite your best efforts, but the harm can be reduced by preparing ahead of time. To keep damage to a minimum, get to know your plants; inspect them regularly, and treat problems as soon as you notice them.

Fortunately, woody plants by their nature are fighters. They will tenaciously try to struggle through even the worst injuries or infestations. With you alongside, doing what you can, woody plants can live through some of the worst of gardening calamities and thrive again.

Pruning

Perhaps no other aspect concerning trees, shrubs, and vines confuses amateur gardeners as much as pruning. When to prune? What to prune? How to do it? These are just a few of the questions asked.

When to prune depends on several factors, notably the type of plant and the reason for pruning. Pruning can actually stimulate growth. Pruning back a weak branch in late winter or early spring will often cause the new growth that replaces it to grow much faster. To slow growth down, prune in early summer. These are the two basic principles of pruning, but there are numerous exceptions.

Trees, shrubs, and vines that bloom in spring (blooming on branches formed the previous year) are usually pruned immediately after they finish blooming. This stimulates fresh new growth that will produce more flowers the next year. Those that bloom on new wood (usually summer-bloomers) can be left until the following spring. Most formal hedges can be pruned in any season, as needed. It is preferable not to prune at the very end of summer since this can promote new growth that will be susceptible to winter damage. Informal hedges may be pruned after blooming.

There are two kinds of coniferous plants that require different types of pruning. The first are those that put out their entire year's new growth all at once, in late spring. This group includes pines, spruces, and firs. They can be pruned by removing up to two-thirds of the new growth while it is still fresh and pale green. Do not prune them back to old wood because they will not produce new shoots from those sections. Conifers that grow throughout the summer, such as yews, arborvitae, and junipers, are pruned once in early summer and again, if necessary, later in the season. They can also be pruned more heavily, down to old wood if necessary.

What to prune depends a great deal on the effect you want to create. There are major differences between the way to prune shrubs and the way to prune trees.

Except under rare circumstances, ornamental trees should be left to take their natural shape and appearance, resulting in little need for pruning. They are usually pruned only to remove damaged or diseased branches or ones that cross, rub together, or form an overly acute angle with the trunk. Suckers (also called water sprouts) should also be removed. Suckers are upright, unbranched sprouts that often appear at the base of the tree or on the lower trunk. Sometimes the upper limbs of overly dense shade trees can also be thinned to open them up, allowing more light to reach the garden below.

Large branches require a pruning saw and should be removed back to the trunk or a main branch. Do not leave a stub, or the healing process will be very long. For major branches,

Colorful rhododendrons add interest to this hedge border. Pruning away older branches will stimulate new growth and blooming.

use the three-cut method. In most cases, major pruning on a large tree should be left to a professional arborist, especially if there are nearby electrical wires or if a ladder is needed.

Different pruning techniques are used on shrubs, depending on the desired effect. Formal hedges, topiaries, and other closely clipped forms are sheared, which means all branches are clipped to the same length. Some shrubs that bloom on new wood are also sheared back annually to the base to encourage a maximum number of branches and thus more flowers.

When a more natural shape is desired, shrubs are generally thinned. Older or excessively long branches and weaker secondary branches are removed down to a main branch or to the base of the plant. This allows room for younger branches to grow to their best advantage. Thinning is usually the preferred method for spring-flowering shrubs and is carried out as soon as the year's flowers have faded.

In general, vines should be treated in the same manner as shrubs. Vines grown for their foliage often produce overly exuberant growth, especially once well-established, and need to be pruned regularly. They can be pruned back any time except late summer or early fall; pruning at that time of year can result in new growth that doesn't harden properly.

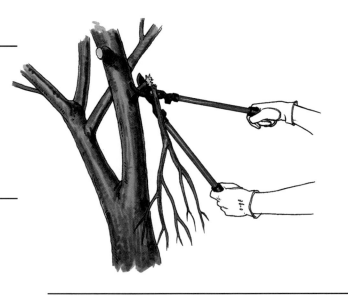

Trees
Once young trees are established, they can be pruned to remove weak growth and give them a better form. When the tree has attained a fair height, any lower branches that interfere with human movement can be removed, preferably over a two- to three-year period.

Shearing
Shearing is the most common form of ornamental pruning for hedges. Shrubs or small trees are planted closely together—only one to two feet apart—forming a wall or screen. Formal hedges are trimmed into geometric shapes and require frequent shearing, often up to four times a year (less for conifers). The base of the hedge should be wider than the top, or the lower branches will be shaded out and die. Shrubs that bloom on new wood can also be sheared.

Thinning

Spring-flowering shrubs should be thinned by cutting one-third of the oldest stems to ground level each spring. This will encourage new growth from the base of the shrub, producing a heavy flush of flower buds for the next bloom season.

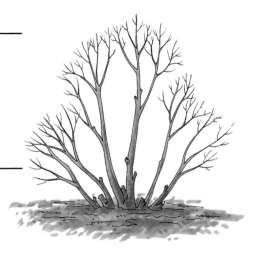

Three-Cut Method

1. Undercut the branch halfway through to prevent the weight of the branch from tearing the bark down the trunk.
2. Cut from above, slightly beyond the first cut.
3. Cut from above, parallel to the collar, to remove the stub.

Topping

One common technique in tree pruning is topping, or heading. This is not a recommended pruning technique. Topping involves pruning back the large branches of deciduous trees in an indiscriminate fashion to change the tree's natural shape into that of a ball. This causes all sorts of problems, including wounds that heal poorly, severe dieback, and increased danger of wind damage. It also destroys the tree's natural symmetry.

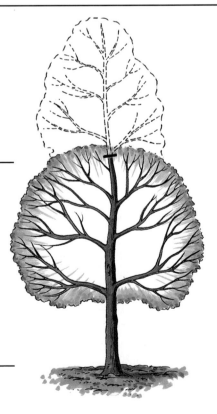

Environmental Hazards

Something is obviously wrong with your plant. Your natural reaction is probably to reach for the nearest can of insecticide. Don't do it. First, analyze the situation to determine what is causing the problem. Only afterward should you search for a solution. Most problems with trees, shrubs, and vines are not caused by insects or disease, but rather by an inappropriate environment.

Some areas seem chronically dry. Even when rainfall has been abundant, plants suffer from scorched leaf margins and wilt frequently. This problem is common with newly planted trees and shrubs on slopes and in clay soils. It is caused by not enough water reaching the roots. When planting, leave a water dam around the root ball for the first year or so. This will help hold the water in place so it can soak in. Clay soils hold water readily when damp but are hard to remoisten once they dry. Water slowly over a long period of time to make sure the root ball is thoroughly moistened.

A tree or shrub may actually choke itself to death if the roots continue to encircle around themselves. Especially prevalent with container-grown plants, the cause of the problem is often discovered only when the plant dies and is removed. Carefully inspect your plants during planting, and straighten or prune away any encircling roots. A girdling root on an established plant, especially a large tree, can be difficult to remove and requires the assistance of an experienced arborist.

Compacted soil will cause general slowed growth. Compaction is especially frequent following new construction; therefore, whenever heavy vehicles or machinery are used in the yard, make sure that a predetermined path is followed and that trees and shrubs requiring special protection are roped off. Prevention is better than correction around established plants.

If the ground is very hard, or if water runs off before seeping into the ground, the soil is seriously compacted. Verticutting or aerating may loosen up the soil in the surface area if that is where compaction has occurred. Machines can be rented or lawn specialists hired to perform this task.

🐚 *Drought has damaged the tops of these conifers. It is crucial to keep woody plants deep-watered during dry periods. Superficial watering can do more harm than good.*

The most common winter injury is due to the drying effects of cold winds (windburn). Especially obvious on broad-leaf evergreens, windburn is best prevented by planting susceptible plants in a protected area. The problem can become worse if the plants do not receive generous amounts of water throughout the fall and winter seasons.

Sunscald is caused as the bark heats up on a warm winter's day and freezes rapidly at night. Vertical cracks may form on the south side of a trunk, especially on trees or shrubs with thin bark. These cracks provide a path for diseases and insects. Sunscald can be prevented by wrapping the trunk in a protective covering for the winter.

Salt Toxicity

Salt toxicity is common in areas where de-icing salts are used in the winter. The worst damage occurs right where the salt is applied, near roads and walks. Plants will display general dieback, yellowish foliage, and weak growth. Environmentally safe compounds are now available that are not harmful to plants.

Girdling

Girdling occurs when a plant's own roots wrap completely around its base. Sometimes the girdling root is visible at the surface of the soil, but often it is hidden from sight. Nylon labels and packing twine must also be removed at planting to prevent girdling of the trunk or limbs.

Winter Injury

Windburn is a common winter injury, turning leaves and needles reddish brown and causing them to fall off in spring or summer. In severe cases, branches die back. If windburn is a recurring problem, set up burlap barriers to the windward side of these plants. Another option is to plant a windbreak of tough trees and shrubs.

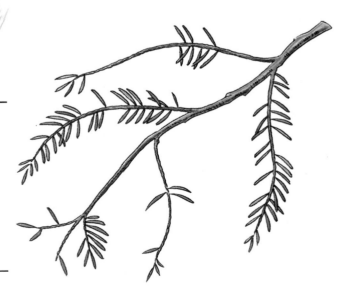

Pests and Diseases

There are a great many potential pests and diseases of trees, shrubs, and vines. Fortunately, most are relatively innocuous, causing no long-term damage and only minor aesthetic damage. This is just as well since it can be difficult to treat pests on woody plants, especially large trees, because sprays don't reach the upper branches.

The first step in treating any pest problem is prevention. Give your plants the best conditions possible and that includes planting them in places where they are likely to grow healthily. Buy varieties noted for their disease resistance. When a problem does become noticeable, try to determine what is causing it. The chart below should be of some help in this regard. If you can't ascertain the cause of an infestation, have it identified by an expert. Applying pesticides indiscriminately can do more harm than good. The following pests and diseases include those most commonly found on a variety of ornamental trees, shrubs, and vines in North America.

Even a few small pests can cause considerable damage.

INSECTS AND ANIMALS

SYMPTOM	CAUSE	CURE	PLANTS
Small brown spots appear on leaves, often coalescing, giving the leaf a scorched look. Leaves may drop.	*Anthracnose*	Keep trees growing healthily. Remove badly diseased foliage. Apply Bordeaux mixture when buds are first opening.	Ash, Flowering Dogwood, Sycamore, Weeping Willow, others
Tiny pear-shaped, soft-bodied insects in green, brown, red, or black appear in clusters on stems and leaves. They often leave sticky secretions on the ground below.	*Aphids*	Spray with insecticidal soap, repeating as necessary.	Most trees, shrubs, and vines

INSECTS AND ANIMALS

SYMPTOM	CAUSE	CURE	PLANTS
Stems and shoots die back. Holes, sawdust, or droppings are visible on trunks or branches. Wormlike, legless, cream-colored larvae are found in holes.	*Borers*	Keep plant healthy. Prune off infested branches. For insecticide treatment, check with county Cooperative Extensive office to determine proper product and period.	Fruit trees, Birch, Dogwood, Lilac, Mountain Ash, Rhododendron, others
Large discolored spots appear on stem, becoming dry and dark or light. Black fungal spots appear in dead areas. Stems or trunk may die back.	*Canker*	Avoid pruning during wet weather. Prune out and destroy infected stems. Sterilize pruning shears between cuts.	Apple, Ash, Beech, Honey Locust, Mountain Ash, Pear, Poplar
Leaves are partly or entirely consumed; the entire plant can be defoliated. Soft-bodied, wormlike insects, which can be smooth or hairy, are observed. Weblike tents may be visible. Adults are moths or butterflies.	*Caterpillars*	Cut down and burn webs. Spray with *Bacillus thuringiensis*. Direct spray toward offending organisms only.	Most trees, shrubs, and vines
Plants have blackened terminal shoots and oozing stem cankers that result in plant death.	*Fireblight*	Avoid pruning during wet weather. Prune out and destroy infected stems. Sterilize pruning shears between cuts. Select resistant varieties. Spray with bactericide.	Plants in the rose family: Apple, Cotoneaster, Hawthorn, Mountain Ash, Pear, others
Leaves and shoots wilt suddenly and turn brown. Plant growth is stunted.	*Fungal blight*	Avoid moistening foliage. Improve air circulation around plants. Prune out infested sections.	Clematis, Lilac, others
Leaves are chewed, even skeletonized. Flowers may be frayed. Hard-shelled, oval to oblong insects may be visible. Roots may also be eaten by the larval stage of the same insect.	*Leaf-feeding beetles*	Spray with insecticidal soap, repeating as necessary.	Grape, Linden, Rose, others

INSECTS AND ANIMALS

SYMPTOM	CAUSE	CURE	PLANTS
Papery, meandering paths and blotches are found in leaves. Leaves may drop. Small, soft-bodied grubs are found within leaf. Adults are flies or beetles.	*Leaf miners*	Damage is largely aesthetic since plants are rarely weakened, even by heavy infestations. Remove severely infested leaves. Chemical sprays are largely ineffective.	Ashes, Boxwood, Holly, Lilac, Privet
Leaves and stems are covered with a grayish, powdery coating. Leaves may be deformed or fall off.	*Powdery mildew*	Increase air circulation. Regularly thin infected trees and shrubs. Treat with appropriate fungicide.	Apple, Euonymus, Lilac, Rose, others
Stems are covered with small, waxy, soft- or hard-bodied "scales" (stationary insects) in shades of white, brown, black, or gray. Growth is stunted. Leaves are yellowed.	*Scale insects*	Spray in spring with dormant oil spray before growth begins.	Beech, Camellia, Euonymus, Horse Chestnut, Magnolia, others
Leaves appear pale and dry from a distance; up close they seem to be covered with small yellow dots. Fine webs may be present. Tiny eight-legged arachnids are seen in profuse numbers on leaves and stems. Plant may be stunted.	*Spider mites*	Spray regularly with water on both sides of leaf.	Arborvitae, Peach, others
Plant growth stunted. Leaves become crinkled, mottled, or deformed.	*Viruses*	There is no cure. Destroy infested plants. Buy only disease-free plants.	Many trees, shrubs, and vines
Progressive wilting. Leaves turn yellow. Infected branches or even entire plant may die. Often transmitted by insects.	*Wilt (fungal or bacteria)*	If only a few branches are infected, remove them. Destroy heavily infested plants.	Maple, Smoke Tree, Sumac

Directory of Popular Trees, Shrubs & Vines

Once you have an idea of the kind of conditions your yard has to offer, the sort of landscaping needs you want woody plants to fill, and the amount of care you are willing to put into your landscape, there is only one thing left to do—actually pick out the actual trees, shrubs, and vines you would like to grow.

You'll find that woody plants require less attention than do annuals, perennials, and lawns. They give your garden structure, and (once well established) will continue to grow with little demand into permanent features in your landscape. The following section highlights a few of the sturdiest trees, shrubs, and vines that you might like to try. The choices cover varieties suitable for most climates in North America as well as growing conditions of all sorts (from deep shade to full sun). The profiles also include all the types and categories of woody plants: flowering and foliage; deciduous and evergreen; needled and broad-leaf. Read the profiles over carefully and take a few notes on the plants that strike you as the best adapted to your needs; then visit a local garden center. You shouldn't have any trouble picking plants that will fit in perfectly with your lot.

American Beech
Fagus grandifolia
Zone: USDA 4a to 9a

This majestic species is one of the most remarkable trees of eastern North America, where it forms dense groves in deciduous forests.

Description: A tall, massive tree, the American beech can grow to more than 80 feet, providing dense shade. It has a beautiful ghost gray bark, the nicest coloration of all the beeches. The deciduous leaves are oval and pointed, toothed on the edges. They are dark green in summer, turn golden bronze in fall, and often persist much of the winter. The edible nuts are protected by a prickly outer coating.

How to grow: The American beech does best in full sun, but tolerates partial shade. It likes relatively moist, yet well-drained, soils.

Uses: The size of this tree limits its use to large gardens, where it quickly becomes the focal point. It is a domineering tree, and its dense shade and shallow roots eliminate all competition.

Related species: The European beech (*Fagus sylvatica*) has smaller leaves and darker gray bark and is less hardy.

Flowering Dogwood
Cornus florida
Zone: USDA 5b to 8b

This native of the eastern United States is perhaps the king of all the flowering trees.

Description: The flowering dogwood is a deciduous tree of medium size (20 feet in most areas) with a spreading, layered habit. It produces large white bracts surrounding insignificant flowers. The blooms appear before the foliage, making for a spectacular display. The leaves are showy when they turn bright scarlet in the fall.

How to grow: The flowering dogwood grows best in a rich, acidic, but well-drained soil in partial shade or full sun. It will not tolerate prolonged drought.

Uses: The flowering dogwood's year-round beauty makes it a perfect accent plant. Because of its modest size, it suits the smaller lots of modern homes.

Related varieties: There are many varieties of flowering dogwood. 'New Hampshire' is the hardiest form, often flourishing where other flowering dogwoods have failed.

Crape Myrtle
Lagerstroemia indica
Zone: USDA 7b to 9a

This is a dazzling summer flowering tree with showy flower panicles in electric colors that sizzle across the branches.

Description: The crape myrtle is a broad-crowned tree that is variable in size, averaging about 20 to 25 feet, but potentially much taller. Often multi-stemmed, it has smooth, sculptured gray bark that gently exfoliates, showing multi-shaded underbark. Dappled shade allows for the growth of complementary ground covers beneath its leaf canopy. The petals are crinkled, like crepe paper, and vary from white to red, pink, lavender, or purple. They appear recurrently July through September.

How to grow: Transplant container-grown or balled-and-burlapped plants into slightly acidic, well-drained soil. The crape myrtle will not flower well in the shade, where it is subject to powdery mildew. It can get tip blight if planted north of Zone 7b. Encourage recurrent blooms by tip pruning spent flowers.

Uses: Used as a tree or shrub, crape myrtle is a good choice as a specimen plant, for borders, or to plant near a corner of the house.

Douglas Fir
Pseudotsuga menziesii
Zone: USDA 4b to 6a

Douglas fir is native to western North America, a cone-bearing member of the pine family, and favored as a cut Christmas tree in some areas of the country.

Description: This pyramid-shaped ornamental tree has wingy branches and a unique, youthful habit in which the upper branches are ascending, while the lower branches descend. It is distinguished from other narrow-leaved evergreens by its scaly, long, pointed terminal buds and curious cones. No other cones of native conifers have persistent scales with conspicuous, protruding three-pointed, forked bracts. The Douglas fir has flat, blunt needles with two white lines on the underside of the leaf, which are variable in color.

How to grow: This tree needs humid conditions and moist, well-drained acidic to neutral soil. It will not survive arid, thin, infertile soil and dry atmospheric conditions.

Uses: The Douglas fir makes a fine specimen tree and can be used as a screen. It holds its short needles when used as a Christmas tree.

Washington Hawthorn
Crataegus phaenopyrum
Zone: USDA 4b to 8b

The Washington hawthorn is quite possibly the best of all the ornamental hawthorns—and that's saying a great deal, since they are a particularly showy group of trees. It is especially functional because of its resistance to fireblight, a disease that severely limits the use of many hawthorns.

Description: As a tall shrub or small tree, it grows to about 25 feet. Growth is rather columnar at first, eventually becoming rounded. The clustered spring flowers are white and numerous. The Washington hawthorn forms a thorny, dense mass of dark green, lustrous foliage. The leaves turn orange-red in the fall, then drop to reveal an abundant crop of bright red berries.

How to grow: Full sun and most soil conditions suit it best.

Uses: An excellent city tree, it is important to prune away thorny lower branches so they will be out of the way of human contact. The tree's thorny nature makes it a good hedge for security purposes. The fruits not only attract birds but are delicious to eat.

European Hornbeam
Carpinus betulus
Zone: USDA 5a to 7a

An outstanding small, multi-purpose landscape tree, the European hornbeam is under-used in North America. It is attractive in all seasons, adaptable, and easy to grow.

Description: European hornbeam attains only 40 feet in height. Allowed to grow naturally, the plant takes on a pyramidal form in youth, becoming rounded in maturity. The deciduous foliage is dark green and oval with toothed edges. It has an attractive fall color—golden yellow.

How to grow: European hornbeam is quite tolerant of most soils, including moderately acid and alkaline ones; however, it prefers well-drained conditions. It does best in full sun to light shade.

Uses: This species makes an excellent small landscape tree and is useful for screens, hedges, and patio boxes. It can be pruned heavily if needed and, in Europe at least, is often trained into an arbor form.

Related species: The American hornbeam (*C. caroliniana*), native to eastern North America, is a choice plant for fall color—a bright yellow to orange-red. It can be difficult to transplant.

American Holly
Ilex opaca
Zones: USDA 6a to 9a

This is the best of the native evergreen hollies. It has been widely planted both within its native east coast range and well beyond it.

Description: American holly is extremely variable. More than 1,000 varieties have been named. It is generally a slow-growing tree, reaching up to 50 feet. Densely pyramidal in youth, it becomes more open with age. The leaves are typical of our image of a Christmas holly—thick and dark green, with spiny edges. The berries are red and produced on female plants in the fall.

How to grow: Like many evergreen hollies, this tree is particular about its needs. It prefers deep, rich, well-drained acidic soils. Partial shade or full sun are fine, but drying winds should be avoided. One male should be planted for every three females so fruit will develop.

Uses: Smaller clones are often used as evergreen shrubs and patio trees; standard size selections can become outstanding landscape specimens. The American holly makes an excellent privacy screen and security fence and can easily be pruned to hedge form.

Juneberry
Amelanchier arborea
Zone: USDA 3b to 8a

The juneberry is native to eastern North America but has abundant and similar relatives in other parts of the continent.

Description: This small, often multi-stemmed, deciduous tree or tall shrub grows to 25 feet tall. It offers color in all seasons; in winter, with smooth gray bark delicately streaked with longitudinal fissures; in spring, with its delicate white flowers, appearing just as the leaves start to burst out; in summer, with its red berries that gradually turn black; and finally, in fall, with its beautiful orange-red oval leaves.

How to grow: Juneberry is tolerant of various soils and exposures, although it blooms most heavily in full sun.

Uses: It can be trained as a small tree or encouraged to develop multiple trunks by pruning. Juneberry is often planted in naturalistic landscapes, not only for its appearance but because it attracts birds.

Related species: There are several similar *Amelanchier* species, some more shrublike than the species mentioned. They are all interesting landscape plants.

American Linden
Tilia americana

Zone: USDA 3a to 8a

This is the native eastern North American species of linden, also known as basswood.

Description: The American linden is a tall, stately tree, growing to more than 100 feet. Pyramidal in youth, the tree develops a more rounded crown at maturity. It has gray to brown bark and large, toothed, heart-shaped, deciduous leaves. They are dark green above and pale beneath, turning yellow or yellow-green in the fall. The yellow flowers would not be particularly noticeable without their pervading fragrance.

How to grow: This tree transplants readily and does best in deep, rich, moist, well-drained soils with full sun or partial shade. Never plant the American linden over a parking lot; the sticky nectar dripping from the flowers can damage car paint.

Uses: American linden is a good choice for a specimen tree or for naturalizing large lots and parks.

Related species: A smaller-leaved linden, the European linden (*Tilia cordata*), is the most widely planted ornamental species and offers many varieties.

Maidenhair Tree
Ginkgo biloba

Zone: USDA 4b to 8b

This ancient oriental, single-species genus is believed to be the oldest flowering plant in existence, although it is now apparently extinct in the wild.

Description: Variable in height from 40 to 80 feet, the ginkgo's foliage has the unusual habit of hugging spur branches instead of forming a broad crown. This results in branches that grow in every direction. The exotic, parallel-veined, green leaves are fan-shaped, but often deeply notched at the outer margin's center. They turn butter-yellow in autumn. Male and female flowers are on separate trees. Naked seeds, produced in late summer and fall, are plum shaped with a fleshy outer coat that smells like rancid butter when decomposing. Curiously, the seeds are considered gourmet fare and highly touted in the Orient.

How to grow: This survivor is tough enough to tolerate differing soil pH, many soil types, moisture variations, and light exposures. The ginkgo needs little pruning, and is virtually free of pests and diseases.

Uses: To avoid fetid fruit, plant only male trees as specimens or shade trees.

Honey Locust
Gleditsia triacanthos inermis

Zone: USDA 4b to 9a

Honey locust is a tall, pod-bearing shade tree with striking, ornamental foliage.

Description: This deciduous short-trunked tree bears lacy, medium- to fine-textured foliage. Its mature size is variable, growing in the 30 to 70 foot range, taller in the wild. Honey locust is a rapid-growing tree whose fall foliage is clear-yellow to yellow-green. Its fruit is a long, reddish-brown, straplike, curved pod produced in late summer.

How to grow: Plant honey locust in full sun and limey soil. It's adaptable to a range of conditions including drought and high pH, and is tolerant to road salt spray.

Uses: To avoid thorns and litter problems, use an unarmed, podless selection as a shade tree. Webworm is this plant's worst enemy. Leaflets are small and break down quickly.

Related varieties: 'Shademaster,' a superior podless cultivar with a vase-like form, is fairly resistant to webworms. 'Skyline' is noted for its golden fall color and upright form.

Southern Magnolia
Magnolia grandiflora

Zone: USDA 7 to 9

This is a splendid, broad-leaved evergreen tree, native to southeastern United States. The standout qualities of the magnolia include its large, flamboyant flowers and attractive, tropical-looking leaves, both of which add distinction to the garden landscape.

Description: Southern magnolia is a handsome, low-branching tree, reaching heights of 60 to 80 feet. It displays wooly, young buds and eight-inch-long, thick, shiny leaves. The huge, solitary blooms are white and exude a lovely fragrance. Its fruit is three to four inches long and conelike, revealing red seeds when opened.

How to grow: Plant container-grown or balled-and-burlapped plants in spring. The soil should be fertile, deep, well-drained, and slightly acidic. This tree tolerates high soil moisture, but should be protected from wind. Avoid transplanting once it is situated. It can be pruned after flowering, if needed. Pests are not a particular problem.

Uses: Southern magnolia is used in the South as a specimen tree, but it does have a good deal of leaf litter. It is best used where it has ample room to develop without having to cut off the lower limbs.

Sugar Maple
Acer saccharum

Zone: USDA 3b to 7b

Sugar maple (also called hard or rock maple) is a popular choice for its razzle-dazzle red, orange, and yellow fall color. Native to the northeastern United States, this selection is best known as the legendary source of maple syrup.

Description: A short-trunked, large, and spreading tree, the sugar maple can reach heights of 50 to 70 feet or more, but grows somewhat slowly. The pointed leaves are four to six inches across, with five lobes. Non-showy, chartreuse flowers appear in early spring preceding the leaves.

How to grow: The sugar maple requires a well-drained, fertile soil and plenty of room to grow. Do not plant in dry, compacted soil, or too close to streets where road salt is used.

Uses: This plant is best used as a shade or specimen tree. It is resistant to storm damage.

Related species: Among the larger-growing maples, the Norway maple (*Acer platanoides*) is particularly popular. This species offers many varieties, including some with deep purple, red, or variegated leaves.

Eastern White Pine
Pinus strobus

Zone: USDA 3a to 9a

This was once among the tallest trees of eastern North American forests. Unfortunately, today it is rare to see one any taller than 100 feet.

Description: Young white pines are pyramidal in shape, but lose their lower branches as they age and take on a wind-beaten look, rather like giant bonsais. The tree is attractive at both stages. Its persistent needles, soft for a pine, are grouped by fives and are bluish-green in color. The cones are large and decorative.

How to grow: This pine is easily transplanted. It grows best in fertile, moist, well-drained soils; and, although it prefers full sun, it can tolerate some shade. It can be pruned into an attractive evergreen hedge.

Uses: The eastern white pine is an exceedingly handsome landscape tree; some rate it as the best ornamental conifer. Given lots of room, it makes an unforgettable impression as a landscape plant. It is not a good city tree because of its susceptibility to pollution and salt damage.

Related species: The Japanese white pine (*Pinus parviflora*) is a slow-growing, smaller pine.

White Oak
Quercus alba

Zone: USDA 4b to 9a

Not only does this tree grow to a massive size—up to 150 feet with an 80-foot spread—but it can reach a great age: 800-year-old trees have been known to exist.

Description: The white oak has a pyramidal form when young, but becomes broadly rounded in maturity. The oak leaves, narrow at the base, have five to nine rounded lobes. They are dark green in summer, turning red before falling.

How to grow: The white oak is slow growing and must be planted as a small tree, since its deep tap root makes transplantation difficult. It prefers full sun and a deep, moist, well-drained soil that is slightly acidic. Its leaves tend to acidify the soil over time.

Uses: The white oak makes a splendid specimen tree for parks and large terrains.

Related species: A good substitute for the white oak in moist soils, the swamp white oak (*Quercus bicolor*) has leaves that are broad and undulated on the edges rather than lobed.

Western Yellow Pine
Pinus ponderosa

Zone: USDA 3b to 8a

The species name "Ponderosa" is Spanish for ponderous (heavy, enormous), a name given to this tree for its huge size at maturity.

Description: Western yellow pine bears bundles of two to three persistent needles from 5 to 11 inches long. They are an attractive yellow-green. This tree grows as a narrow pyramid when young, then develops a bare trunk with a cluster of branches at the tip forming a cone or flat-topped crown. It reaches more than 100 feet in ideal conditions.

How to grow: This pine prefers a deep, moist, well-drained loam. It needs full sun and is tolerant of alkaline soils.

Uses: This is a good tree for windbreaks, as well as a specimen plant for dry climates.

Related species: The lodgepole pine (*Pinus contorta*), a closely related species, has a straight trunk that was once used by Plains Indians to construct their teepees. It is a better choice for damp soils than the western yellow pine.

Sour Gum
Nyssa sylvatica

Zone: USDA 5a to 9a

The sour gum is a beautiful shade tree with fire engine red fall foliage. Native to eastern United States, it is a favorite plant of bees. This water-loving plant is also known as tupelo, pepperidge, and black gum.

Description: Sour gum grows pyramidally in youth, but with maturity forms an irregularly rounded crown. With cultivation it grows to about 25 feet by age 30. One of the first trees to show color in fall, sour gum's glossy, green leaves turn scarlet. Its bitter, fleshy, blue-black fruit is favored by bears and birds, and follows pollination of female trees. Older trees have dark, blocky bark.

How to grow: Moist, acidic soil is required. This tree needs protection from the wind, and light shade will decrease its spectacular show of autumn leaves. For best performance, transplant in spring, using local stock. Tap-rooted sour gum transplants poorly unless balled-and-burlapped or container-grown plants are used.

Uses: Sour gum is used as a specimen, shade, or street tree, also naturalized or in mass plantings.

Japanese Zelkova
Zelkova serrata

Zone: USDA 6a to 9a

Used as a replacement for the disease-ridden American elm, Japanese zelkova is an attractive landscape tree and well worth planting.

Description: This is a fast-growing, round-headed tree in its youth, becoming moderate in growth in middle age and taking on a vaselike silhouette. It can reach up to 50 feet in height. The bark, cherrylike on younger trees, exfoliates on older trees, leaving an attractively mottled pattern. The elmlike deciduous leaves turn yellow or yellow-brown in the fall.

How to grow: The Japanese zelkova is easily transplanted. It prefers moist, deep soil and full sun. It is wind and drought resistant once established and is not bothered by air pollution. Susceptible to some elm diseases and pests, it is generally immune to Dutch elm disease.

Uses: This is a good choice for a lawn or street tree, providing good shade relatively quickly.

Related varieties: 'Village Green' has an elmlike form and rusty red fall leaves. 'Green Vase' is similar but with orange fall leaves.

Norway Spruce
Picea abies

Zone: USDA 3a to 7b

With its perfect shape, the Norway spruce makes a fine live Christmas tree for the yard.

Description: Norway spruce form a pyramidal silhouette, never rounding out with age like many pines. It is rather stiffly formal in its youth, but older branches produce pendulous branchlets, giving it more charm as it ages. Its needles are dark green year round. The cones, borne sporadically, are particularly large for a spruce. It can reach more than 100 feet in height, even under cultivation.

How to grow: Grow in full sun in just about any soil, although moist, sandy, well-drained soils are preferred. The Norway spruce does best in cool climates. Give this tree plenty of space, because it will lose its lower branches—and much of its charm—if crowded or shaded at its base.

Uses: This tree makes a striking specimen plant or an excellent windbreak.

Related species: The Colorado blue spruce (*Picea pungens glauca*) is renowned for its blue needles.

Bridal-wreath
Spiraea x vanhouttei

Zone: USDA 3b to 8b

The genus Spiraea is a highly popular one in the garden. Most are spring-bloomers with numerous tiny white flowers.

Description: The Vanhoutt spirea grows 6 to 8 feet in height, spreading 10 to 12 feet in diameter. It has a distinctly fountainlike growth habit, with a round top and arching branches recurving to the ground. Its leaves are greenish-blue, turning plum-colored in the fall.

How to grow: Although the shrub will grow well in medium shade, full sun produces more flowers. The bridal-wreath adapts well to most soils. To keep the shrub in top shape, prune back one-third of the old flowering wood annually after it finishes blooming.

Uses: An excellent accent plant, the bridal-wreath is also good for informal hedges or screens and is well suited to mixed shrub borders.

Related species: The garland spirea (*Spiraea x arguta*) is similar to the bridal-wreath but has less pendulous branches and a better covering of flowers in spring. The bumald spireas (*Spiraea x bumalda*) are summer-flowering spireas with pink to whitish flowers.

Red-osier Dogwood
Cornus sericea (formerly Cornus stolonifera)

Zone: USDA 3a to 8a

The red-osier dogwood gets its name from its purplish-red stems and its former use in making wicker baskets ("osier" is French for wicker).

Description: The red-osier dogwood is a tall shrub that grows to 10 feet in height and has an even greater spread. Young branches are smooth and attractively colored in red; older ones are woody and less charming. Its smooth, pointed leaves are medium green, turning purplish red in fall.

How to grow: The red-osier dogwood seems to adapt to most soils. It does best in full sun.

Uses: Excellent for mass plantings and shrub borders, it is also useful in erosion control and makes a good container plant.

Related species: The Tatarian dogwood (*Cornus alba*) is nearly indistinguishable from the red-osier dogwood. Most variegated-leaved varieties belong to this species.

Related varieties: 'Flaviramea' is a popular yellow-stemmed variety.

Michigan Holly
Ilex verticillata

Zone: USDA 4a to 9a

This shrub, with its deciduous, spineless leaves, is a rather unhollylike holly. Nevertheless, it's an attractive plant since leaf drop better reveals its spectacularly colored, long-lasting berries.

Description: Michigan holly's densely foliaged shrub has an oval form and numerous branchlets. The leaves, 1½ to 3 inches long, are dark green and shiny, turning yellow in the fall. The flowers are insignificant but are followed by scarlet red berries, which last right through the winter if not eaten by the birds.

How to grow: Michigan holly does well in full sun or partial shade and moist, rich soils. This is an acid-loving plant that will do poorly in neutral or alkaline soils.

Uses: The shrub makes a good accent plant for spots where its winter color will be appreciated. It is a fine choice for mass plantings and wildlife gardens. At least one male must be planted for fruiting to occur.

Related varieties: 'Sparkleberry' is one of the more spectacular selections, with numerous, long-lasting berries.

Dwarf Fothergilla
Fothergilla gardenii

Zone: USDA 5b to 9a

The dwarf fothergilla, native to the southeastern United States, is a low-growing shrub with intensely fragrant, fluffy, white, bottlebrush flowers that bloom in the spring.

Description: The tip of each of the spreading branches, rarely more than three feet tall, is decorated in spring with an erect cluster of white, petalless flowers, creating the typical bottlebrush appearance of the shrub. Its leaves, rounded but somewhat irregular, don't appear until later. They are dark green, turning a combination of yellow, red, and orange before dropping in the fall.

How to grow: This shrub requires an acidic, peaty, sandy loam with good drainage. Although it does well in partial shade, it only blooms and colors abundantly in full sun.

Uses: The dwarf fothergilla is a choice plant for borders, foundation plantings, and mass plantings. No pruning is required.

Related species: The large fothergilla (*Fothergilla major*) is similar to the dwarf, but can attain heights of up to 10 feet.

Oakleaf Hydrangea
Hydrangea quercifolia

Zone: USDA 5a to 9a

This species is an exception among hydrangeas, since it blooms quite well in a lightly shaded garden.

Description: This hydrangea forms upright, nearly unbranching stems, spreading at the base from stolons to make a mounded colony. Its flowers, borne in terminal clusters in early summer, are of two types: sterile and fertile. The sterile flowers, found at the base of the cluster, are 1 to 1½ inches in diameter. They are white, changing to purplish pink then brown in the fall. As the name suggests, the deeply cut leaves are oaklike. They are dark green in the summer, changing to a spectacular mix of red, orange-brown, and purple in the fall.

How to grow: Plant in partial to half shade, although full sun is tolerated. This shrub does best on rich, moist, well-drained soils. Mulch to maintain the cool, moist conditions the roots prefer. Pruning mainly consists of removing faded flowers and cutting out dead wood.

Uses: Oakleaf hydrangea is a good shrub for planting in wooded areas and in shrub borders.

Drooping Leucothoe

Leucothoe fontanesiana

Zone: USDA 5b to 9a

This southeastern United States native is an excellent low-growing shrub or ground cover, offering a combination of evergreen foliage, often with fall color, and attractive flowers.

Description: A graceful evergreen shrub reaching 3 to 6 feet in height and width, the drooping leucothoe gets its name from its spreading, arching branches, which are almost weighted down by the pendulous fragrant clusters of creamy white flowers. The leaves are leathery and dark green, 3 to 6 inches long. They often take on a bronzy to purplish color in fall and winter.

How to grow: This shrub is a good choice for partial to full shade, although it will tolerate sun if mulched and protected from drying winds. It prefers moist, well-drained, organic soils and acidic growing conditions.

Uses: Drooping leucothoe is a good ground cover and is excellent for mass plantings. It nicely hides the base of other shrubs that become leggy over time, especially rhododendrons.

Sweet Mock Orange

Philadelphus coronarius

Zone: USDA 4a to 7b

The sweet mock orange is a tall, deciduous shrub that develops abundant fragrant summer flowers.

Description: It forms a large rounded shrub up to 12 feet in height with an equal spread, although it is often kept much shorter by pruning. The leaves are medium green, ovate, and lightly toothed, with little fall interest. Its flowers, borne in early summer, are sweetly scented, much like orange blossoms. They are white and 1 to 1⅖ inches across.

How to grow: Sweet mock orange is easily transplanted. It needs full sun to partial shade and tolerates most soils (although it prefers moist, organic, well-drained soil). Prune after flowering, either lightly to stimulate new growth, or heavily to rejuvenate older specimens.

Uses: It can be used singly as an accent plant, or grouped in shrub borders or mass plantings.

Related varieties and species: 'Aureus' has bright yellow spring foliage, turning yellow-green in summer. A great many hybrid mock oranges exist, most of which retain their sweet perfume.

Common Lilac

Syringa vulgaris

Zone: USDA 3 to 7

The common lilac's dense clusters of highly perfumed, lavender flowers are an essential part of the landscape, especially in colder climates.

Description: This species of lilac is an upright, leggy shrub that grows to about 15 feet with a spread of 12 feet. Its heart-shaped, dark green leaves are up to five inches long. The flowers are produced in dense, pyramid-shaped clusters at the end of the branches in spring. They are light lavender in this species.

How to grow: Full sun is best, although lilacs will grow in medium shade. They prefer neutral soils with good drainage. Remove old trunks and unwanted suckers occasionally.

Uses: The lilac is a good spring accent plant, offering little interest the rest of the year.

Related species: There are many other species of lilac, some earlier or later bloomers and many with equally interesting perfumes. They are often used to extend the common lilac's all-too-short flowering season.

Related varieties: The so-called French hybrids contain all of the improved forms of *Syringa vulgaris*.

Eastern Redbud

Cercis canadensis

Zone: USDA 5b to 9a

This small tree, native to eastern North America, is popular for its long-lasting spring flowers that grow directly from the trunk and branches.

Description: The eastern redbud generally forms multiple trunks, developing a flat-topped or rounded crown of 20 to 30 feet in height, slightly more in spread. The heart-shaped leaves are reddish purple when they open, fading to dark green. The pea-shaped flowers are small but numerous, appearing before the tree is in leaf. They are reddish-purple in bud, opening to pink.

How to grow: The redbud does best in full sun or light shade and deep, well-drained soils. It is, however, quite adaptable to varying soil conditions, from highly acidic to slightly alkaline, and moist to dry. It will not take waterlogging. Pruning is rarely necessary.

Uses: The eastern redbud makes a good accent tree or can be grouped by threes or fives. It makes a nice addition to the shrub border and naturalizes well in woodland settings.

Related varieties: There are many selections with flowers ranging from white to purple. 'Forest Pansy' is grown for its purple leaves.

Smoke Tree
Cotinus coggyrgria

Zone: USDA 5a to 7b

This tall shrub from Europe and Asia is popular for its often striking summer and fall colors and plumelike inflorescences.

Description: This is a multi-stemmed, deciduous shrub with an open, spreading form. The smooth, satiny leaves are nearly round and are blue-green in color in the species. The flowers are borne in large, long-lasting, fawn-colored, feathery inflorescences, appearing in summer and lasting through fall.

How to grow: Full sun is best, especially for the purple-leaved varieties. The smoke tree tolerates just about any soil. Pruning this shrub is a compromise between two goals: obtaining dense foliage growth (best obtained by heavy annual pruning) or stimulating abundant flowering (since blooms only appear on wood three years old).

Uses: The smoke tree is good for shrub borders and mass plantings. The varieties with colorful foliage make nice accent plants.

Related varieties: Many purple-leaved varieties exist. 'Royal Purple' is a particularly choice specimen.

Jackman's Clematis
Clematis x jackmanii

Zone: USDA 4 to 6

This old-fashioned hybrid is still the most popular clematis in gardens and is a parent of several of the more modern large-flowered varieties.

Description: The plant's 4- to 7-inch, deep violet flowers with four flattened sepals appear on new wood all summer until frost and can be extremely abundant. The Jackman's clematis climbs by wrapping its leaf petioles around narrow objects and can reach 12 feet. Its leaves are dark green and pinnate.

How to grow: Plant so that the roots are in a cool, shady spot but the upper growth is in full sun. The soil should be light, organic, and well-drained, but not constantly wet. In cold climates, mound plentiful soil at the base of the plant for the winter.

Uses: Jackman's clematis is spectacular for use on rock walls, trellises, fences, or in shrubs and trees.

Related varieties and species: There is an entire series of large-flowered clematis similar to Jackman's clematis. The colors range from white to pink, red, purple, and blue. Some varieties have bicolored or double flowers.

Common Witch Hazel
Hamamelis virginiana

Zone: USDA 4a to 9a

This plant is usually grown as an ornamental tree or shrub for its fall flowers.

Description: Common witch hazel is a small tree that grows up to 20 feet in height and spread. It is remarkable for its fall flowers, usually being the last shrub of the year to bloom. The flowers are yellow and fragrant, bearing four straplike petals. They are borne in loose clusters and the display can last from 2 to 4 weeks in late autumn. The leaves are irregular in shape—nearly rounded but with toothed margins. They are medium green in summer, turning golden before dropping in the fall.

How to grow: Witch hazel does best in full sun to light shade and adapts to most soils. In the wild, it prefers moist situations.

Uses: The common witchhazel is used as an ornamental woodland tree or as the back of a shrub border.

Related species: The vernal witchhazel (*Hamamelis vernalis*) is similar to the common, but blooms in winter, often while the ground is still covered with snow. Its flowers are yellow to red.

Trumpet Honeysuckle
Lonicera sempervirens

Zones: USDA 4 to 9

This climbing vine, native to south-central United States, is evergreen over much of its range, becoming deciduous only in the coldest sectors.

Description: This twining vine can grow to a height of 50 feet. The leaves are blue-green, and tubular red flowers are produced in clusters at the tips of the branches throughout the summer. Unlike many flowering vines, they are scentless. Bright red berries appear at the end of the summer and last through much of the fall.

How to grow: Plant in full sun to partial shade and ordinary to poor but well-drained soil. Overly rich soils tend to promote excessive stem growth while reducing flowering.

Uses: Trumpet honeysuckle makes both a good ground cover and climbing vine for trellises, pergolas, and fences. It requires a strong support on which to grow. Harsh pruning tends to create a more controlled, attractive plant, while stimulating bloom.

Related species: Of the climbing species, the choicest is the woodbine honeysuckle (*Lonicera periclymenum*) with its two-tone flowers.

Master Gardener Q & A

Commonly Asked Questions

Q: Why does my wisteria never bloom? It grows so quickly that it must be pruned often.

A: You may be pruning off next year's flower buds. Encourage short side shoots for flower buds by partially pruning the longest side branches. To avoid excessive growth, do not fertilize wisteria. Wisteria blooms best with ample exposure to the sun. Root pruning may shock the plant into flowering—in June, use a spade to cut a six-inch deep circle about two feet from the base of the plant.

Q: When should I prune my trees?

A: Pruning shade and ornamental trees not only adds to the aesthetics of the landscape, but prolongs the life of the tree. Prune to thin out branches in late winter when the sap is rising. The sap "bleeding" helps prevent disease organisms from entering the wound and the tree will heal quickly at this time of year. Limbs that need to be removed because of storm or disease damage can be pruned any time of year.

Q: To receive more light into the yard, should I have the trees topped?

A: Topping not only disfigures a tree aesthetically, but drastically degrades its long-term health. The large, open wounds that topping creates will not heal completely, allowing easy entrance to disease-causing organisms. Rapid, dense, shoot growth (called suckers) grow to the original height of the tree, consequently defeating the purpose of topping. The new growth will not be as structurally sound as normal branching, becoming more susceptible to storm damage.

Q: I have several hydrangeas, all of which are the same kind. Why are some blue flowering while others are pink?

A: The availability of aluminum in the soil, determined by the soil's pH, determines the color of your type of hydrangea. If the pH is high (7.0 or above), the flowers will be pink. Blue flowers develop from acidic soil (4.5 to 5.5), and purplish flowers in between. To ensure blue flowers, lower the pH with a sulfur-based product. Raise the pH with lime for pink blossoms.

Q: Can a live Christmas tree be planted after the holidays?

A: Yes. Prepare the hole well before the ground freezes. Amend the loose soil as you dig so it will be ready for planting, and store the soil where it will not freeze. Choose a tree with a tight, solid root-ball and wrap the ball in plastic to keep moist while it's in the house. A cool room for no more than a week is advised. Plant the tree as soon as possible; mulch and water well.

Q: What causes the bark of young trees to crack, and how can it be corrected?

A: The vertical cracking, or sunscald, appears on the southwest side of the trunk; where the tree heats up on warm, sunny, winter days, and freezes rapidly when the sun sets. Young trees are most prone to sunscald because of their thin bark. These cracks provide a path for diseases and insects. Sunscald can be prevented by wrapping the trunk in a protective covering for the winter. Expandable, white plastic tree wraps are available at garden centers.

Master Gardener Q & A

Commonly Asked Questions

Q: What makes some hollies produce berries when other don't?

A: Hollies are either male or female; only the females produce berries. A pollen-producing male plant needs to be growing nearby to pollinate a female, otherwise berries will not form. Although some species can pollinate other species, it's generally necessary to have both a male and a female of the same type. Other reasons for lack of fruit include a shortage of sunlight where the female is planted, or severe drought while berries are forming.

Q: Is it possible to transplant trees from the woods to the yard?

A: Although it's possible, the success rate is low. Forest tree roots are quite entangled with other trees; either with wide-spreading shallow roots, or a deep taproot, depending upon species. The tree is already acclimated to the woods exposure. Both the shock of transplanting and the loss of roots often kill the tree. Nursery-grown trees have been tended by root pruning to encourage the development of a small but concentrated root system, making transplanting more successful.

Q: Is it possible that road salt is killing the shrubs at the end of my driveway?

A: Salt toxicity is common in areas where deicing salts are used in winter. The worst damage occurs right where the salt is applied, near roads and walks. Plants will display general dieback, yellowish foliage, and weak growth. Wash salt residue from plants with a hose, and soak the soil to leach the salt from the beds. Don't use salts around the home. Some fertilizers can be safely used to melt ice and will not harm nearby plants.

Q: Is it necessary to stake newly planted trees?

A: If the crown of the tree is relatively large compared to the size of the root ball, staking may be needed to prevent the tree from tilting as it settles. Be sure the root ball sits on a firm soil base. Tie with flat plastic guy string or wire covered in old garden hose to protect the bark from being cut or wounded. Remove stakes and wires as soon as the tree roots become established. Evergreen trees do not usually require staking.

Staking is not recommended unless a tree is unstable. In most cases, two or three stakes will suffice.

Index